EQUESTRIAN EXCELLENCE

EQUESTRIAN

EXCELLENCE

*The Stories of Our Olympic Equestrian
Medal Winners From Stockholm 1912
thru Atlanta 1996*

⸻

BARBARA
WALLACE
SHAMBACH

Half Halt Press, Inc.

Boonsboro, Maryland

Equestrian Excellence: The Stories of Our Olympic Equestrian Medal Winners, From Stockholm 1912 thru Atlanta 1996

© 1996 Barbara Wallace

Published in the United States of America by

Half Halt Press, Inc.
P.O. Box 67
Boonsboro, MD 21713

The Publishers thank Editors Eileen Thomas and Beth Baumert for their invaluable help with this project.

Book and cover design by Jim Haynes, Graphics Plus, Inc.

Printed in the U.S.A.

Shambach, Barbara Wallace, 1941
Equestrian Excellence: The stories of our Olympic medal winners, from Stockholm 1912 thru Atlanta 1996 / Barbara Wallace Shambach: general editor, Eileen Thomas
p. cm.
ISBN 0-939481-47-2
1. United States Equestrian Team-Biography. 2. Horsemen and horsewomen-United States-Biography. 3. Olympics-History. 4. Horse sports-United States-History.
 I. Thomas, Eileen.
 II. Title.
SF294.85.U55S48 1996
798.2'092'273--dc21
(B)   96-46233
                                                                CIP

Dedication

This book is dedicated to my daughters Nancy
and Susan, and would not have been written
had it not been for them.

TABLE OF CONTENTS

THE UNITED STATES ARMY EQUESTRIAN TEAM MEDAL WINNERS

NOTE TO THE READER

The three organizations most vitally involved in American international equestrian sports are listed below. They are all commonly referred to by their initials. The actual titles of these organizations are as follows:

AHSA = American Horse Shows Association—the governing body of horse-show sports in America, which formulates rules for all domestic equestrian competition and is our official member of both the FEI and the United States Olympic Committee.

FEI = Federation Equestre Internationale—the Brussels-based governing body of international equestrian sports, which formulates the rules under which all international equestrian competition is conducted.

USET = United States Equestrian Team, Inc.—the nonprofit, voluntary organization that exists for the express purpose of training, selecting and financing the amateur equestrian teams that represent the United States in world competitions, including the Olympics.

•

The United States' equestrian involvement at the Olympics began with the U.S. Army Equestrian Team's participation at the 1912 Olympics in Stockholm. When the Army phased out its cavalry unit and advanced to more sophisticated technology, the Army's Equestrian Team disbanned. Cooperative effort between Army and civilian horsemen was responsible for the development of what we know today as the United States Equestrian Team.

ACKNOWLEDGEMENTS

There are a number of people I owe credit to for the encouragement and accomplishment of this book.

My daughters and I met Michael Page, who was then the chief 'd' equipe of the USET Three-Day Event, at the 1990 Rolex. He not only encouraged me to proceed with my idea for the book, he recommended that a good beginning would be to attend the World Championship Games in Stockholm in 1990, to start my interviews of the riders there.

The following people helped sponsor my trip to Stockholm: Jim and Paula Bauer; Dr. G.B. Lopez; Dr. and Mrs. Frederick and Kathy Sawchuk; Dr. John Schwarz; Dr. Chihsing Chen; Dr. and Mrs. Richard and Pat Allen; Dr. Charles Seifert; Dr. John Chadwick; the late Lt. Col. Richard Fox; Dr. Raakesh Bhan; Dr. and Mrs. Leandre and Tild Bautista; Harold Kelley; Dr. and Mrs. John and Pat Huntington; Dr. Norman Amos; and Dr. Monte Gould.

Jim Ortman at Krum's Photography in Battle Creek, Michigan worked with me from the beginning. My hat is off to his patience and expertise.

It was from Max Ammann, Director of the World Cup, that I received my press pass to gain access to the grounds and the events at the World Championships in 1990. He has been a wonderful contact and has shared statistics and pictures that he has carefully kept organized over a wide span of years. He is a believer in people and a horse lover in the truest sense.

In researching the Army years the following sources provided invaluable information and/or contacts:

U.S. Cavalry Museum, Special Collections, Fort Riley, Kansas; The U. S. Military History Institute, Special Collections Branch; The U. S. Military Academy at West Point; The U.S. Horse Cavalry Association; The University of Michigan's Library of Cavalry Journals; Mrs. Hiram Tuttle. She was 94 years old when I first spoke with her. She was baking cookies that morning to entertain her Literary Society in the afternoon. She was as sharp as a tack, and her memories of her husband were fond and clear in her recollection of their days at Fort Riley. She was delightful and I will never forget her. She has since passed away.

Also, Col. Clarence Edmonds; the late Colonel Charles Anderson was an invaluable help in providing information and pictures from the military era. He, also was a devoted collector of statistics, pictures and information, in addition to being a writer about equestrian events.

William McKale, Museum Specialist, U.S. Cavalry Museum; Michael Winey, Curator of the U. S. Army Military History Institute; J. R. Spurrier, President of the U.S. Horse Cavalry Association; Col. Richard L. Gruenther; James McEnery, Library Technician Special Collections, U.S. Military Academy; Alfred R. Kitts; the late Brigadier General Franklin Wing, Jr.; Major General Jonathan Burton and Jack Fritz, who were the first two who read and reviewed my writing covering the military riders and offered encouragement and helpful comments; Col. Morris J. Herbert, Assistant Executive Vice President, U.S. Military Academy. My interview with Maj. Bob Borg will always remain a treasured memory and created what could almost be referred to as a reverence for the riders and their commitment in that era. Maj. Borg also did the first review of the section on dressage.

The entire USET Headquarters staff were generous with their time and one of my best resources: Mickey, Inga, Rhonda and Jamie, along with Finn Caspersen and Robert Standish.

My Aunt and Uncle, Gene and Joyce Brooks provided my transportation from Battle Creek Michigan to the USET Headquarters and they and their daughter and son-in-law, Joan and Steve Peterson, provided lodging for me while I was in the area. I am indebted to their generosity and hospitality.

Thanks to Kathy Kusner who first reviewed the section on Grand Prix Jumping; and to Karen Stives who first reviewed the section on Three-Day Eventing.

A very special thanks to Bill Steinkraus, who not only gave me an interview, but also reviewed my book when it was about two-thirds completed and put me in touch with a publisher, Elizabeth Carnes at Half Halt Press. His words of encouragement and generosity have touched my heart, and have done more to make this book a reality than any other contact.

David Wallechinsky and his inspiring book, *The Complete Book of the Olympics*, shared statistics and allowed me to use some of the personal excerpts from his book in mine.

Thanks to Liz Hoskinson from the AHSA, and Nancy Hobson from the USOC for reviewing the manuscript and making excellent editorial suggestions. Thanks also to Linda Sears at Classic Saddlery in Galesburg, Michigan for being a willing resource, and to Classic Communications for timely info and bios on the 1996 Olympic competitors.

The team mangers of the equestrian disciplines in the '96 Atlanta Games made it possible for me to interview the riders after their "across the board successes": Jim Wolf, three-day eventing; Kathy Roberts, dressage; and Sally Ike, show jumping.

I am grateful to Brother Anthony at the Holy Spirit Abbey, a Trappist Monastery, for putting me in touch with George and Cindy Corless family as my host family in Conyers for the '96 Games, who were wonderful and generous. A special thanks must go to the people of Conyers and their Horse Park facility; the friendliness of the people in this town would be hard to surpass.

I would also like to thank the typists that helped me both to edit and to finish the text: Holly Byrd, my husband Mason Shambach and his daughter Jennifer, and son Stephen. In finishing the 1996 Atlanta stories and updates my husband was indispensable. His support to me and hours of careful proofreading far exceeded the "through thick and through thin" vows we made to one another for a lifetime; my daughter Susan Stewart, who in addition to typing, was a major support to me through the six years it took me to complete the book.

Special accolades to the expertise and knowledge of the section editors: Eileen Thomas on three-day eventing and Beth Baumert on dressage, in addition to my publisher, Elizabeth Carnes. They are the ones who took the manuscript and picture collections of a first time writer and transformed them into a finished and readable book. Their interest and dedication in seeing this project through to the finish is appreciated beyond words.

It is apparent from this long list that no one person ever writes a book of this nature without tremendous help from many sources. The writing of these stories has been a great adventure. I hope you enjoy them.

PREFACE

This book really started with a trip to the Rolex Kentucky Three-Day Event in Lexington. It was the final qualifying competition for the USET to go to the World Championships in Stockholm in 1990. I went with my two daughters, Nancy and Susan. All three of us were horse lovers. After ten years of battling against a foe that wouldn't be stopped, Nancy's most recent diagnosis was that her Hodgkins disease had metastasized into the bone. We realized this would be our last big vacation together. We were unanimous about what we wanted to do, and we had an absolutely wonderful time together doing it.

It was being at this event that kindled a genuine interest on my part to learn more about the riders and equestrian sport. From working with Kentucky Educational Television to review nine years of their Rolex videos and catalog the different horses and riders participating in each year, I learned a great deal from the commentaries and the competitions I reviewed. The more I learned, the more I wanted to know. I found very little information on the individual horses and riders that I was looking for, either in the library or in the book stores. This is when I conceived the idea to write a book about the personal interest stories of the Olympic medal winners, as representative of the hopes and dreams of all equestrians. My goal from the onset has been that, in the sharing of their stories and the other information I learned along the way, the readers of my book would gain the same understanding and respect that I have acquired for the outstanding job the USET has done.

I knew also that I wanted to dedicate my book to my daughter, Nancy, as an ongoing tribute to her love of horses and people.

She had dreams of being a top rider that would never be fulfilled in this life.

I have always held in the highest regard those special people who strive to excel in the goals they have set for themselves, and who keep focused in spite of hardships and drawbacks. How often we forget that these very set-backs, disappointments and failures are often our best teachers. I've always been fond of the story about Thomas Edison who had hundreds of failures before he perfected the electric light. An interviewer once posed the question to him, "After so many failures, what kept you going?" to which he replied, "You don't understand. What you are calling failures, I regard as times I successfully proved how not to do it." Equestrian riders who reach the Olympic level also demonstrate the patience and persistence of Thomas Edison in their striving for excellence. Their tenacity of purpose, to be the best they can be, is a quality that I found highly motivating in the writing of this book.

Not all equestrian Olympic history in the United States is included in this book. It deals rather with the highlights and milestones of that history as the stories of the riders are progressively told from their own perspective. You need to know, also, that all of the riders in this book have scores of other competitive credits to their names that are not mentioned here. No one reaches Olympic status without long lists of honors. I elected, for simplicity's sake, to focus primarily on the Olympics.

Writing this book has been the greatest adventure of my life. I hope you learn as much along the way in the reading of it as I did as I researched and interviewed for it.

Barbara J. Wallace Shambach

DESCRIPTIONS OF THE DISCIPLINES

OLYMPIC DRESAGE

Dressage is a French word which means "training." Although it can apply to the basic training of any horse, it often refers to the advanced stages of training the horse where there are virtually no limits when it comes to talent and time. From the root word *dressuer*, the dressage training of horses aims at the physical and mental improvement of the animal by natural means through logical sequential exercises, progressing in difficulty as the horse progresses in ability. Centuries old, dressage is based on the classical training methods developed by the finest European equestrian institutes, such as the French Cavalry School at Saumur, the Imperial Riding School in Vienna, and the Cavalry Schools of Sweden and Switzerland. Dressage had its beginning in the educational training of cavalry horses when they played a vital part in warfare.

Grand Prix dressage at the Olympic level is elevated to an art form. It lies well beyond the realms of ordinary, practical horsemanship. The pursuit of the ideal is a passionate quest of the riders at this level. Realizing that perfection is never attainable, they are, nonetheless, always striving to come as close as possible. Horses with the ability to execute the precise maneuvers required by the Grand Prix test at the Olympics are as rare and special as their riders, who must be willing to devote a lifetime to the pursuit of a flawless and harmonious performance by horse and rider.

The ultimate goal of dressage is complete harmony between horse and rider. Years of patience and hard work are needed in order to refine the communication between horse and rider through the use of the aids, which are the legs, the seat, the weight and the hands of the rider. The rider's legs create energy from the hindquarters and define the bend of the horse's body. The rider's seat helps to establish balance and, along with precise changes in the distribution of the rider's weight, the horse understands that he is to respond in a given way. The rider's hands, as the receivers of his horse's energies, make it possible to steer by pointing the way. At all times the aids should be used consistently and in perfect coordination with each other. As a result of the rider's clear and consistent use of the aids, the horse learns obedience. The aids that the rider gives the horse are so subtle that they appear to be invisible to the observer. The horse's performance looks so effortless that it appears that he is executing the movements himself with no help from his rider.

Here is a description of the aids for a flying change, as written by Marguerite Henry in her book, *Album of Horses*: "If he wishes his horse to take a left lead, he brings back the calf of his right leg, but only a trace. He turns his horse's head toward the left, but only a hair's breadth. He shifts his weight onto his right seat bone. He brings back his left shoulder. But all of these signals are so fine, that only the horse is the wiser." Years of patience and correction precede the achievement of smooth transitions and brilliant action in the movements of a dressage partnership. The young rider learns the most from the fully trained horse, and the green horse from the experienced master.

In Olympic competition, the judges are looking for consistency. The supple horse who bends and turns with ease, has a cadenced gait and a cooperative rapport with his rider consistently throughout the whole test will score higher marks than the one who flashes off and on in occasional movements of brilliance. If a horse is resistant to the bit it is a grave fault. When the horse is "on the bit" or "through" (which is the ideal), he has a roundness to his frame. This means that all the energy, created by the active hindquarters in response to the rider's leg, is pushing through into the bridle to be controlled by the rider's hands, allowing horse and rider to function as a unit. The action of the hind legs should match the action of the front legs. There should be a regular cadence to the horse's gait.

The movements of the dressage test require bending and turning, and collection and extension from the horse. The rider must commit the sequence of the test to memory, paying particular attention to the markers at which certain movements begin or end. The rider's strategy in riding the test will include deciding the precise distance from each marker at which he must begin to prepare his horse in order to ensure smooth execution of the transition into another movement. He must anticipate where he is most likely to have problems. A difficulty foreseen is probably more than half corrected.

A description of some of the most difficult and beautiful movements that the dressage test encompasses are:

The passage

is a forward springy, slow motion trot in which the horse should produce a graceful hesitation between one trotting stride and the next. Diagonal legs strike out in unison. The hesitation gives the impression that the horse is floating above the ground, and that his feet approach rather than touch the earth.

The piaffe

is from a French word meaning to prance. In this trot-like movement in place, the even rhythm of hoofbeats, the forelegs higher than the hind legs, and all legs leaving the ground in a brief moment of suspension, are all present.

The pirouette

is a 360 degree turn on the horse's hindquarters ridden at the canter. You should see the horse's hind legs striking the ground separately, just as they do when he is cantering forward. His hind leg base should remain stable throughout the turn  which, ideally, he should take six to eight strides to complete. The horse is asked to turn around his inside hind leg by gently bending around the rider's inside leg toward the direction of the turn.

Flying changes

require the horse to change his lead leg in the air. It is referred to as "in the air" because the horse does the change during the fourth, or silent, time of the canter, which is the brief moment when he has all four legs off the ground. During this fraction of a second, he reverses the relative position of all of his legs. He does this with unfailing accuracy and smoothness, without acceleration or deceleration. The rhythm of the canter is undisturbed and it is merely the lead that changes. The horse doing this maneuver has the gracefulness of a ballet dancer, supple and precise, as he jumps through each lead change.

Half pass

is where the horse steps sideways in a diagonal line across the ring with graceful bending.

In the Grand Prix dressage test, each rider must perform a set pattern of movements. Each movement is marked independently by a panel of three to five judges known as the Ground Jury. Collective marks are given by the judges which represent their judgement on each of the movements of the test regarding:

a) Gaits (freedom and regularity).

b) Impulsion (desire to move forward, elasticity of the steps, suppleness of the back, and engagement of the hindquarters).

c) Submission (attention and confidence, harmony, lightness and ease of the movements, acceptance of the bridle and lightness of the forehand).

d) Rider's position and seat (correctness and effect of the aids.)

The maximum number of points each rider can achieve for each movement is 10. Collective marks represent the subjective part of the dressage scoring system. The judges are not judging one horse against another, but rather are evaluating the horse's movements in relation to the ideal. The system of marking is as follows:

10..............Excellent
9................Very Good
8................Good
7...............Fairly Good

6...............Satisfactory
5...............Sufficient
4...............Insufficient
3...............Fairly Bad
2...............Bad
1...............Very Bad
0...............Not Performed

The test must be executed from the rider's memory. Errors of the course or a wrong sequence of movements, whether correctly performed or not, are penalized as follows:

first error................2 marks
second error..........4 marks
third error..............8 marks
fourth error...........elimination.

At the Olympic Grand Prix level, when there is harmony and effective communication between the horse and the rider and the movements are brilliant and correct, the performance commands respect for the magnificence of the horse from casual observers, as well as from seasoned horsemen.

OLYMPIC THREE-DAY EVENT

Endurance and versatility are the two hallmark qualities required of an event horse. On the first day of the competition it must be calm and obedient in the precision maneuvers of the dressage test. On the second day it must be fast and adaptable in jumping solid obstacles across all sorts of uneven ground and through water on the cross-country course. Then, it must still be resilient enough to come back on the final day to do stadium jumping with reliable continuity. Few horses qualify to reach the Olympic level due to the rigorous demands of the test.

Three-day eventing has its background in the training program for military horses. By the nature of their duties, cavalry chargers needed to be prepared for the difficulties encountered on the battlefield, as well as dangerous runs to dispatch information behind enemy lines. In addition to these requirements, the discipline of control was also needed in the movement of troops from one location to another and in the pageantry of parades. Due to its military background and the high physical requirements of eventing, the FEI did not open the Olympic competition to

women until 1964.

Because the competition covers a span of three days, it was very aptly named the Three-Day Event by the British.

Day 1: The Dressage Test

Day 2: The Speed and Endurance Test, comprised of four phases:

Phase A: Roads and Tracks. A short warm-up before the Steeplechase. Usually about 6,000 meters long, the Time Allowed is based on a speed of 220 meters per minute, enabling horse and rider to trot and canter for about 20 minutes.

Phase B: The Steeplechase, which tests the horse's ability to jump at speed over eight to ten brush fences. The course is just over 3,000 meters and is run at a speed of 690 meters per minute.

Phase C: A Longer Roads and Tracks (about 9,000 meters), ridden at 220 meters per minute. This is a recovery phase for the horse after its exertion on the steeplechase and a test of horsemanship for the rider, who must arrive in the Vet Box at the end of Phase C with the horse in a fit state to start on the final phase, the Cross-Country.

The Second Horse Inspection, a mandatory ten-minute rest period, takes place in the Vet Box at the end of Phase C. At this point the horse's physical condition is carefully checked by the Ground Jury (judges) and veterinarians. Horses that pass this inspection are then allowed to start on the Cross-Country.

Phase D: The Cross-Country is comprised of approximately 40 jumping efforts over challenging fences, banks, ditches, and water obstacles. It is approximately 7,500 meters long and is ridden at a speed of 570 meters per minute. During the entire Speed and Endurance Test, horse and rider are out on the course for almost two hours, covering a distance of nearly sixteen miles.

Day 3: The Jumping Test. Performed in an arena over colored obstacles, with poles set in cups so that they may knock-down and count as faults against the competitor. There are about fifteen jumping efforts over an 800 meter course, ridden at a speed of 400 meters per minute.

Veterinary examinations and inspections are made throughout the course of the competition. The Ground Jury and an official veterinarian will determine whether or not each horse is fit as they inspect it. They are looking for signs of lameness or unfitness no matter what the cause. If the committee decides that a horse is unfit, they are responsible for ordering the immediate withdrawal of the horse from the competition. No appeal is allowed. In addition to these precautions, at the 1996 Atlanta Games there was a veterinarian at every fence to give immediate assistance if needed.

Denny Emerson, a former international competitor, wrote an article entitled "The Event Horse is Special" which appeared in the January 12, 1990 issue of *The Chronicle of the Horse*. In the article he says, "The event horse is a special kind of competitive animal with courage and stamina. It is the kind of horse that may go down on its knees at a jump, recover, look up and say in as much as a horse can, 'Damn it, where's the next obstacle?' and then start moving towards it." Tad Coffin, a former Olympic three-day event rider, compares the horse's participation in stadium jumping the day following the strenuous competition on the cross-country course to a human athlete running the Boston Marathon one day and getting up the next morning to play five sets of tennis. Tremendous mental and physical preparation and fitness are required to achieve this level of competition.

The cross-country part of the second day of testing is indeed the most exciting and demanding segment of the speed and endurance test. Here are just some of the things the horse will be required to do, once again quoting from Denny Emerson's write-up in the *Chronicle*. "Jump over ditches. Jump up and down banks. Jump into water. Jump down a 7' drop. Jump up three steps, bouncing each one. Jump about 30 obstacles. Do this after having already done twelve miles of roads and tracks and steeplechase in the preceding hour, and having completed a precision test the day before. Jog out sound the next morning to do stadium jumping on no drugs."

Riders have a number of decisions to make on how they will ride the cross-country course. They are permitted to walk the course to analyze it and to plan their strategy. At some of the more difficult obstacles on the cross-country course, alternative ways of taking the jump are offered. These choices present weighing of talent and risks and help sort out the top horses and riders from the rest of the competitors. Weather conditions are another factor that must be calculated into the rider's decision as to how he will negotiate the obstacles. If the track is slippery from rain, or heat and humidity are present, riders may elect to guard their horse's well-being by choosing to take the time penalties that the longer but safer route represents.

All cross-country horses are required to carry 165 pounds minimum weight to ensure a fairness in this difficult part of the test. At the finish of phase D (cross-country), the rider must go to the steward in charge of weighing-in. Being below weight can be grounds for elimination. If the rider is underweight, he may include the bridle worn by the horse in addition to the saddle, girth and the pad. If he is still below minimum weight, he is eliminated.

A judge is stationed at every obstacle on the cross-country course to further ensure fairness.

Additional rules for the cross-country part of the test include:

- first refusal, run out, circle of horse at obstacle........................**20 penalties**
- second refusal, run out, circle of horse at same obstacle...............**40 penalties**
- third refusal, run out, circle of horse at same obstacle.................**elimination**
- fall of horse and/or rider at obstacle........................**60 penalties**
- second fall of horse and/or rider at obstacle during the steeplechase phase............................**elimination**
- during the cross-country phase............................**elimination**
- error of course, not rectified..................**elimination**
- omission of obstacle or red or white flag......................**elimination**
- retaking an obstacle already jumped..........................**elimination**
- jumping obstacles in the wrong order............................**elimination**

The order of go, (which horse and rider go when), is established by a draw. It remains the same for both the dressage and the speed and endurance test. On the third day, however, the stadium jumping test is run in reverse order of the point standings; that is, the last-placed horse goes first and the first-placed horse goes last.

The international rules best define the purpose of the third day of stadium jumping:

"It is not an ordinary show jumping competition, nor a test of style and endurance. Its sole object is to prove that, on the day after a severe test of endurance, the horse has retained the suppleness, energy and obedience necessary for them to continue."

At first the jumping course may appear to be fairly simple, but the pattern of the course is irregular and winding, with changes of direction to create a test of handiness and cooperation between horse and rider. Once again the rider has the opportunity to familiarize himself with the course beforehand, but the horse sees the jumps for the first time when its number is called and it goes out on course to compete. Refusals and falls are penalized as in the cross-country course, but not as severely. Knockdowns of the rails, which are set in jump cups, also incur penalties.

Scoring is as follows:
• knocking down an obstacle or a rail at the jump...............**5 penalties**

• first disobedience at an obstacle.................**10 penalties**

• second disobedience in the whole test.............**20 penalties**

• third disobedience in the whole test........................**elimination**

• first fall of horse and/or rider......................**30 penalties**

• second fall of horse and/or rider.................**elimination**

• jumping an obstacle in the wrong order.....**elimination**

• error of course not rectified............**elimination**

To obtain the final placings, a rider's penalty marks for each of the three days are added together, the winner being the one with the lowest score. In a team competition, the scores of the three best riders in each team are counted.

It is no understatement to say that three-day eventing is the ultimate test of ability and durability of both horse and rider. The Olympic three-day event is an international showcase of the most capable and versatile horses and equestrians in the world, representing their respective countries in both individual and team competition.

The range from precision elegance in the dressage test, through the breathtakingly, grueling efforts of horse and rider on the cross-country course, to the resilient continuity of these outstanding athletes on the third day of stadium jumping, presents a test of unmatched demands. Only superior athletes of the most competitive and courageous kind qualify for this discipline.

OLYMPIC SHOW JUMPING

Olympic Grand Prix Show Jumping encompasses the ultimate in beauty, speed, excitement, and risk as the top horses and riders from different nations are brought into one skillfully laid out jumping arena to compete and determine which partnership and/or nation is the best in the world.

To take a visual scan of the course alone exposes the viewer to approximately fifteen challenging obstacles of beautifully painted jumps decorated with shrubs, greenery and flowers. Each fence asks a question regarding the most expedient efforts required to safely and clearly negotiate that jump, given the abilities of the individual horses and riders.

The skill of the course designer is seen in setting a course of jumps that are just the right dimensions and distances from each other, and placing them in just the right order to sort out the top horses and riders, while at the same time making the course as safe as possible for the less experienced. Add to this scene one partnership after another of magnificent top jumpers and their dedicated riders striving for superiority against one another for the cleanest, fastest round, jumping fences approximately 4' 9" to 5' 11" high and with spreads of 6 to 7 feet. Each horse and rider partnership represents tremendous investments of time, money and hard work, plus an outstanding commitment to and love of the sport to have arrived at this top level of competition.

The competition consists of two rounds and a jump-off if necessary to determine the winners. Action and excitement are accelerated in the second round and the jump-off when fences are raised and the course is shortened. The jump-off is where the riders "go against the clock." They want to travel the shortest route possible at the fastest pace possible, and still leave all the jumps standing. Refusals, falls of both horses and riders, eliminations, last minute soundness problems of the horse, plus spectacular clear rounds over a difficult course are all factors that emotionally involve and excite the fans.

In show jumping, distances between fences are critical in determining the rider's strategy for riding the course. This is one of the main reasons why riders are permitted to walk the course before the competition, so that they can analyze the number of strides between fences and the distances in combinations. A horse's long cantering stride averages about twelve feet. Pace of approach, the number of strides and finding the right takeoff point, along with the horse's natural ability and instinct to jump cleanly, are all determining factors in whether the horse makes a clean, effortless jump. The poles on the course are set in half cups and can be dislodged by a rap of the horse's hooves. While the rider has the advantage of walking the course before the competition, when the horse enters the arena it is the first time it has seen that particular course.

Olympic Show Jumping rules are governed by the regulations laid down by the Federation Equestre International (FEI) the international equestrian rule-making organization. In the first round of each jumping competition, there is a preset time allowed. Any horse going evenly and well, with economical turns, should complete the course in this time

allowed. If it exceeds the time allowed, it will be penalized one-quarter a fault for each second or part of a second over this predetermined time.

In addition, it will be penalized:
- **4 faults for each knockdown**
- **3 faults for the first refusal**
- **6 faults for the second refusal**
- **elimination for the third refusal**

In the case of a fall, the rider may remount and continue the course, but time will run on throughout and there will be a penalty of eight faults. A fall of the horse does not mean elimination, as it does under the American Horse Shows Association rules.

Jump-offs are judged on the basis of time and jumping faults as follows:

Jumping faults are judged in the same way as in the first round.

Time is considered along these lines:

1) If one or more horses have clean rounds, the faster time wins.
2) If one horse has a clean round in a slower time, and another makes a fault in a faster time, the clean round wins.
3) If two horses have an equal number of jumping faults, the one with the faster time wins,
4) A horse with fewer jumping faults in a slower time beats a horse with more jumping faults in faster time.

Jump-offs are held to determine first place only. The lower places are either determined by time, when the jumping faults are equal, or they are placed equal when the jumping faults are equal.

Anyone who loves horses and intense action, and has an appreciation of riders committed to being the best they can be, will find Grand Prix Show Jumping at the Olympic level irresistible

GENERAL BENJAMIN LEAR

Born May 12, 1879 • Died November 1, 1966

Cavalry Journal

Benjamin Lear, Jr. was born in Canada on May 12, 1879. He was nineteen years old when he began his military career on May 1, 1898, in Denver, Colorado, where he became the 1st sergeant of Company C, 1st Colorado Infantry. He served with the Colorado Infantry until 1899 when he was commissioned a first lieutenant and went to the Philippines to serve under the distinguished cavalry leader, Colonel J. Franklin Bell, who later became Chief of Staff of the Army.

In September, 1901, he was commissioned a second lieutenant of cavalry in the Regular Army. He was a student at The Mounted Service School at Fort Riley from 1910 to 1911. He was a member of the Cavalry Rifle Team in 1911 and distinguished himself in this capacity. He also became the officer-in-charge of the Training School for Farriers and Horseshoers in June of 1911. He was a member of the first U.S. Army Equestrian Team that participated in the Olympic Games held in Stockholm, Sweden, in 1912.

At the 1912 Olympics he competed in the Military Competition, better known today as the Three-Day Event. He had an individual ranking of sixth place competing against 27 other riders, only fifteen of whom finished the course. He had the highest American score. He rode the Army horse named Poppy and helped the United States Team to win the bronze medal. Benjamin Lear also competed in the Grand Prix Jumping competition, along with his teammates, and they placed fourth among the six teams that competed. He rode Poppy in this event also.

In 1913, Captain Lear wrote a very informative article for *The Rasp*, an annual school publication on which he served in the capacity of assistant editor. The article was a detailed description of the preparation of the first U.S. Army Equestrian Olympic Team, beginning on January 24, 1912, when the War Department designated five officers to represent the United States in the Olympic Games in Stockholm in July of the same year. The brief six months' preparation was hampered by a number of factors including: 1) Frost and snow on the ground during those winter months, thereby limiting outdoor work; 2) Three of the officers were instructors who were required to maintain their regular duties in addition to preparing the horses and; 3) Finding horses that were capable of competing in the rigors of the military tests. Captain Lear said "The horses we started working with had practically none of the qualities of a thoroughly trained military animal, except in the rough, and all of them had to be developed within three months - and this at a time of the year not well suited for the work."

"The horses left for New York by express on June 10, arriving there on June 12, and were loaded on board the 'Finland' on June 14. On board the ship they were very comfortable, with plenty of fresh air and, during the trip, were exercised by being led from one to one and a half hours a day around a small circle in the lower deck, about twenty five yards in circumference."

"The ship arrived at Stockholm on June 30. The horses were unloaded and taken to the military stables of one of the artillery regiments. The competitions were to start on July 13, which gave us thirteen days to get our horses into condition for these severe tests. We found the horses very soft after their trip and capable of doing nothing but slow work for some days. This we tried to make as hard as possible by climbing hills, going through mud and various things to gradually draw out and harden the muscles. Each animal was required to carry 176 1/2 pounds." The general conclusion was that, in view of the brief preparation and the fact that the European horses outclassed the Army-bred horses ridden by the U.S. team, that they had indeed given an honorable showing in spite of the handicaps they encountered.

Benjamin Lear had a long and distinguished career in the Army. He held a number of positions in the cavalry, including that of Senior Instructor of the Department of Equitation in 1919 and then the Director of Equitation at the Cavalry School at Fort Riley until 1921.

He had risen to the rank of lieutenant general just before America's entry into World War II. It was in July of 1941 that an incident occurred that dubbed him with the nickname of 'Yoo-Hoo.' Known as a strong believer in discipline, on this particular day in July he happened to be out playing golf on one of the Memphis courses. Within sight of the range where he was playing were some young ladies in shorts, also playing golf. All was well until a motorized regiment, returning from Middle Tennessee maneuvers to Camp Robinson, Arkansas, drove past the Memphis golf course. The soldiers whistled and shouted "Yoo-Hoo" at the young women. Lieutenant General Lear witnessed and heard all of this. He stepped out and ordered the regiment to proceed immediately to Camp Robinson - and then ordered the troops back to Memphis, a round trip of 300 miles.

Fifteen miles outside Memphis, Lear halted the convoy of 325 officers and men, and the men were ordered to march the rest of the way under the blazing sun. The incident reverberated in Congress, where there was criticism of "grouchy old golfing generals" and an inquiry into the military precedent for "mass punishment of guilty and innocent alike."

General Lear defended his action and explained that he felt that the soldiers' conduct was a "disgrace to the Army." He went on to say, "A high state of discipline is the foundation upon which all military attainment is based. Loose conduct and rowdyism cannot be tolerated among personnel of any army. I am responsible, also, that members of the Second Army treat the civilian population with respect and consideration."

The 'Yoo-Hoo' incident followed Lear during the war. When the General returned from Europe in 1945, hundreds of GIs on the Boston pier shouted "Yoo-Hoo" as he stepped ashore. Lear was Deputy Commander under General Dwight D. Eisenhower during the latter part of World War II. He retired from the Army in December of 1945 and moved to Memphis.

Lt. Benjamin Lear on
Fencing Girl

Courtesy Col. C. Anderson

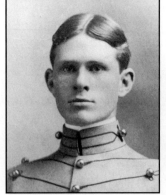

CAPT. JOHN CARTER MONTGOMERY

Born 1882 • Died June 7, 1948
West Point Class of 1903

John Carter Montgomery, known by his West Point classmates and most of his friends as 'Cit', was born in Kentucky. Quite naturally, from his earliest years, he was interested in anything that had to do with horses, and nothing else in the Army or in business during his entire life quite took equal rank in his mind.

He entered West Point in 1899. A natural leader and one with great energy, he sometimes found himself in hot water, as was bound to happen when a young man of his nature was surrounded by the restrictions then placed on cadets. He was a good student who could have graduated considerably above the middle of his class, where his marks placed him, had he been more serious about his studies. However, where horses were concerned, he always shone brilliantly and was considered the best horseman of his class. He played on the polo team and rode in exhibitions.

Upon graduation he was assigned to the 7th Cavalry at Fort Riley. He was a member of the first Army Equestrian team that was sent, in 1912, to Stockholm to represent the United States at the Olympics. In Stockholm, he competed in both the Three-Day Event and Grand Prix Jumping on a horse named Deceive. He helped the U.S. Three-Day Event Team win a bronze medal and, in Grand Prix Jumping, he and Deceive contributed to a fourth place team standing. Captain Montgomery also played for the Army in international polo competitions and won a bronze medal as a member of the 1920 polo team at Antwerp.

Montgomery served in World War I and was awarded a battlefield promotion to Colonel by General Pershing. No similar promotion on the battlefield was made by General Pershing during the war. Later in his life he became Financial Vice-President and Director of the First Boston Corporation which grew to be the largest investment banking firm in America.

The U.S. Army Equestrian Team, bronze medal winners in the "Military Championships," now called the Three Day Event, 1912 Stockholm Olympics. Benjamin Lear on Poppy, John Montgomery on Deceive and Guy Henry on Chiswell.

MAJOR GENERAL GUY V. HENRY, JR.

Born January 28, 1875 • Died November 29, 1967
West Point Class of 1898

Guy Henry accumulated innumerable credits to his name as a horseman and as a pioneer in equestrian training and competitions while serving in the Cavalry. His military career spanned a period of fifty years, during which he fought in the Spanish American War, in World War I and in World War II. He was awarded the Silver Star for gallantry in action against insurgent forces at Balantang, Panay, in the Philippine Islands in November 1899. When he died at the age of 92, he had some 87 years of riding activity behind him. In 1906 he was the first of many U.S. officers to attend the full course of equitation at the French Cavalry School at Saumur. This course influenced him significantly in preparing a program of instruction which came to be used at Fort Riley and which established continuity in instruction and training. He was also a strong influence in promoting advanced equitation courses at the Cavalry School, and was creator of the modern U.S. Army doctrine in equitation.

In the summer of 1911, when Guy Henry, Jr. was serving as the Head of the Department of Equitation at Fort Riley, and as such was the senior instructor of equitation, the United States Army agreed to take on the task of preparing an equestrian team to compete in the 1912 Olympics in Stockholm, Sweden. The responsibility of organizing this first Army Equestrian Team fell, quite naturally, into the capable hands of Captain Henry, who assumed the task in addition to his instructional duties.

The few possible team candidates that were available trained hard under Captain Henry's supervision, and the team gradually began to take shape. The Army sent them to the 1911 Olympia International Show in London and, although it was an indoor show, it gave the U.S. team insight into the European rules and a glimpse of how they themselves compared

with other more experienced teams. On their return from London, they knew their work was cut out for them. With determination, hard work and a strong desire to represent their country honorably, they proceeded with their training.

In his autobiography, "The Guy V. Henry, Jr. Papers", the following reference was made regarding the trans-Atlantic shipping of the Olympic team to Stockholm. "We sailed from New York on the 'Finland'. This ship was chartered by the Olympic Committee, and all American participants in the Games were aboard her. This made the trip interesting, as training continued throughout, each sport doing its best to keep participants in good physical condition. The track and field men exercised around the deck; the bicyclists, on stationary bicycles with brakes on them; the swimmers, in canvas tanks with belts whereby the coach could put proper resistance against the swimmer; the shooters, at targets on the stern of the ship. We exercised our horses by leading them for about an hour, twice a day, on a small track around one of the hatches. The horses got stale and sick of being led around this small track. My horse, Chiswell, showed his resentment one day by just touching Lt. Graham's nose with a full length kick. A fraction of an inch more, and it would have been a dead Lt. Graham. As it was, he simply suffered a broken nose. When the grooms became seasick, the officers and some of the wives, including Mrs. Henry, had to assist in caring for the horses and in their daily exercise. The trip lasted about fifteen days. The 'Finland' was the largest ship that had ever entered Stockholm's harbor."

"The 'Military' event consisted of an Endurance Phase, a Jumping Phase and a Training Phase. I rode Chiswell in this event. On one portion of the endurance phase I was riding at speed over the steeplechase course, and two British competitors who had gone

Guy Henry on the remarkable Chiswell.

Courtesy Col. Richard Gruenther

before me had been killed. One of the obstacles was a pretty big bank. As I approached this obstacle, I knew Chiswell could not jump it and that he didn't even want to try. I determined Chiswell was at least going to make an effort to jump this bank. As he took off, my heart was in my mouth, because I knew he could not clear it. However, almost like a cat, he jumped onto its narrow top and down on the other side. I only got a small penalty for his failure to actually clear the bank whereas, if he had refused, or if I had received a fall, the penalty would have been very heavy. Chiswell continued this attitude in the cross-country phase, which was filled with ditches. We went over them all by my driving."

At the 1912 Olympics, Guy Henry, Jr., rode in all three competitions - Dressage, the Three-Day Event and Jumping. When the competition was over, the United States had won a bronze team medal in the Military (the forerunner of the present Three-Day Event), and had placed fourth as a team in the Grand Prix Jumping; a very respectable showing indeed for a team inexperienced in competing against

horsemen from nations having a far greater number of years of tradition and training behind them.

Quoting once again from his autobiographical papers, Captain Henry expresses, "It was a great pleasure to us personally to receive, as representatives of the U.S. Army, our bronze medals from the King of Sweden."

Born into a family with a long line of distinguished Army officers, Guy V. Henry, Jr., entered this world in a primitive log and canvas hut in the freezing cold of a January winter at Fort Robinson in the Nebraska Territory. Some of his first visitors in this remote area were a number of friendly Sioux Indians. The Army at that time, with Guy's father serving as captain, was trying to protect the Indians' land from an increasing number of prospectors pushing west and showing very little respect for the Indian ways or their land. Within six months the great Sioux uprising would occur but, on the night of Guy Henry's birth, they did a dance to celebrate the birth of this 'white baby with the lusty cry.' Guy's early years were spent as an officer's son at Fort Robinson.

During this formative time in his childhood, his primary association was with soldiers, Indian scouts, frontiersmen and Indians. It was through their influence that he developed his initial knowledge and skill in riding. His fast pony, Prince, was the envy, not only of the other post children, but also of the Indians. Riding at full speed across the open terrain had a profound bearing on his equestrian participation later in life.

From the age of seven, young Guy had set his sights on going to West Point. When he entered the Military Academy in June of 1894, he fully realized the limitations of his schooling in one remote outpost after another. He found the academic work of his four years there very strenuous. On the other hand, he was far ahead of most of his classmates in equitation and practical soldiering. Over his lifetime he held a number of interesting positions and his influence was significant. Without ever having written a book on horsemanship he was, nonetheless, one of the creators of the methods and training systems used by the Cavalry.

In 1905 and 1906 he was an aide to President Theodore Roosevelt prior to his duty as Commandant of Cadets at the USMA. He was Director of Equitation at the USMA in 1916. He became Chief of the Cavalry in 1930 and served in that office until 1934. From 1935, until his retirement in 1939, he served as the Commandant of the Cavalry School at Fort Riley, Kansas.

In his later years he was a judge in many top level competitions, including two Olympic Games. He was a director of the civilian United States Equestrian Team, as well as the American Horse Shows Association and New York's National Horse Show Association. From 1930 to 1938 he was President for four years and then Vice-President for another four years of the Federation Equestre International. He was the first and only American to hold this position. In those days the office of President of the FEI was given to a qualified horseman from the country that was hosting the next Olympic Games. Guy Henry held this position in preparation for the 1932 Los Angeles Olympics and, as such, it was he who directed the equestrian events for these Games.

Guy Henry's involvement and influence spanned the entire period when equestrian Olympic competitions were open only to military personnel. Starting with his role as captain and organizer of the first U.S. equestrian team at the 1912 Stockholm Olympics, he was also coach for two Olympic Games, chairman of the U.S. Olympic Equestrian Committee, a judge at two Olympic Games, and Chef d'Equipe for the U.S. 1948 Olympic team, which ended the military era. He dedicated his entire life to participation in and promotion of equestrian sport and was held in high esteem in equestrian circles throughout the world. The members of the USET who have followed him continue to benefit from his far-reaching contribution.

USMA Library

LT. EPHRAIM FOSTER GRAHAM

Born August 10, 1881 • *Died December 23, 1962*
West Point Class of 1903

Ephraim Foster Graham was born in the rolling hills north of Nashville, Tennessee, where his grandfather had established his home after moving from the original family settlement in North Carolina. He grew up in this environment and never once left his native state until his entry into the U.S. Military Academy in September of 1899. The continuity of those early years stamped him indelibly with an integrity, a love of good sportsmanship, and a sense of chivalry that characterized the Old South.

At West Point he found the ideal environment for expression and development of his strength of character which was so clearly evident throughout his life. His athletic ability led him into a variety of sports as a cadet and carried him to the captaincy of the baseball team of 1903.

Upon graduation he was commissioned in the Cavalry and the following years afforded additional opportunities for participation in many competitions that were the hallmark of the cavalryman. His service included assignments with the 10th and 14th Cavalry, Aide at the White House during President Taft's administration, and riding instructor at his Alma Mater.

Whenever he could find the opportunity, he played polo, steeplechased, and rode in horse shows that included some of America's finest competitions. He also earned renown abroad as a member of the U.S. Army Olympic Team in Stockholm, Sweden, in 1912, where he rode the horse, Connie, and was on the three-day event team that won the bronze medal. He also participated in the International Horse Show in London on the occasion of King George V's coronation.

In 1916 Colonel Graham was in a tragic accident during a polo game, which left him critically injured. He was serving as a riding instructor at West Point at the time. His recovery was a tribute to his determination and to the loyalty and encouragement of his family and friends who saw him through this difficult time. Despite a resulting handicap, which he carried with him the rest of his life, he carried on to complete 16 more years of active duty in the service that he loved. The years before his retirement in 1922 included tours at Ethan Allen, Vermont; Schofield barracks, Hawaii; and Forts Bliss and Sam Houston in Texas. After retirement he remained on active duty until 1932, serving in ROTC work in Tennessee and Missouri. In 1933 he made his home in San Antonio. Among the highlights of this period were his visits to the Military Academy for the 45th and 50th reunions of his classmates of 1903. During his last years he fought valiantly and uncomplainingly against the ravages of age and his old injuries and lived to enjoy his golden wedding anniversary in 1962.

Ephraim Graham on Connie
U.S. Military History Institute

Colonel Sloan Doak

Born January 28, 1886 • Died August 10, 1965
West Point Class of 1907

Although born in Taylor, Texas, Sloan Doak came from a long line of distinguised Virginian ancestors. His father, A.V. Doak served as surgeon with General Lee's cavalry throughout the Civil War and surrendered with him at Appomattox Court House.

During his early years in Texas, Sloan developed a life-long interest in horses. At West Point, he played on the cadet polo team and became known for his horsemanship. A classmate once recalled, "There were stirring days in the riding hall at West Point, when Sloan's superb horsemanship was displayed taking four horses abreast over the jumps, dismounting and mounting at the gallop, and facing to the rear as four horses cleared the obstacles. It was to no one's surprise that, upon graduation, he chose the cavalry." Subsequently, the greater part of his service was to be spent as an instructor in equitation at the Cavalry School at Fort Riley, Kansas. While at Fort Riley, he played polo extensively and was a member of the winning Western Circuit Championship Team, in Chicago, in 1915.

He represented his country three times at the Olympics as a rider in 1920, 1924 and 1928. At the 1924 Games in Paris, he won an individual bronze medal in the Three-Day Event on a horse named Pathfinder, taking first place in the steeplechase portion of the course. Colonel Doak was Captain of the U.S. Three-Day Event Team in the 1928 Olympics in Amsterdam.

In 1932 he served as chairman of the Ground Jury which judged all the Olympic equestrian events at Los Angeles and was the first American to be so honored. From 1931 through 1941 he served as a judge in nearly all the top horse shows on the East Coast, including Madison Square Garden in 1941. He also served as Zone chairman for the American Horse Shows Association for many years.

Colonel Hiram E. Tuttle

Born December 22, 1882 • Died November 11, 1956

Shelburne Studios

Hiram Tuttle was born on December 22, 1882, in Dexter, Maine. He grew up on a farm. His love of horses began with riding on the back of his father's plow horse, as his father worked the field, and it continued throughout his lifetime.

His musical education started at the age of eight, and he later studied violin under the direction of the solo violinist at the Boston Symphony Orchestra. He also studied orchestral and choral directing and used these skills to earn money to put himself through college.

He became a member of the state bar and practiced law in Waltham, Massachusetts, just outside Boston. Hiram Tuttle was a versatile and talented man. In addition to being a lawyer, he was also a master mechanic, a talented violinist, a watchmaker, and was skilled in dramatics. While at Fort Riley, he was a leader and director of the Drama Club productions for several years.

When he realized that war was imminent, he enlisted in officers' training. When World War I was officially declared, he was commissioned a second lieutenant in the National Army and served throughout the war as a Motor Transport officer in the Brownsville, Texas district. His selection of the cavalry branch of service and his business experience eventually saw him transferred to the Quartermaster Corps. After the war, Colonel Tuttle attended the Troop

Officers' Class at Fort Riley in 1923 and 1924, and then served in remount work at Fort Robinson, Nebraska. While there, he was in charge of buying and overseeing the breaking of horses and mules for the Army to make them suitable for the service for which they were intended.

It was as a dressage rider that Colonel Tuttle gained his greatest fame. He represented the United States team in the Olympic Games at Los Angeles in 1932, and at Berlin in 1936. In addition to his individual bronze medal in 1932, he also contributed strongly to achieving the team bronze medal in dressage that same year.

The horse Colonel Tuttle rode at the Los Angeles Olympics was a Thoroughbred from France. Hiram once spent a summer vacation on Long Island, working with E.Q. McVitty's polo ponies. Hiram wouldn't hear of taking pay for his work. McVitty, however, figured out another way to show appreciation for the work his friend had done. When Hiram was back at his job in the remount office in

Hiram Tuttle on the great dressage horse Olympic, who lived up to his name in the 1932 Games.

Courtesy of Mrs. Gladys Tuttle

26

Col. Tuttle demonstrating the "backwards canter" on Vast. Their exhibitions together raised money for the early Olympic teams, and included command performances for Franklin Roosevelt and Winston Churchill in 1943.

U.S. Cavalry Museum, Ft. Riley, Kansas

Washington D.C., a courier delivered a message which read, "Your horse has been delivered. Please pay $1.00." He paid the fee and this is how he acquired Olympic, the horse which lived up to the destiny of his name at the 1932 Olympics, where he won the individual bronze medal.

For years, Hiram Tuttle was known as the outstanding rider of dressage in the United States. It was at Fort Riley that he developed such great dressage horses as the famed Olympic, Vast, Si Murray and Peter Brown. At exhibitions he demonstrated his horses' skill and training before hundreds of spectators at the National Horse Show in Madison Square Garden, New York, and he was a featured attraction at other horse shows and livestock exhibitions across the country. One year he raised $8,000 from his dressage appearances to help finance the Olympic team. Colonel Tuttle's horse, Vast, became widely known at these exhibitions because sometimes he used

only silk thread instead of reins during the performance. These exhibitions were so highly regarded among the horse-loving populace that, in the fall of 1943, Colonel Tuttle was called to Washington for a command performance before President Franklin D. Roosevelt and British Prime Minister Winston Churchhill.

Hiram Tuttle owned all the horses he rode. They were like members of his family. He refused to sell any of his highly trained animals. When he retired from the Army, he got special permission from Washington to keep his horses, at no expense to the Army, at Fort Riley, only five miles from his home in Junction City. As long as he was able, after his retirement, he worked with his horses daily at Fort Riley. Later, after he became ill, he still went as often as possible to see his beloved mounts.

Colonel Tuttle died on November 11, 1956. He was buried at Fort Riley Cemetery with full military honors.

USMA Library

Col. Earl F. "Tommy" Thomson

Born August 14, 1900 • Died July 5, 1971
West Point Class of 1922

Col. Earl F. Thomson competed in three Olympic Games and won five medals in the process. (To date, Mike Plumb is the only rider from the United States to win more Olympic medals, with a total of six). In 1932, on a mare named Jenny Camp, Colonel Thomson won an individual silver medal and a team gold medal in eventing. In 1936 he won another individual silver medal in eventing, once again riding Jenny Camp. In 1948, at the age of 48, he won a team silver medal in dressage on a horse named Pancraft and a team gold medal in eventing on a horse named Reno Rhythm. He and Frank Henry are the only Americans to have won medals in both the Three-Day Event and the Grand Prix Dressage competition in the same Olympic Games. There can be little doubt that he was the most successful American military rider of all time. His service spanned three Olympic Games and yielded two gold medals and three silver. In 1952, he officiated at the Olympic Games.

Earl Thomson was born in Cleveland, Ohio. After his retirement from the Army he became a mathematics teacher and obtained his Masters Degree in Science from Purdue University in 1959. In the early 1960s, he went on to do his graduate study at both the University of California in Santa Barbara and the University of Southern California. His extra curricular activities included polo, show jumping, sailing and golf.

Earl Thomson was an outstanding all-round horseman whose partnership with the Army-bred bay mare, Jenny Camp, remains an example of the high achievements a great horse and an outstanding rider can reach together. Jenny Camp was related to Democrat, the great Army

Olympic show jumper. Both horses were born at the Fort Robinson Remount station and shared the same sire, Gordon Russell, who was donated to the Army by the American Racing Association. Jenny Camp was a responsible partner in helping to win three Olympic medals for her rider.

At the 1936 Olympics in Berlin, Jenny Camp was the United States' best mount. She was an exceptionally fine event horse. Standing 16.1 hands, she was ten years old in 1936 and at the peak of her condition. The United States Army team was a heavy favorite to win the Three-Day Event in that year.

The organizing officials of the Berlin Olympics, under Hitler's direction, were naturally out to show the supremacy of their athletes, especially that of their military equestrian riders. To a large majority of the foreign competitors it seemed that the course had been set up to favor the German team, although there was never any sound proof to confirm this suspicion.

About one-third of the way through the cross-country course, there was an obstacle that required the horse to jump over a post and rail fence, land in a pond and then jump out the other side over another fence. Such obstacles were normally constructed with an even bottom in about two feet of water and considered to be more of a mental, rather than a physical, challenge.

"Tommy" Thomson on Jenny Camp, who helped win three Olympic medals for her partner.

Courtesy Col. Charles Anderson

28

The approach to this obstacle was on a turn and, to save precious time, almost all the non-German horses attempted to take the direct approach into the water. The horses taking this approach had great difficulty keeping their footing on the landing, and there was a great deal of flailing and struggling on their part, and on the part of the riders, to prevent going down. There was speculation as to whether several horses taking the direct approach had caused a treacherous hole in the pond's bottom, or whether one had been deliberately dug by the German course designer. One thing was known for certain - several horses had a difficult time at this obstacle.

The first American horse to negotiate the pond was Trailolka, ridden by Captain Carl Raguse. Raguse was nearly unseated on the landing, but clung to the gelding's sides and managed to hold on as he struggled out. The next American partnership to approach this jump was Slippery Slim, ridden by Captain John M. Williams, an experienced veteran. It was Slim's last fence, for he broke a foreleg struggling to recover his balance in the water and had to be destroyed. This heartbreaking incident eliminated the Americans from the team competition because of the requirement that all three riders and horses had to complete all three days of the test.

The last U.S. competitor to approach this controversial jump was Captain Thomson, riding Jenny Camp. On the landing, the pair went completely under water, but Captain Thomson was able to hold onto the reins and, with difficulty, was able to remount and continue.

All three of the German riders approached this jump slowly and jumped it near the opposite side, where the water was much more shallow and the bottom even. Why did they all take this longer but safe approach? Was it coincidence or insider information? No one was ever to know for certain. On the day after the competition, because of several objections by foreign competitors, the water from this jump was drained away. No hole was found; only a sloping away of the ground

from the jump was seen to explain the difficult footing for the horses. It had rained the night before the cross-country event, making the water deeper. Although there had been an order to drain off the excess water, this had not been carried out, and no one could explain why this had not been done.

The jumping portion on the third day of competition was anti-climatic. The Germans were sure winners. Due to exhaustion and stiffness from their exertion at the pond obstacle, many of the other horses were not up to their usual form and some riders, like Captain Raguse, chose not to push their horses to rally for a lost cause.

Captain Thomson presented Jenny Camp on the final day of competition. Determined that the Germans were not just going to be handed the honors without earning them, and disappointed at the toll the cross-country course had taken on the American team, he and Jenny Camp were at the in-gate to contend with when their number was called. Even though she was tired and muscle sore, Jenny Camp remained a horse that gave 100%. The mark of true greatness is often seen when an athlete, be it human or equine, gives beyond what can reasonably be expected and excels in performance. Such was the case on that August day in 1936 when Earl Thomson and Jenny Camp won the individual silver medal in eventing, showing without a doubt their versatility and durability under gruelling circumstances and their brilliance as a partnership.

Colonel Thomson retired from the Army on August 31, 1954. During his army career he was decorated with the Silver Star, the Legion of Merit and the Bronze Star Medal with Oak Leaf Cluster.

Aboard Jenny Camp at the 1932 Olympics. He was captain of the gold medal team in the Three-Day Event in Los Angeles.

Courtesy Col. Charles Anderson

USMA Library

BRIG. GEN. HARRY D. CHAMBERLIN

Born May 19, 1887 • Died September 29, 1944
West Point Class of 1910

Harry Chamberlin was an outstanding horseman and trainer. He participated and excelled in hundreds of equestrian events. In fact, he was an all-round outstanding athlete, being also a competent performer in boxing, track and football. In the 1909 Army vs. Navy football game, Chamberlin ran 95 yards for a touchdown in the last few minutes of play to win the game for Army.

He had a long and brilliant military career and was admired as an outstanding line officer and a keen strategist on the battlefield. In recognition of his equestrian skills, the Cavalry sent him to the French Cavalry School at Saumur, and to the Italian Cavalry School at Tor di Quinto, to help him gain an even greater expertise and an insight into European equestrian training methods. On his graduation from Tor di Quinto, the Italian Commandant remarked, when he handed him his diploma, "The pupil has surpassed the master." In rounding out his study abroad, he also had the privilege of being an observer at the English Cavalry School in Weedon.

In 1919, as a member of the Army Equitation Team in the Inter-Allied Games in Paris, he won second place in the Three-Day Event. He competed in three Olympic Games - 1920, 1928 and 1932. At the 1932 Olympics in Los Angeles, riding Pleasant Smiles, he was captain of the Three-Day Event team that won the gold medal. During these same Olympics he also won the individual silver medal in the Grand Prix Jumping, riding a mare named Show Girl. Harry was also an avid polo player.

He served at Fort Riley as the head of the Department of Horsemanship. His influence there added much to the organization of their Cavalry School. After a thorough study of the best points of all types of riding seats, General Chamberlin determined that the forward riding and jumping seat served both the horse and rider's efforts in competition better than any other. Some feel that the legacy of the forward seat (sometimes called the Chamberlin Seat) was the greatest of his achievements and the overall most important contribution from the military era of riders. Many of the West Pointers from the thirties and forties may still have in their attic a two-page description of the forward seat.

Harry Chamberlin wrote several articles on riding, horsemanship and training. He was also the author of two highly respected books entitled *Riding and Schooling Horses* and *Training Hunters, Jumpers and Hacks.*

Harry D. Chamberlin on Pleasant
Smiles, members of the gold medal
team in the 1932 "Military."
Courtesy Col. Richard Gruenther

COL. ISAAC LEONARD KITTS

Josepho Studios

Born January 15, 1896 • Died April 1, 1953

Isaac Kitts was born in Oswego, New York. He had finished three and a half years of seminary when World War I broke out and he decided to join the Army. It was not until 1940, after continued study, that he became ordained as an Episcopal priest. During his army career, he assisted the Episcopal Chaplains wherever he was stationed and would conduct the Sunday service when the Chaplain was unavailable.

The article 'The Two Colonels' by Glencairn Bowlby, covers that fact that both Colonel Isaac Leonard Kitts and his son, Colonel Alfred Kitts, became leaders in dressage when this discipline was new in our country. The following is an account of Colonel Isaac Kitts' equestrian involvement while he was in the Army.

"He attended the Army Equitation Schools at Fort Riley and Fort Sill, eventually taking the Advanced Equitation Courses. Later, he returned to teach Advanced Equitation in both places. Len, as Kitts was called by his friends, was a pretty good polo player too. He become good friends with Will Rogers, the cowboy star, who once captained an opposing team, and they often played against each other in Oklahoma. (Mrs. Kitts also rode well and she became a member of the Army's only ladies' polo team.) Another talent of Len Kitts' was show jumping and he rode with the Artillery team."

"In 1931 he started to study dressage,

working from books, (translations of French dressage writers Baucher, L'Hotte, Beudant and Fillis) and from limited experience at the Artillery and Cavalry Schools. He and Colonel (then Captain) Hiram E. Tuttle got together and taught each other, since there were no other experienced instructors in the United States at that time. The Army assigned Kitts a Thoroughbred mare called American Lady, who had been badly injured in steeplechasing and was a bit of a rebel. On their first ride together she ran away for eleven miles in the wide open stretches of Fort Sill. Finding that her rider was still with her at the end, she decided to be more cooperative from then on. Although never an easy mare, she became one of the top dressage horses of her time."

"Incredible as it may seem, Len Kitts and American Lady, with no previous dressage experience, and no qualified experts to help, worked up to Grand Prix level in one year! In 1932 the team of Captains Tuttle, Kitts and Alvin H. Moore, with their three horses, repre-

Isaac Kitts on his American Lady, at the 1932 Los Angeles Games.

U.S. Cavalry Museum, Ft. Riley, Kansas

Col. Kitts and American Lady. The mare had been badly injured in a steeplechase accident and was known for being difficult, once running away with Col. Kitts for eleven miles! She went on, however, to be one of the top dressage horses of her time.

H.C. Elmore

sented the United States. This green team managed to win the bronze medal. (Due to the post war recession and the general economic climate of 1932, only three teams competed in dressage in 1932.) The winning of the bronze medal did inspire them and, when they returned home, they continued to work on dressage with their eyes on the 1936 Olympic Games.

"In 1936 the entire Kitts family, consisting of father, mother and three sons, sailed for Europe on the SS Roosevelt with American Lady. They all lived in Berlin while Len and Lady gained more experience competing in some of the European dressage shows - there being none in the United States." The United States Team for the 1936 Olympics again

included Tuttle and Kitts, with Stanley Babcock as the third member. No American rider finished in the individual placings this time, and the team placed ninth in a field of nine teams competing.

Len Kitts joined the ROTC unit at Culver Military Academy from 1939 until 1942, when he was sent to China as Chief of Staff of Z Force. After the war he specialized in equestrian sports, such as jumping, polo and hunting. In 1946 he returned to the United States to retire from the Army. Not long afterwards, he rejoined the staff of the Culver Military Academy in Indiana, this time as Director of Horsemanship. He remained there until he died in 1953. He is buried in Arlington National Cemetery.

CAPTAIN ALVIN H. MOORE

Born November 11, 1891 • Died (unknown)

Courtesy Col;. Charles Anderson

Captain Alvin Moore was a member of the dressage bronze medal winning team of the U.S. Army Equestrian Team at the 1932 Olympics in Los Angeles. He trained with Captain Hiram Tuttle, riding a black Thoroughbred horse named Walter Pat. Together they placed seventh individually and third as a team. Only three teams competed at this event, and the American team was drawn first in the order of go. The captain of each team, in turn, assigned the order in which the members of his team would ride. Captain Moore was the first rider to compete.

A quote from *The Horse in the 1932 Olympiad* by Captain Lara P. Good states, "The natural inclination to nervousness or stage fright on an occasion of a first competitive exhibition of its kind in America might have been with Captain Moore but, if so, no one was able to detect it."

Participation in the 1932 Olympics was the lowest it had been, even though the level of competition was excellent. Two major factors accounted for this - the Great Depression and the geographical isolation of California. Even though the United States was in the midst of Prohibition, an exception was made for the French, who claimed that wine was an essential component of their diet. Automatic timing and the photo-finish camera were introduced at the 1932 Olympics.

Captain Moore was the reserve member of the dressage team at the 1936 Olympics, but did not compete.

Capt. Alvin Moore, at 1932 Los Angeles Olympics, on Water Pat.

U.S. Cavalry Museum, Ft. Riley, Kansas

LT. EDWIN YANCY ARGO

Born September 22, 1895 • Died March 10, 1962

Courtesy Col. Charles Anderson

Edwin Yancy Argo was born in Alabama. He entered the United States Military Academy in June of 1915 but he did not graduate from the USMA. As an inexperienced young fellow from the deep south, life as a "Plebe" was not altogether an easy experience for him. While he could take mathematics and science in his stride, it was his poor foundation in English that gave him so much trouble and caused him to feel that he was not USMA material. Even though he was scheduled to return the following fall, he elected instead, against his parents' wishes, to put himself through Alabama Polytechnic Institute.

In the spring of 1917, Eddie enlisted in the National Guard and was soon called to duty as a private, driving a two-mule garbage wagon. He decided he could do better than that. By the light of a kerosene lantern in a tent, he studied and passed, with ample success, the examination to become a Second Lieutenant in the Field Artillery of the United States Army. Although he often considered it, he never obtained a college degree. He did, however, improve his use of the English language and became a successful public speaker.

Eddie was a graduate of both the Cavalry School Advanced Class in Horsemanship and the Italian Cavalry School. He was a member of the first Field Artillery Horse Show Team from 1929 to 1934 and was the team captain throughout those five years.

In the eulogy by Eddie's wife at his funeral, one of the riding stories that she related about him was the following:

"The Army Horse Show team was in New York and about to embark for contests overseas. From experience, they knew that the horses required several days to regain their equilibrium after balancing from the ship's motion for the time of the crossing, plus a regaining of condition from lack of exercise, and they didn't have that time."

"Somehow, Eddie 'finagled' from storage the treadmill used on the stage set of the play 'Ben Hur.' Every day on the ship, the horses were exercised. At first it took some handling and persuasion but, when they landed, the horses were ready for the contests."

Lieutenant Argo was a member of the 1928 and the 1932 Olympic teams. In 1932, as a team member in the Three-Day Event competition, he placed eighth in a field of fourteen competitors with only nine of them finishing. He rode a Thoroughbred chestnut mare named Honolulu Tomboy, a 15.2 1/2 hand, six-year-old who had been bred at Fort Reno. Eddie always referred to her as "a lovely mare."

The following excerpt is from an article written about the 1932 Games by Major W.M. Grimes, who was an assistant to Major General Guy V. Henry. This article appeared in the issues of both *The Cavalry Journal* and in *The Field Artillery Journal* after the 1932 Games.

"Prior to the team's departure from Fort Rosencrans, (the Southern California training area used by the 1932 team for about six months before the Olympics), Lieutenant Argo slipped and fell on a staircase and dislocated his shoulder. When he rode in the 1932 Olympics, he had his shoulder strapped to his side. The training (dressage) test caused him no difficulty, but the water jump on the steeplechase was a disastrous fence for him. Here Argo's shoulder popped out once more. The excruciating pain caused intense suffering, and it was only by the greatest display of grit and determination that Lieutenant Argo carried on, riding a distance of approximately twenty miles and negotiating some forty odd fences. He scored high enough to warrant an individual classification of eighth for the endurance phase. After the water jump, it became necessary for Lieutenant Argo to radically change his seat in order to ease the strain from his injured shoulder."

"Captain Argo, riding Honolulu Tomboy in the Stadium Jumping phase, made a remarkable performance; not a fault at any of the jumps -

only a time penalty of 0.75. He finished first in this last competition!"

Along with teammates, Captain Earl Thomson and Major Harry Chamberlin, who placed second and fourth individually, Lieutenant Argo helped the United States to win the Three-Day Event team gold medal at the 1932 Los Angeles Olympics.

After the 1932 Olympics, Eddie turned his attention to the military side of soldiering. Eventually he had to retire due to physical disability from injury to his knees during his riding years. Prior to his retirement he was Commandant of Cadets and Professor of Military Science and Tactics at Louisiana State University and both organized and directed the Department of Student Life while he was there. However, because of his injured knees and the complete absence of elevators, he was unable to access the upper floors of the university.

After resting for a while, he was employed in the Public Relations Department of the International Paper Company and became manager of the Shreveport office, which was the first district office outside New York. He continued in this position until his death from cancer on March 10, 1962.

LT. COL. FRANK SHERMAN HENRY

Born December 15, 1909 • *Died August 25, 1989*
West Point Class of 1933

Frank Henry is the only member of the United States Equestrian Team to have won three Olympic medals at one Olympic competition. At the 1948 Games in London, he was on the silver medal-winning dressage team, in addition to winning both the individual silver medal and the team gold medal in the Three-Day Event. Frank Henry and Earl Thomson were three-day event riders who trained with Bob Borg to learn dressage so that the U.S. could also have a dressage team. Neither of them had been on a Grand Prix dressage horse before, but both were outstanding riders. When Frank Henry's horse for the three-day event went lame, he was placed on Colonel Anderson's spare horse, Swing Low, a horse that had been his remount back in 1938 and 1939. The horse he rode in dressage was Bob Borg's horse, Reno Overdo. Thus, in the two Olympic competitions in which he rode in 1948, he had not trained on either horse prior to arriving in London about one month before the Games, and yet he still won three medals.

He was born in Cambridge, New York, but he was not related to Major General Guy V. Henry, Jr. He graduated 33rd in a class of 347 from the United States Military Academy Class of 1933. In the USMA Year Book he is described as being a quiet, unassuming, but forceful young gentleman from upstate New York. From the beginning it was apparent that this young man would have no trouble with the Academic Department. "'Hank' has always been one who could prepare even the hardest and the longest lessons in the shortest time. He seems to have a knack for doing things well with the least amount of effort."

He distinguished himself as a horseman from his early days at the USMA, and then as a member of the United States Army Equestrian Team, both nationally and internationally. He retired from the Army in 1963 as a Brigadier General.

MAJOR ROBERT BORG

Born May 27, 1913

Courtesy Col. Charles Anderson

Bob Borg recalls sitting on his first pony at the age of three. His first riding challenge (and that of many other young riders) was how to keep the pony's head from going down to graze! Bob's early years were spent in the Philippines. His father was an Army officer and his mother was Spanish, which accounts for his fluency in that language also. When his family moved back to the United States they located in Oregon, where he grew up with horses on the family's farm. After he graduated from high school, he went to the Warm Springs Reservation to help catch wild horses to keep the population down for grazing purposes. This led to breaking horses and eventually to training them.

The beauty of dressage and the unity of communication between horse and rider first captured Bob Borg's attention at the 1932 Olympics in Los Angeles when he was nineteen years-old. Unable to obtain tickets for the actual competitions, he watched the schooling sessions and was completely enthralled by them. Later on he hunted up some books on the subject and set about training a horse of his own in dressage.

In 1940, Colonel Hiram Tuttle, the famous dressage trainer and rider from the 1932 Olympic Games, came to Oregon as part of his tour to give Grand Prix dressage exhibitions. Bob was more than a little excited and, when the time came, he was not only in the audience, but he was in line after the performance to speak with Colonel Tuttle about his own interest and involvement in dressage. Bob's enthusiasm about dressage was obvious to Colonel Tuttle and, when the young man invited him to visit his farm after the exhibitions were over to evaluate his dressage efforts, he accepted. Without any outside help, Bob had progressed to quite an advanced level with his horse, and the Colonel was both surprised and pleased with what he saw. He gave Bob some help and encouraged him to continue his work. A warm friendship began between the two men, which gave Bob renewed energy in his desire to continue with dressage.

Very close to this time, World War II broke out and Bob enlisted in the Army. He

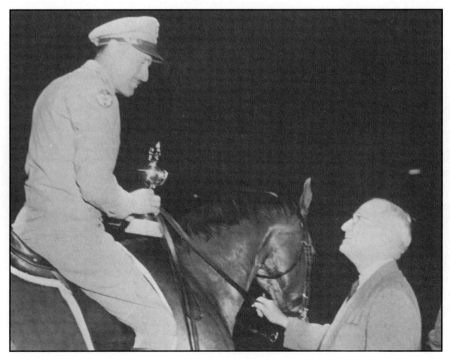

Bob Borg being congratulated by Harry S Truman.

Courtesy Col. Charles Anderson

36

carries the distinction of being the last enlisted man to be assigned to the Cavalry. When this knowledge was certain, he wrote to Colonel Tuttle and expressed his desire to have the opportunity to train with him in dressage. Colonel Tuttle's exact response to him was, "I'll show you the ladder, but you have to do the climbing."

In 1943, Bob Borg was sent to Fort Riley as an instructor in horsemanship to train the troops. He renewed his friendship with Colonel Tuttle and credits him with his own further advancement of dressage knowledge and skill. In the fall of 1947, Bob outscored Colonel Tuttle in the Army Olympic Trials. For Bob it was 'awkward,' but the truth is that a teacher can never be diminished when his student excels.

Another very talented and dedicated horseman Bob had the good fortune to work with was the German dressage trainer, Otto Lorke, who had prepared outstanding Grand Prix horses for some of Germany's Olympic teams. Before the 1948 Olympics in London, the United States Army Equestrian Team set up its training quarters in Munich, Germany. Otto Lorke was in charge of the dressage horses at the Vornholz Stud Farm at this facility. The two men, through their love and interest in dressage, quite naturally became friends. They shared and compared ideas as they trained their respective horses. Bob Borg liked Lorke's philosophy that there was no limit to what was possible when striving for quality in a performance.

Bob trained four horses in preparation for the 1948 Olympics, in addition to working with and training both Colonel Earl Thomson and Colonel Frank Henry. Both of these men were three-day event riders who had agreed to ride in the Grand Prix dressage competition so that the United States would have a team for that event. This dressage team won the silver medal. To this day, this is the only silver medal in dressage that the United States has won at the Olympics. Credit reflects directly back to the man who pulled it all together, spending countless hours preparing both horses and men to perform at the Grand Prix level at that competition.

In the individual dressage competition at the 1948 Olympics, Bob Borg placed fourth. One judge who placed his own countrymen first, second and third, ranked Bob in ninth place. Of the other two judges, one had him marked as the first place winner, and the other had him in second place. To many discerning and qualified observers, the one low score that dropped Bob to fourth place was an unfair call, depriving him of the individual medal they felt he deserved at his Olympic debut. Bob and the chestnut horse, Klingsor, competed in a field of nineteen competitors representing nine nations from around the world.

In addition to training his own horses for the United States first civilian Olympic team in 1952, Bob was also placed in charge of the young three-day event team, working particularly on their dressage training. The members of this team had little knowledge of what dressage was all about, but they were strong in their love of horses and the desire to do well. Once again, Bob Borg simultaneously developed both horses and riders, who grew to respect and admire the talents of their teacher, which they related to me in my interviews with them. The resulting team bronze medal at the Helsinki Olympics speaks for itself and is a reflection of the caliber of Bob Borg as a horseman and teacher.

At the 1955 Pan-American Games in Mexico City, Bob had the pleasure of seeing Walter Staley, one of the young three-day event riders he had trained in dressage, win America's first individual three-day event gold medal. In the Grand Prix dressage competition at the same Games, Bob won the individual silver medal on a horse called Bill Biddle, named after the General, Bill Biddle.

After his third Olympic competition in 1956, Bob and his good friend, Frank "Red" Duffy, whom he had met at Fort Riley, looked at a farm in Michigan and began plans to establish a horse farm there. They went into business together with the purchase of the farm and named their acreage Red Bob Farm.

On October 1, 1959, Bob Borg had a riding accident that changed his life dramatically. The horse he was working with backed onto one of the lettered boxes that marked the dressage arena. The horse reared up. This was nothing new for Bob. He'd handled rearing

Maj. Borg's dressage team's silver medal at the 1948 Olympics to date remains the only silver medal in dressage the U.S. has won at the Olympics. Much of the credit goes to this man.

Courtesy Col. Charles Anderson

horses throughout his career as a horseman; he knew what to do. The difference this time was that he came down on the marker, making it virtually impossible to maneuver his body to safety before the weight of the horse fell on him. He lay there for three hours before help came and he was rushed to the hospital. For four days his life hung in the balance before he began to come around. Nerve damage from his injuries left his legs paralyzed.

When I asked him how long it was after the accident before he made the decision to continue working with horses, his reply was, "It never once occurred to me that I wouldn't continue working with them." He also related that, when he spoke to his doctor about riding again, he was patted on the shoulder and told that that wasn't going to be possible.

During the long months of healing and rehabilitation, while he was learning to adjust to his altered body and keep it healthy, he was also working on devising a platform with bars from which he could mount a horse by swinging over onto it, using the strength of his upper body. When he reached the point of being able to do this, a picture was taken of him on his horse and sent, with a letter, to the doctor who said he would never ride again. With the help of a special circular platform he was also once again able to work with the horses. By standing in a protective box with his leg braces locked and his body supported, the platform

rotated by the weight of the horse moving. In this position, Bob was able to hold the reins, with whip in hand just above the saddle and move with the horse. When I asked him who had developed this special equipment, he said, "I did and I also helped build it!"

Talk about personal courage and determination! You cannot help but be touched by a man who does not look to others for help when things go wrong, or wait for them to fix everything and make it all right. This man looked within and literally began to rebuild his life. At his home, strategically placed bars in the driveway and within his house assist him with transfers in and out of his wheelchair. This man may be physically handicapped, but there is no way that he is disabled! For him there was no other way to go, but we all know that the pathways of coping with major disasters are many, and not all of them are positive. Somewhere along the line, I believe Bob Borg looked adversity in the face and said in a calm, certain inner voice, "You are not going to get the best of me."

The following story about Bob Borg as a dressage judge tells much about him. (Since he can't ride as he used to, he chooses not to judge any more.) After every competition he judged, Bob would always issue an open offer to anyone wishing to discuss their dressage performance to meet him in the ring after the last test. He remembers one young woman who met him in the ring after a competition at Stephens

College in Missouri. She wanted to know why her horse hadn't scored higher. In his mind Bob recalled not being able to see an appreciable lengthening of stride during the extended trot. He asked her if her horse was nearby. "Yes, it was." She was then instructed to bring the horse to him and he would show her. She did, and he then got on her horse and reversed roles. She was now the judge. Bob rode her horse across the ring very much as the young woman had and then he asked her how she would score the ride. He then gave the horse some more definite aids and rode it across the ring in a lovely extended trot. The young woman was asked how she would score the second ride. Could she see the difference? Of course she could. Bob Borg had shown her what was and what could be.

When he related this story to me, his eyes had a sparkle in them and his voice became more animated. I recognized the signs of a man who loves to teach and realized that his pleasure was derived from enabling students to see the possibilities and by inspiring them to want to strive for the attainment of higher skills.

He went on to talk about what he referred to as the sovereign law of teaching, which holds true for both man and beast. This law is, "to gain confidence and instill kindness with a will that is calm and inflexible." He went on, "The principles that inspire man to excel in what he does, require that he observe, remember and compare. All of the implications of learning stem from doing these things and asking questions such as, 'How did I get out of this problem yesterday? Do I see someone else doing something which yields a better result?' For the horse, the principles require that it learn to be calm, straight, and forward. The groundwork must be completely and carefully developed. The horse must be able to stand well before it

can walk well, before it can trot well, before it can canter well. When the basics are soundly in place, then you can move to an advanced level and there is no limit to how far you can go. If you have trouble with any steps along the way, go back to each preceding step and then work the horse forward as each step is firmly re-established." Simple truths and great wisdom have a way of coming from great teachers.

Bob Borg is still a very active man and is just beginning to let go of a few things that used to be more physically easy for him to do. He continues to teach young riders who want to specialize in training dressage horses. A few weeks before this interview, he was very involved with a horse sale held at Red Bob Farm. He explained to me that, as owners, they are always upgrading their brood mares. They keep records of how well the foals do at the race track when they grow up. The mares that produce winners are kept, while the others are sold.

Looking back at his life, in addition to his Olympic achievements, Bob Borg is especially proud that he was the very last man to have had the privilege of being in the Cavalry, that he was an instructor in the Department of Horsemanship at Fort Riley, and that he trained all of the horses and all of the men that performed in dressage at the Olympics during his time on the United States Equestrian Team, first as a military officer and then as a civilian.

Life has not always been kind to Bob Borg, but he is a man who is at peace with himself; a man who has the satisfaction of knowing that at every turn of the road, whatever befell him, he gave 100% of himself to make the situation the best it could possibly be. As I drove home after this interview, there was no doubt in my mind that I had been in the presence of a gifted and exceptional horseman, teacher and human being.

Courtesy Col. Charles Anderson

COLONEL CHARLES ANDERSON

Born October 24, 1914 • Died May 27, 1993
West Point Class of 1938

Colonel Charles Anderson rode on the last Army Olympic Equestrian Team to compete for the United States at the 1948 Games in London. He placed fourth individually in the Three-Day Event and his score, coupled with teammate Frank Henry's second place ranking and Earl Thomson's twentieth in a field of 45 competitors, earned them the team gold medal in eventing.

The 1948 Olympic Games were the first to be held after World War II, twelve years after the last Games in 1936. The intervening two Olympic Games (1940 and 1944) had to be cancelled because of this tremendous conflict. (It is interesting to note that, in the early years of the Olympic movement, it was war that was cancelled in order to allow all nations to participate in the Games; not the reverse which is the case today.) In the U.S. nearly all of the Army mounted units were eliminated in 1942. After the war there were no plans to revive these units or the related equestrian activities. In fact, the winds of change were moving in the direction of terminating the cavalry altogether and replacing it with more sophisticated means of mechanized fighting.

It was probably pressure on the Army from influential civilian horse enthusiasts in the East that eventually led to Chief-of-Staff, General Eisenhower, accepting the responsibility of sending an equestrian team to the 1948 Olympic Games. He, in turn, delegated this responsibility to the Commanding Officer at Fort Riley. Then came the real challenge - finding suitable riders, horses and equipment to form the nucleus of the 1948 team, plus the hard work and dedication needed to bring them up to top form before the Games. When the final decisions were made, it was Colonel Earl Thomson who was designated as Team Captain in charge of this task.

As their captain, Colonel Thomson was the one who made the horse/rider assignments, based on which rider was best qualified to match a horse's temperament, strengths and weaknesses. If the combination didn't work out, a reassignment was made. The team captain was also responsible for posting training schedules ahead of time so that each rider knew which horse he would be riding and which discipline he would be working on.

Colonel Anderson had a string of three horses for the London Games. When Frank Henry's horse, Reno Ike, went lame, Colonel Thomson consulted with Colonel Anderson to determine which of his two spare horses could be assigned to Colonel Henry. It was decided to give him Swing Low, who had been Colonel Henry's remount back in 1938. Consideration was also given to the fact that Colonel Henry did not want to ride Reno Palisade!

Colonel Anderson remembers how important the team concept was to the military riders. "We only had three members on the team and, in order to achieve a team score, all three riders had to finish all three days of competition, or your team was disqualified. It would have jeopardized the team if any of the three riders had tried any fancy heroics or risky shortcuts in order to gain high individual scores. It was a time when you thought as a team, you worked as a team, and you won or lost as a team. There was no fourth member of the team to allow for discarding the lowest score as there is now."

The horse Colonel Anderson rode in the 1948 Olympics was a nine-year-old, 16 hand Thoroughbred bay mare named Reno Palisade. She was an Army-bred, Army-trained horse that had been brought up as a remount. Together they were a worthy partnership, ranking fourth among 45 competitors, and giving strong assistance in claiming the gold medal.

When I asked Colonel Anderson if Reno Palisade, Reno Ike and Reno Rhythm were related, he explained to me that the similarity in names did not necessarily mean that they were related. Although it was possible that they

The 1948 Olympic
U.S. Equestrian Team.
Front row:
Lt. Col. Charles Anderson,
Lt. Col. Charles Symroski,
Capt. John Russell,
Capt. Jonathan Burton.
Back row:
Lt. Col. Frank Henry,
Col. Franklin Wing,
Col. Tommy Thomson,
Col. Andrew Frierson and
Lt. Col. Harvey Ellis, team
veterinarian.

shared either the same dam or sire, this did not always hold true. What their names indicated, instead, was that they all came from the Fort Reno Remount Station in Oklahoma; all the horses bred there had Reno as the first part of their name, plus a second name which started with a letter of the alphabet, depending on the year in which the horse was born. This meant that Reno Palisade was born seven years after Reno Ike, and Reno Rhythm two years later.

Colonel Anderson's love of horses can be traced back to his boyhood days of growing up on a farm where plow horses were standard equipment and learning to work with horses and ride them was part of this young lad's life. His interest in horses was also fueled by stories of cowboys and Zane Grey novels.

At West Point he had to relearn how to ride, using the military 'forward seat' instead of the 'western.' At that time all cadets received three and a half years of instruction in horsemanship. Colonel Anderson's first choice had always been the Field Artillery and at that time he had no particular interest in going into the Cavalry Branch of the Service. His first assignment was at Fort Sill, Oklahoma where he was a member of the 18th Field Artillery, a horse-drawn light artillery regiment. His first Regimental Commander was Colonel C.P. George, who had competed in the 1928 Olympics as a three-day event rider. He ordered all new officers to participate in the many equestrian events there, such as jumping, racing, steeplechasing, polo,

and fox hunting. Colonel Anderson's aptitude for horses became known and, two years later, he was enrolled in the Advanced Equitation Course at Fort Sill. Shortly thereafter the U.S. entered World War II.

Colonel Anderson's participation on the Army Olympic Equestrian Team provided him with memories he will never forget. Reassignment from the Military Academy to the team at Fort Riley came as a sudden surprise in late December, 1946. Then followed nine months of intensive training at Fort Riley, culminating in the full-scale trials from October 1st to 3rd, 1947. With almost no warning the team was ordered to Europe to complete the pre-Olympic training. The shipment was complicated because of the need to send a jumping team to the fall circuit of indoor shows. Colonel Thomson flew alone to Frankfurt, and six other riders followed in two groups by sea to Bremerhaven. Two shipments of officers, enlisted men and horses docked in Antwerp. All travelled by rail to Munich, where training began in earnest in the former SS Riding School, after the horses had a much needed three-week rest.

At the opening ceremonies of the 1948 Olympics, the equestrian team members marched into the stadium with the other U.S. athletes. In accordance with the past custom, the equestrian teams wore military and not Olympic uniforms and marched at the head of the column of the other athletes. This practice was discontinued after the 1948 Olympics.

The members of the 1948 United States Army Equestrian Team knew they would be the last of the military competitors to ride for their country and they wanted to honor it. They were well aware of the acquired knowledge that had been gained since the Army's equestrian Olympic debut in 1912 in Stockholm. Once again they had come to the Olympic scene by hard work and determination. They came away with a silver team medal in dressage, a silver individual and a team gold medal in eventing, fourth place individual scores in Grand Prix jumping, dressage and eventing, plus an eighth place individual ranking in dressage. Not only had they honored their country, but they left to future representatives of the United States Equestrian Team a legacy of high achievement in horse sports.

Colonel Anderson was rightfully proud of being a member of the final U.S. Army Olympic Team. Through the years he had been a careful historian and had kept pictures and records that were compiled into a book entitled *The United States Army's Olympic Equestrian Teams* which documents the Army Olympic equestrian activities, achievements and contributions. His primary goal since his retirement, however, was to develop an Educational and Training Program for Artistic Equitation. Unfortunately this work was not completed by the time he died in May of 1993. He was an invaluable resource to me in providing pictures and information about the military era of U.S. equestrian competitors.

CHARLES "CHAMP" HOUGH

Born May 3, 1934

Courtesy Charles Hough

At the age of eighteen, Charles 'Champ' Hough was the youngest rider to compete in the 1952 Olympics. He was chosen for the team at age seventeen and turned eighteen just in time to be eligible to compete in the Games. The horse he rode, Cassavellanus, was only six years old and also shared the record of being "the youngest to compete." In spite of their inexperience at the 1952 Olympics in Helsinki, they placed ninth in the three-day event individual scores out of 59 competitors from around the world. They had the highest American score and thus led the United States' first civilian equestrian team to the team bronze medal honor.

Champ's love for horses had surfaced by age six when he scavenged for Coke bottles which, when turned in, enabled him to have money for rides at a local stable. He had par-

ents who were supportive of his interest. By age ten, he was taking regular lessons to improve his riding ability and, by age twelve, his folks had moved the family to a small ranch. Two years later a small, elegant black gelding, named Craigwood Park, was purchased for him. It was Champ's outstanding riding ability, and his partnership with this horse, that not only got him recommended for consideration to be on the first civilian equestrian team to go to the Olympics, but also got him selected.

After being chosen to train for the three-day event team, Champ went to Fort Riley in Kansas to begin preparation in May of 1951. It was in October of that same year that the actual tryouts were held, with members of the Olympic Committee present. In less than six months a very novice group of young riders put in a very creditable performance at the October trials and were given final clearance to represent the United States in Helsinki at the

The beginning
of a career!

Courtesy Charles Hough

1952 Olympics. Because Champ had not yet graduated from high school, he continued his education by going to school for several hours each day in nearby Junction City and also by taking home study courses.

In the 1950's, three-day eventing and dressage were practically unheard of in the United States, and opportunities to train for either of them were almost non-existent. The center of advanced equitation training was at the Cavalry School at Fort Riley and, fortunately, the Army allowed the first civilian team to train there. With the indispensable knowledge and teaching of 'Gyp' Wofford and Bob Borg, both Army cavalry officers, the young team in eventing was taught to understand the ground work and techniques required for each of the disciplines in three-day event competitions.

Champ Hough pays high tribute to Robert Borg "who was, and is the greatest horseman that I've known personally in my lifetime. Bob Borg is an extremely gifted individual and horseman. He inspired my ongoing love for horses and taught me what being a dressage rider is all about. He worked with all of us and all of our horses in our Olympic dressage preparation. He did this on top of preparing his own horses for competition and in addition to putting in a full day of military duties when we were at Fort Riley."

The horse Champ rode to win the team

bronze medal in eventing at the 1952 Olympics was a five-year-old that needed further breaking and training when Champ first saw him at Rimrock, the Wofford's family farm. Gyp Wofford had invited the riders to come out to his farm in their spare time to break and school any of his horses that looked as though they had some potential. Cassavellanus, nicknamed 'Cass,' soon showed good form in dressage. He and Champ worked so well together that it was decided that Cass would be his mount for the Olympics. Champ's own horse, Craigwood Park, was originally designated to be ridden by reserve rider Bill James but, because of a technical error with the entries, he ended up being ridden by Walter Staley. Before going to the Olympic Games, Cass had never been away from the farm at Rimrock. Champ remembers this young horse as having a good disposition, being very responsive and having a good mind.

When he walked the cross-country course at the Helsinki Olympics, Champ recalls that, "In all honesty, I anticipated three refusals and three falls. I was trying to be realistic. I was well aware of how green Cass and I were. We had never been called upon to do anything quite as demanding as that course looked. Fortunately, probably even miraculously, none of these things occurred. When I was finishing the course, I remember galloping by the group of American riders who called out the two best words any competitor can hope to hear. 'You're clean!' they yelled. I was in a near state of shock."

At the Olympic medal ceremony Champ admits that, "It was very emotional. Tears accompanied a sense of both pride and awe. Of the nineteen teams and nations represented, nobody had expected 'the baby-faced American team' to fare as well as we did. The average age of all the other riders on the other teams was 39. The truth is that nobody had been intimidated by the U.S. event team whose riders were age eighteen, twenty, and twenty-one. We were even surprised at ourselves. It was great!"

As a young man, Champ lived in Burbank and was well-known in California as a point-to-point rider. Champ feels that the horse business has been very good to him and has given him an opportunity to be involved with many great horses. For 27 years, Champ operated his own show barn in Northern California, making his

name with such model horses as Showdown, Sutton Place, Mr. Spindletop, Emmett Kelly and the top hunter, Modest Man. He currently lives in Ocala, Florida, and is now in the race horse industry. Employed by Fasig-Tipton, he does appraisals for the major yearling markets. He sold his race horse training farm in Florida and is no longer involved in showing horses, other than to give his full support to his daughter's show jumping efforts. He is very proud of his daughter, Lauren who, at age fourteen, was the youngest rider George Morris had taken on for training. In 1993 Lauren was International Grand Prix Rider "Rookie of the Year."

Champ used to write the"Conformation Clinic" for *Practical Horseman*. He and George Morris, who writes the "Jumping Clinic" for the same publication, share a laugh together as they speculate that they are probably better known for their articles in *Practical Horseman* than for their Olympic achievements.

WALTER G. STALEY, JR.

Born October 20, 1932

A dream can be inspired and may grow from many different sources. For Walter Staley, the dream to be a top level equestrian competitor was brought to life in the living room of his boyhood home when two of his father's West Point classmates came to visit and shared stories and pictures of their Olympic competitions. Walter will never forget the excitement generated by the experiences that the renowned Olympic rider, Harry Chamberlin, and his teammate friend, William Greer, shared about the Army's Equestrian Team. Being a young boy whose love of horses had always been present as far back as he could remember, no one could place a limit on his desire to excel as a horseman after Harry

Chamberlin saw him ride and commented to his father, "The young fellow has a lot of talent."

It was not by happenchance, therefore, that in his late teens he was entered in the regional trials at the county fair in Mexico, Missouri, where selection events were being held to determine candidates for the first civilian team to represent the United States in the 1952 Olympics. While the trials were primarily to select the jumping team, for which he did not qualify, his ability as a rider did not go unnoticed, and he was invited to go to Fort Riley to begin training for the three-day event team. The fulfillment of his dream was about to unfold.

Walter remembers sitting down with a book to learn what three-day eventing was all about for, back in the early 1950's, the disciplines of eventing and dressage were virtually unknown to most riders in the United States.

Colonel 'Gyp' Wofford was their teacher in eventing. It was through him that the novice civilian team learned the value of patient, repetitive work. They came to realize that regularly walking their horses up and down steep hills helped to build the wind and stamina required for an event horse. Colonel Robert Borg trained the young team and their horses for the dressage phase of the competition. Once again, repetitive elementary work was required in order to teach the subtle aids needed for a smooth dressage performance.

Within a fourteen-month period, this young, inexperienced eventing team was transformed to a level of competency strong enough to enable them to win the team bronze medal in the Three-Day Event at the 1952 Olympics in Helsinki. This award was a credit to both their instructors and to their own discipline and determination to succeed. General Guy Henry

is quoted as saying that the ages of all three of the U.S. team members, combined with the ages of their horses, only equaled 80. They were indeed a young team; Charles Hough was eighteen, Walter Staley nineteen, and Jeb Wofford only twenty one. What they accomplished was nothing short of amazing.

Walter Staley recalls the unusual sequence of events that ended up placing him on Champ Hough's eight-year-old black gelding, Craigwood Park, for the Olympic competition. The original plan was for him to ride Reno Palisades, the mare Colonel Anderson had ridden in the 1948 Olympics. However, during a loading accident at Fort Riley, his horse injured herself, had to be left behind and eventually was put down. Walter was then placed on Reno Rhythm, Captain Earl Thomson's mount from the 1948 Games, but she went lame shortly after the final entries were filed. At this point, arrangements were set in motion to scratch Walter and to put Bill James on Craigwood Park as the third rider. However, due to a technical problem and late timing, Bill James' name was never changed from alternate team rider, so he did not qualify to compete. This quirky turn of fate left Walter as the third rider on a horse that he had only four days to get acquainted with.

"Craigwood Park was a light-weight, black Thoroughbred with a steeplechasing background. He was experienced and well trained, albeit a little highly strung," Walter commented. He summarized their competition experience this way, "I regarded our dressage test as 'somewhat tense' and not really reflective of what the horse could have done with a rider that was familiar with him. After a couple of refusals early in the cross-country course, Craigwood Park was delightful and a breeze to ride. The third day we had two knock-downs in the stadium jumping. All in all we did pretty well with such a short time to get to know each other."

Walter Staley laughs easily today about another circumstance he found himself in as a novice Olympic participant. Being the last

The 1952 Olympic Three Day winners. The young American team took the bronze. From the left, Walter Staley, Jr., Champ Hough, and J.E.B. Wofford. *Olympic Photo Ltd.*

45

member of the U.S. team to ride, he had gone out to the steeplechase area to watch Champ Hough and Cassavellanus. Much to his chagrin, when he returned to the stable area to catch a bus back to the Olympic Village in order to change into his riding uniform for the cross-country, he discovered that all the buses had been reassigned and were now delivering spectators out to the cross-country course. He grabbed the nearest bicycle and began to pedal, like a mad hatter, five miles to the Olympic Village, and then another five to return to the stables. As it happened, the bike he grabbed belonged to Bill James and the seat was set lower than Walter was accustomed to. It was the most fatiguing bicycle ride of his life. Meanwhile, Craigwood Park's groom had the horse all ready to go. Walter's teammates were beginning to get anxious as they scanned the horizon for a frantic bicycle peddler. With minutes to spare, he wheeled up. "At least I didn't have time to get nervous about my cross-country ride," he muses.

Walter Staley rode in a total of three Olympic Games. He was also the first USET member to win an individual gold medal in the Pan-American Games in Mexico City in 1955. He rode for the USET for most of its first decade. This placed him in a position to appreciate the difficulties faced in making the transition from a military to a civilian equestrian team. He states that, "Moving from the caliber of full-time horsemen, represented by the Army officers who had the advantage of organized training at the best facility in the United States (Fort Riley), to one of civilian riders scattered throughout the country, with no organized competitions, was bound to present its share of problems."

Through the years, gradual improvements helped make the situation better and better. Walter believes several things were responsible. The formation of the U.S. Combined Training Association in 1959 promoted the growth of eventing in the U.S. At the same time the USET hired a full-time three-day event coach and kept a nucleus of horses and riders at their training center. These developments generated dividends of success for the U.S. three-day event team.

He described the Olympic medal ceremony with these words, "It was extremely emotional, intensive, incomparable; a tremendous thrill encompassing self-achievement, gratitude, and national pride. I had to pinch myself to make sure it was really happening to me and not just a dream."

After his participation in the 1960 Olympics in Rome, Walter Staley retired from the equestrian team. He then went to Pennsylvania State University, where he earned a Ph.D. in solid state science. In addition to this accomplishment, he also acquired degrees in geology and in geological engineering, knowledge helpful when he joined the family business started by his maternal grandfather. A.P. Green Industries is a firebrick refractory company, producing material (the high intensity clay is mined from the Missouri land) that is used to line the processors to melt down steel and glass.

Walter's last competitive effort as a horseman was in 1975 when he was the high point rider at a dressage event in Kansas City. Back trouble, and eventual surgery in 1976, forced him to alter his life's activities and required a reduction in his work schedule from a full-time occupation to one of a consulting nature. He plans to continue in the business until retirement and then to spend more time enjoying his favorite things - his family, reeling in a bass in the summer, and bagging a duck or quail during hunting season. And, because of his love for horses, he would also like to attend top level three-day event and dressage shows when time permits.

Courtesy Jeb Wofford

JOHN EDWARD BROWN "JEB" WOFFORD

Born April 11, 1931

In 1952, John Edward Brown 'Jeb' Wofford, the eldest son of the famous Colonel John 'Gyp' Wofford, rode in the Helsinki Olympics as a member of the United States' first civilian equestrian team. He was on the Three-Day Event team that won the bronze medal and was coached by his father. Also assisting John's father in handling the team was Robert Borg, whose 1948 Olympic involvement, advice and counsel, gave the team access to an indispensable resource in dressage expertise, as well as in international competition. The United States won team bronze medals in both the Three-Day Event and in the Grand Prix Jumping - a pretty respectable showing for the civilian team's first Olympic competition.

Pulling a civilian team together had not been easy. With the disbanding of the Cavalry came a termination of any government funds to help finance an equestrian team. But finance was not the only problem. Developing an organizational structure, delegating responsibility, seeking out top level riders and horses willing to commit themselves to rigorous training schedules, and providing opportunities to compete, plus the logistics of shipping the horses across the Atlantic, and the need to arrive on the European scene in time to compete in at least a few horse shows; these were just a few of the challenges that had to be met.

Jeb Wofford remembers the officers from Fort Riley discussing these problems when they came over to his father's adjacent farm to socialize during their off-duty hours. It is to these men, plus others from the East Coast and the National Horse Show group, that we owe thanks for taking on the responsibility of piecing together a civilian team. They had foreseen the end of the cavalry era and cared enough about having a U.S. team to roll up their sleeves and combine their knowledge and financial support to develop a plan. They wanted to see the proud record, established by the U.S. military, carried on in international equestrian events. Jeb Wofford's father became the first president of the International Equestrian Competition Corporation, the forerunner of our present United States Equestrian Team.

The horse that served the young John Wofford well in the 1952 Olympics was a bay Thoroughbred named Benny Grimes, a horse born on his father's farm. Young John broke the horse and trained him. They grew up together, an uncommon occurrence with Olympic riders and their mounts. Jeb describes Benny Grimes as "being sound, having a good disposition and being a strong competitor." I asked him about the horse's name. "My father was fond of naming some of his horses after his friends. My horse, Benny Grimes, was named after General Benny Grimes, who was then Chief of Cavalry and who also was my Godfather."

Jeb believes that many good riders could achieve Olympic status if only they had a 'great horse.' "In order to reach the top, ability, hard work and luck are essential, but without a 'great horse' it's just not going to happen."

When I asked him about the greatest horses he has had the privilege to see, he mentioned two that came to his mind right away. The first was Democrat, an Army-bred jumper, whose story is included here in both Bill Steinkraus' and John Russell's biographies. The other great horse he was privileged to see compete was a twelve year-old mare named Halla, ridden by Germany's Hans Winkler.

In talking with Jeb, it does not take long to realize that he is extremely perceptive about equestrian sport. Having been a former participant, and now an interested observer, he has a computer-like mind for detail. He knows the people in the sport, most of their trials and triumphs, the year they competed in a particular event and the horses that they rode. He is a most engaging conversationalist.

He commented on two things he has observed in current equestrian competition:
"Today the expense of maintaining a top-

J.E.B. Wofford, shown here in 1957 but still in the form that brought success at Helsinki in 1952.

Stewart's Commercial Photographers & Finishers

level horse and competing him throughout the year, both nationally and internationally, is beyond the reach of several good riders unless they have access to sponsorship or are independently wealthy."

"I believe that the building of equestrian competition courses is underrated as a science. The well-built courses of today are fair and require a lot of thought. There are no easy fences - they are all challenging. It used to be that there were some 'give-away' fences and others that presented problems to several horses (a sure sign that it was an unfair fence!). Today, you aren't going to see several horses having trouble with the same fence but, rather, different horses having problems at different fences, depending on their strengths and weaknesses. Also, today you will see course designers alter a jump if adverse weather conditions occur; this is a definite change from earlier years when, once the course was set, that was it, no matter what happened. Today the courses are thoughtfully designed with enough alternatives to be safe for the less experienced and yet challenging enough to distinguish the top riders and horses."

There is an enthusiasm and warmth in Jeb Wofford's voice that I found refreshing; as in one who perceives and savors the good in life. He impressed me as being both a personable and humble fellow -- a man who enjoys what he does, but whose assistance and support are more often given behind the scenes as opposed to being in the visible front lines.

At a fairly early age, Jeb had to give up riding on a regular basis because of shoulder injuries incurred when competing as an amateur steeplechase rider. To overcome some of the immobility in his shoulders, the clinic he attended recommended swimming. Today, a one-mile swim is part of his daily routine. He belongs to the Master's Club for Swimming and this, coupled with participation in triathalon competitions, has kept him athletically fit through the years.

He currently works for an investment firm, dealing with appraisals. Even though he replaced riding with sports 'less stressful to the human body,' his heart still thrills when viewing the prestigious National Horse Show, and he still enjoys taking in some of the selection trials. He has nothing but good to say about the Badminton Three-Day Event in England. This event, instituted by the Duke of Beaufort in 1949, made incredible strides in popularizing three-day eventing at that time and remains a standard against which other competitions of this discipline are measured. Jeb did comment, however, that "getting in and out of the parking lot at Badminton takes almost as long as the event itself. Well, maybe not quite."

He would like to be remembered for his Olympic achievement and for 'being kind to horses.'

Courtesy Fred McCashin

ARTHUR J. McCASHIN

Born May 5, 1901 • Died September 24, 1988

Arthur McCashin was born in Northern Ireland. He came to the United States with his family at the age of four and settled in Morristown, New Jersey. His love of horses started as a young lad, and it remained a vital part of his activities throughout his life. It was from his riding in steeplechase races and his skillful showing of hunters and jumpers that he came to be known as an all-round horseman.

His keen interest in international equestrian competition brought him into contact with the newly formed International Equestrian Competition Corporation (the IECC), which was the original name of the United States Equestrian Team. The IECC's trials gave him the opportunity to be a contender to go to the 1952 Olympic Games as a representative of the United States' first civilian team. He later became a director of the USET and held that position until 1957.

In an article he wrote for *The USET Book of Riding*, which commemorated the first 25 years of the United States Equestrian Team, he recalled that the 1952 squad was terribly thin in backup horses even though, in 1951, "Gyp" Wofford was able to latch on to the last of the 1948 Olympic horses from the Army for a princely sum of $1.00 a piece. This group of horses included six jumpers. Although they had a lot of age and physical problems, they also had invaluable experience with European competition.

Arthur McCashin qualified for the 1952 Olympic Team aboard Totilla and Paleface. Due to a turn of fate, he ended up riding another horse entirely in his Olympic competition. In the winter of 1951-1952, the FEI voted to maintain their ban on allowing women to compete, in spite of strong petitions from both the United States and Great Britain pressing for women's rights to be competitors. This decision eliminated Carol Durand who had also been chosen to

represent the U.S. team. She gave Miss Budweiser, the horse August Busch had loaned her, to Arthur to ride in the Helsinki Olympics, as neither of his horses were able to compete due to lameness and age. Miss Budweiser's original name had been Circus Rose until Busch renamed the mare. The FEI now prohibits this kind of advertising, but when Miss Budweiser was the only one, nobody paid much attention.

The pre-Olympic European shows were at Wiesbaden, Dusseldorf, and Hamburg. McCashin's perception of these shows was that they showed what novices the Americans were compared to the European experts, both in terms of course design and riding techniques. In spite of this fact, he felt that the Americans held their own competitively. In fact, in the big pre-Olympic team class in Dusseldorf, the U.S. won over Germany. Arthur won an individual class there with Miss Budweiser in which the trophy was a gold ring in the form of Saint George. He wore this ring with pride throughout his lifetime.

Three things were particularly frustrating to Arthur in his 1952 Olympic experience. They were the United States' lack of success in international competition, a lack of organized stable management, and occasional internal friction.

Early career move!
Courtesy Fred McCashin

49

Aboard Miss Budweiser
in 1952 at Helsinki.

Courtesy Fred McCashin

He was quick to add, however, that he knew they were pioneering in new territory and that what they were learning would serve as the basis for making improvements in future years.

As captain of the USET's first civilian show jumping team, Arthur McCashin, riding Miss Budweiser, led them to a bronze medal victory at the Helsinki Olympics. From this experience he gained insights into the lay-out and strategy of international course designing that would change his viewpoint and intrigue him for years to come, eventually becoming a skill he pursued.

In his role as director of the USET, McCashin played a major part in obtaining the services of Bertalan de Nemethy as the team's show jumping coach, a role which de Nemethy filled for a quarter of a century. Having been a member of the Hungarian team, Bert gave the Americans a shortcut to the collaborative experience of the European trainers, in addition to a sound and systematic method of developing horses and riders. With Bert de Nemethy as permanent coach, the team did not disband after the fall circuit, but rather developed a year-round riding program.

Early in the USET's history, Arthur recognized the benefits of a centralized training center. With this realization in mind, he offered his farm, Four Furlongs, as a training center for the team. When the final location was determined to be in Gladstone, New Jersey, he was a major force in establishing an ongoing riding program there. Arthur felt that 1955 was the real turning point for the USET, for this was the time of awakening to what had to be done, and a time to work towards achieving those goals.

In addition to being an international figure in the horse show world, Arthur was also a licensed pilot who flew transport planes for the armed forces in World War II. After the war, Arthur left commercial aviation, obtained his instructor's rating, and taught flying at "Sea Wings," the flying school he co-owned in Westport, Connecticut. Throughout his riding career he also maintained his flying interests and kept an airplane on his farm at Four Furlongs.

Arthur also travelled all over the world to inspect steeplechase courses and to bring the best jump and course design to the growing steeplechase industry in the United States. Each October at Morven Park in Leesburg, Virginia, a memorial race is held in Arthur McCashin's name for his dedication and contributions to the industry.

Arthur McCashin became a sought-after course designer when he retired from competitive riding, and he designed the international courses for many years at the Horse Shows in both Washington and New York. In recognition of his active roles as a competitor and as a leader in international equestrian activities, McCashin was inducted into the National Horse Show Hall of Fame in 1986, and the Show Jumping Hall of Fame in 1990.

One of his four sons, Fred McCashin, a veterinarian and also a pilot, shared the USET veterinary responsibility at the 1975 Pan-American Games, the 1976 Olympic Games and the 1979 Pan-American Games.

Courtesy Col. John Russel

COLONEL JOHN RUSSELL

Born February 2, 1920

John Russell's love of horses began at a young age, helping out with his father's hobby of showing trotters and pacers at county fairs. By the time John was twelve or thirteen years old, there wasn't a horse he could not ride. The first horse he ever owned was a mare named Scarlet O'Hara that he saw at a circus. He was drawn to the horse because it defied its natural fear and jumped over firebars. After the show, John sought out the horse behind the tent. A conversation with the owner ended up with Scarlet O'Hara being sold to John for "a reasonable price." She was the horse he rode when, at age sixteen, he began to show in the big open divisions at the Harrisburg Horse Show. The two of them also caught everyone's attention when he taught her to jump over his convertible.

John Russell was a member of both the last Army Olympic Equestrian Team in 1948 and the first civilian team in 1952. During the second World War, he served in Africa and in Italy. When the war ended, John was working in reconnaissance in northern Italy, where a number of liberated horses were picked up and were eventually commandeered by the Army to help form the next Olympic equestrian team. Before the 1948 Olympics, John requested orders to go to Fort Riley, Kansas, to try out for the team. On the strength of his European horse show record, permission was granted and his orders were cut.

At Fort Riley, John remembers the training of horses as being both varied and interesting. Each rider worked out in all three disciplines; the three-day event, jumping, and dressage. The program was drawn up months in advance and you could tell, by looking at the schedule, when you would be required to ride a dressage test, go cross-country or do stadium jumping, and on which horse. Afterwards you were critiqued on your strong and weak points and given suggestions for improvement.

At the 1948 Olympics in London, John Russell was a member of the Jumping team and rode a horse named Air Mail. In those days there was no discard score for the team, and the U.S. team did not place, due to the elimination of Colonel Frierson on Rascal. Having won almost every big European competition in the Spring prior to the Olympics, including the Grand Prix at Aachen, the Nations Cup in London, and the Nations Cup in Dublin, the loss was a bitter pill to take.

John remembers Air Mail as being somewhere between seventeen and eighteen years old in 1948, a bay with a white blaze down his face. He was not an easy horse. He was a known stopper and required a lot of re-schooling. His redeeming ability was his tremendous scope at negotiating height and spread, and he could sail right over seven-foot fences in puissance classes. He placed 21st in the Grand Prix Jumping at the 1948 Olympics.

There was a genuine sadness amongst the Army's equestrian units when the decision was made to disband further training with horses in lieu of more sophisticated and technological weaponry. It was the end of a grand and colorful era. There would be no more Army Equestrian Olympic Teams. Plans were immediately begun, with collaboration between military equestrian leaders and East Coast horseman, to form a civilian equestrian team before the next Olympics.

Colonel "Gyp" Wofford was placed in charge of this effort and it was his encouragement to John Russell that, once again, prompted him to seek out permission to go to Fort Riley for the equestrian team trials and then, following the trials, to go on temporary duty to train with the team.

On the European circuit before the 1952 Helsinki Olympics, John was the first foreigner ever to win the Hamburg Spring Derby, riding one of the horses on his Olympic string, a Texas-bred Quarter Horse named Rattler. The following year, John's wife, Gabrielle, won the 1953

Col. Russell on
Democrat, 1952
Helsinki.
Foto Tiedemann

Ladies Hamburg Derby on a horse named Lonie. The fact that two Americans from the same family won these events within a year of each other made for a new and unique record. It was no secret that the 1952 U.S. Equestrian Team's string of horses had a lot of age and soundness problems. To have a horse sound enough to go into the ring was a primary concern. Not having access to modern technology and treatments, John recalls that they used Antiphlogistine, mothballs to melt in the horses' feet, and white gas to stand them in.

Democrat was John Russell's mount for the 1952 Olympics. The horse's soundness was so unpredictable that, even though he was John's best horse, he and Colonel Wofford decided against showing him in the United States shows in order to save him for the Olympics. John describes the 16.1 hand Democrat as being "very athletic and having a natural desire to not touch any rails. The horse responded well with just a snaffle bit and had a tremendous scope and ability to jump big fences and combinations. He was an easy horse to ride. Little kids could even hack around on him."

By the last fence, during the second round at the Helsinki Olympics, the nineteen-year-old Democrat was struggling against fatigue, but his courage never gave out. The team of Bill Steinkraus on Hollandia, Arthur McCashin on Miss Budweiser, and John Russell on Democrat won the Olympic bronze medal in show jumping.

Standing on the winner's platform, John remembers feeling, "a great sense of honor that few achieve. One that can only be earned with great dedication."

Another memory from the 1952 Olympics that John will never forget was how much he was touched by the support of one of his fellow competitors, General Humberto Mariles, Mexico's top rider and the individual gold medalist at the 1948 Olympics. When John shared with his friend his concern about Democrat's soundness, Mariles immediately summoned his own veterinarian to give assistance. This particular vet had an outstanding reputation and helped out, both day and night before the competition, to ensure that Democrat would be sound enough to compete. This was all done with Mariles' full knowledge that, on a good day, Democrat was capable of beating him and his own horse.

Years later, John Russell went to visit the controversial Mariles when he was imprisoned on the charge of murder. Mariles died later in a Paris prison. John Russell, to this day, will never forget what an outstanding friend Mariles had been to him.

Having been a member of both the military and civilian teams, John Russell has some insightful comments on the advantages and disadvantages of each: "The advantages of the military team include having a financial underwriting from the Army, in addition to having very organized training, access to facilities and being connected, both nationally and internationally, for transportation and information through government agencies and embassies. When, for example, it came to moving the team and its horses, it was just a simple matter of calling the transportation office and all arrangements were made."

When a military team arrived in any foreign country, it was customary to pay a courtesy call to the U.S. Embassy; this generally guaranteed the athletes' transportation, plus PX and medical support, and a good start on the social side of things. Another advantage of most military teams included a feeling of comradeship. The fact that you and your teammates belonged to the same armed forces may not have made anyone ride any better, but John Russell remembers that it made winning and losing better, and that team members often derived as much pride and satisfaction from a teammate's victory as they did from their own.

On the other hand, the military methods of team selection and assignments could be very unsatisfactory and a definite disadvantage. Top officials made most of the selections and decisions and had rank control. If your immediate commander refused to release you for training with the team, you were stopped in your tracks. It was also very difficult to pursue a riding career and maintain your military promotional status at the same time. Another disadvantage of continuing with Army teams would have been the lack of quality horses. They would have had to put into operation one of the world's largest breeding programs, in order to remedy the deficiency.

With the civilian team system, every professional horseman has the opportunity to develop Olympic-type horses and sell them to prospective Olympic riders or to the team. Riders now have access to both training and buying horses abroad as well as in their own country. Another big advantage of the civilian team system is that the coach starts off with the top riders and horses in the entire nation and they are mostly fully trained and ready to compete at the upper levels. Tryouts are also more open. The selection system has progressed so that it currently ensures fairness to competitors by a points system which more or less eliminates subjectivity.

On the minus side, unless the horse is owned by the team, the civilian coach has little control over the horse and rider, except on tour, where in most cases it is too late or too risky to make any changes. In addition, it is also difficult for a coach to suggest to a rider that he might be better matched on another horse or that another rider might do better on his horse.
One of the biggest disadvantages for individual members who make up civilian team, is that it can be very expensive to own and show horses. Having the money available to train, transport, and compete a horse is definitely more of a struggle individually compared to having military underwriting.

In summary, Colonel Russell feels that it was more comfortable and economical to compete under the military system, but he believes that civilian teams generate more competitors and more winners for the United States.

John Russell ended his own competitive career in 1956 but has remained a part of the international competitive scene as coach of the U.S. Modern Pentathlon Team. 1995 marked his 39th year of directing the equestrian training for the outstanding and versatile athletes who compete in the five events of the Pentathlon. These five events include fencing, pistol range shooting, swimming, cross-country running, and a show jumping competition where they are mounted on horses that they have never ridden before. At the 1979 World Championship Pentathlon in Budapest, Hungary, the United States was the first team ever to win both the individual and team gold medals in Pentathlon.

Colonel Russell trains Pentathlon competitors at the Russells' Equestrian Center in San Antonio, Texas. The Center is also involved in buying and selling horses. At 76 years of age, the Colonel's days continue to begin at 8:00 a.m. and run until 10:00 p.m., and that's just one indicator of the ongoing contributions this professional horseman has made to equestrian sport. His present schedule remains consistent with a man whose career included such highlights as participation in two Olympic Games, training horses for the United States Military for twenty years, judging, course design and his ongoing direction of the equestrian competition for the Pentathlon.

Courtesy Bill Steinkraus

WILLIAM C. STEINKRAUS

Born October 12, 1925

Bill Steinkraus has often been referred to as "a horseman's horseman." This is the highest tribute one horseman can accord to another, for it not only shows a deep respect for the recipient's knowledge of all aspects of the sport, but also testifies to the good character of the one to whom it is given. And in the past four decades there have been few, if any, other riders whose contributions to the world of equestrian sport have had a more significant influence than Bill's.

In 1968 at Mexico City, Steinkraus exemplified the spirit of what it means for a true amateur to excel at the Olympics when he won the first individual Olympic gold medal ever won by a U.S. rider in any of the equestrian events. In an era of "shamateurs," Bill always had a career totally separate from the sport in which he distinguished himself, and was that rare thing, a true amateur.

Bill Steinkraus was born in Cleveland, Ohio with a condition he once referred to as "C.H.E." (Compulsive Horse Enthusiast). He relates that horses quickly became the greatest preoccupation of his youth, transcending baseball, movies and even girls. He began riding at summer camp when he was ten years old, and was able to continue in the fall when he entered a school that had a modest riding program. Although born into a non-horsey family, Bill had a mother who believed that if children were willing to really commit themselves to an activity, they should be encouraged to do so. When both his parents realized how serious he was about horses, they made it possible for him to begin, and then to progress in the sport.

As a young rider, Bill had several different teachers. Following Ada Maud Thompson (who taught at the school), he rode with Gordon Wright (who later was to teach George Morris) and Frank Carroll, who taught him to ride saddle horses and to drive. Then, when he was sixteen, he started to ride in the afternoons with a local horse dealer named Morton W. "Cappy" Smith who was, at that time, perhaps the best jumper rider in America. "Cappy" had a lot of high-class horses. Sometimes Bill would ride as many as six or eight different horses a day, as every three months or so there would be a whole new group of horses to begin working with. This opportunity provided Bill with invaluable experience, in return for which he gladly helped with the chores at the stable. This arrangement lasted for two years until, at age eighteen, he joined the Army, having completed his freshman year at Yale.

In 1942, Bill went into the U.S. Army Cavalry in what he recalls was the next to last increment of the Army that went through basic training with horses. He remembers having pistol practice on horseback and even practicing cavalry charges! He served overseas in Burma, where it had been thought that the

Bill Steinkraus (age 12) and Tweedle Dum, at the 1937 Waccabuc Horse Show.

Earl Picture News

54

At Aachen in 1960
aboard Ksar d'Esprit.

L'Annee Hippique, O. Cornaz

Horse Cavalry could be used to open up the Burma Road. His regiment eventually helped accomplish this task but, having arrived overseas with all their mounted equipment, they went into combat as a dismounted unit, using mules instead of horses to transport their heavy equipment.

After the war, Bill returned to attend Yale and picked up his riding career as well. He did this through a connection with a former wrestling coach from the University, who was also a horse enthusiast. "Professor" I.Q. Winters owned some jumpers which Bill trained after classes and showed on weekends. He graduated from Yale with the Class of 1948.

Bill Steinkraus made his Olympic debut in 1952 as a member of the show jumping team riding Mrs. Wofford's horse, Hollandia. Along with teammates Arthur McCashin on Miss Budweiser and John Russell on Democrat, he shared the team bronze medal at the Helsinki Games.

Bill remembers Hollandia as a big strong chestnut Thoroughbred with phenomenal jumping ability, though quite a hot-tempered young horse. The horse mellowed with the years and had a long and marvelous career as a competitor. Hollandia was by the same sire, Bonne Nuit, as two of Bill's later Olympic mounts, Night Owl and Riviera Wonder, and was the grandsire of Gem Twist.

After the 1952 Olympics, Captain John Russell stayed in Europe on active duty. The horse he had ridden in the Games, Democrat, was offered to Bill to ride for the fall circuit.

Bill was not very enthused with this prospect when it was first presented to him. Although he had admired the horse ever since its brilliant performance at the 1948 Olympics in London, where Captain Franklin Wing had placed fourth with him individually, the horse was now nineteen years-old and starting to show it. In addition, Democrat was also having some soundness problems.

The horse's prime years, unfortunately, had coincided with World War II (Democrat was scheduled to go to the 1940 Olympics and surely would have gone again in 1944 had the Olympics not been cancelled because of the war). The horse was basically turned out to pasture during these years. Bill Steinkraus says that when he was put back in training for the 1948 Games, "Democrat was very much like a fifteen-year-old automobile with only 20,000 miles on it. Although he was fairly old in the chronological sense, he was fresh in other ways, plus he had a vigor and interest that made him a good competitor."

The first competition in which Bill rode Democrat turned out to be an unforgettable event. It was at Harrisburg in the fall of 1952 and there had been an unusual number of clear rounds in both the first and second classes. When the riders complained that the courses were too easy, the head of the Ground Jury, Major General Guy V. Henry, responded by raising all of the fences six inches and increasing the spreads by two feet.

Bill relates that while the course was still

pretty straightforward with the change in dimensions, it was the last fence on the course, a triple bar, that presented the real problem. It had a four-foot single rail as the front element and a five-foot single rail as the last. The spread between the rails was now increased to eight feet.

In the starting order, Democrat was the last horse to jump. As Bill waited at the in-gate, he saw nothing to reassure him. There had been no clear rounds at all, and three or four shattering falls at the triple bar. The horse jumped the early fences well enough, except that his turns were a little rough. As they approached the last fence, Bill remembers not being able to see any way that it could be jumped. The one thought foremost in his mind, as the powerful old horse gathered himself to try, was that he hoped they didn't break anything.

What happened next Bill Steinkraus recalls as being the biggest show jumping thrill of his entire career, carrying all the elements of excitement, amazement and shock. Even though Democrat met the high first rail a bit too long, Bill felt himself "being transported effortlessly aloft, as on a 747 takeoff. The horse landed just as far from the top rail as he'd taken offf, and never touched a hoof to it."

Bill doesn't remember for sure that he even heard the crowd's roar as they landed with the only clear round on the "altered" course. What he does remember is that he had a big grin on his face and that it was some time before he regained his senses. He simply couldn't believe what had happened.

Bill Steinkraus and Democrat went on to win every single individual class they showed in during that fall circuit in 1952, and contributed to several team wins as well.

After the end of this spectacular fall circuit, Democrat was retired with full honors. Everyone who had ever ridden him agreed that no one would ever know just how good he really could have been during his prime years, because they coincided with the war years when he was out of commission. Also, that he would always be remembered as being a generous and consistent horse whose career ended with a memorable winning streak.

Bill rode the amazing Snowbound in the 1968 Mexico Games. They won the first individual gold medal the U.S. had ever won in equestrian events.
Karl Schonerstedt

Bill Steinkraus was the captain for the jumping team at the 1956 Olympics in Stockholm. The U.S. team placed fifth in the team competition. Bill rode Night Owl at this event.

In 1960, at the Olympics in Rome, the U.S. won the team silver medal in show jumping. Bill was paired with Ksar d'Esprit, a huge grey horse with enormous strength and jumping ability. This horse, which had been bred by Hugh Wiley, was loaned to the USET by Eleanora Sears. Ksar had a slight wind problem, which is not unusual in very big horses. It is a flaw that disqualifies them as show hunters, but has little effect on them as jumpers. Ksar was a genuine Olympic horse and a mainstay of the USET from 1958 to 1963. He was an especially brilliant puissance specialist whose strength and courage frequently took him over seven-foot fences in the puissance classes.

1968 turned out to be an extraordinary year in the Olympic career of Bill Steinkraus, for at this event he won the first individual gold medal

56

that the United States had ever won in the equestrian events. The horse Bill rode in Mexico was named Snowbound. Early in his career, this horse seemed a most unlikely candidate to ever achieve Olympic status. A series of unusual and providential events took place to bring about this transformation. Here from M.A. Stoneridge's wonderful book, *Great Horses of Our Time*, and Bill Steinkraus' recollections, comes the story.

"Snowbound, formerly a race horse that went by the name of Gay Vic, suffered recurrent tendon injuries from the age of two. In the races he was entered in, he never showed the slightest interest in being first to the finish line, and was even beaten by as many as sixteen lengths one time. No buyer could be found for him even at the bargain price of fifty dollars."

Bill recalls that the owners contacted Mrs. Barbara Worth Oakford, who owned and managed a leading show and training stable. She told them she would only be interested in him if he could recover from his bowed tendon.

Returning from a horse show one evening, Mrs. Oakford found that Gay Vic had been deposited in one of her empty stalls during her absence. He now had two bowed tendons, not just one. She is said to have looked at the brown horse with the white blaze down his face and stripe on his slightly Roman nose and said, "Good Lord! Gay Vic! With all of your problems you might as well be snowbound as think of being a show horse!" And that is how the future Olympic champion got his new name.

Once in her hands, as fate would have it, she decided to at least give him a chance. After his bowed tendons healed, his first lessons were surprisingly encouraging. Despite his infirmities, Snowbound's basic conformation was well balanced and of a type that Mrs. Oakford liked in show jumpers. Temperamentally, he was highly-strung and nervous, but he was a willing and intelligent pupil who rarely made the same mistake twice.

About two years later, the horse's potential as an international champion was recognized by John Galvin who bought him for his daughter and she, in turn, loaned him to the USET for the 1968 Olympics. His temperament was still on the nervous side and always would be, but he impressed team coach, Bert de Nemethy, and team captain, Bill Steinkraus, with his natural jumping ability. Bill, who was 43 years old at

the time, was considered a specialist in dealing with high-strung horses. It seemed destined that the two of them would become partners.

In the first round, over a tremendously testing course, and riding against 41 competitors representing fifteen nations from around the world, Bill Steinkraus and Snowbound scored one of only two clear rounds in the entire competition. In the second round, with only one fence down, they finished a decisive four faults ahead of their nearest rivals.

After this brilliant gold medal victory in the individual competition, Snowbound pulled up lame and was unable to compete in the team competition. Bill says of him, "He was a very generous horse, often giving everything he had to give and hurting himself in the process. He had tremendous stamina and courage and a remarkable gymnastic ability. In addition, he had so much nervous energy that he was always able to give a little more when asked to." It is for this very quality and reason that Bill Steinkraus still favors Thoroughbreds. He feels that today's courses increasingly demand the scope, courage and gymnastic ability that they specialize in.

At the 1972 Olympic Games in Munich, Bill made his last Olympic appearance. He again rode Snowbound in the individual competition, but the tendon started to give way again and they placed 22nd. For the team event, Bill switched to his alternate horse, Main Spring. This horse was a Canadian chestnut gelding of unknown parentage, donated to the USET by William D. Haggard, III. Bill and Main Spring jumped two brilliant rounds over a very difficult course, recording the best overall score of the day and one of only three clear rounds in the whole contest. Their performance enabled the U.S. to win the team silver medal, finishing only 0.25 faults (representing a one-second time penalty) behind the victorious team from the Federal Republic of Germany.

Main Spring, who was not a Thoroughbred or even close, was a more placid horse and presented Bill with some technically challenging problems. Because the horse lacked that Thoroughbred nervous energy, it was sometimes hard to maintain his impulsion, and he also had a distinctly unclassical jumping style. Bill started out trying to ride him like a Thoroughbred, and the horse let him know he did not appreciate it at all. Work and persistence paid off with some common ground that they found and capitalized on. After Bill retired from the team at the end of 1972, Frank Chapot took over the ride on Main Spring, with whom he won the coveted George V Cup at the White City in London. Bill became President of the U.S. Equestrian Team, then Chairman, and is now, after heading the team's administration for twenty years, its Chairman Emeritus.

Commenting about his jumping style, Bill says, "I like to think of myself as a very economical rider. That is, I try to get the maximum result from the minimum of physical effort. I'd like to be remembered as a rider who didn't appear to intervene very much but who still retained complete control over every situation. I think the best kind of intervention takes place so far back from the fence, and so subtly, that it's not noticeable. I've always aimed at that goal because it's both the most effective style and the most attractive to watch."

He continued, "Before an important competition, I liked to have time to myself, more for technical than psychological preparation. I'd go over the course in my mind many times, analyzing all the different problems and considering situations that might occur, even the improbable ones. I always preferred being able to refer back, while riding the course, to solutions I'd already worked out for every possibility, rather than trust myself to come up with the right answer on the spur of the moment."

Bill Steinkraus is an all-round horseman who has left an indelible mark on the horse world. He has ridden hunters, jumpers, dressage horses, saddle horses and racehorses. He's done fox hunting, driving, judging, television commentary, book writing, and administrating. He has been featured in equestrian video films and been an all-round promoter of equestrian sports. Over the years, he has acquired such a myriad of honors and awards that it would take a separate

book to describe them. He is a member of the Show Jumping, Madison Square Garden, National Horse Show and New York Sports Halls of Fame.

Married to Helen "Sis" Ziegler just after the 1960 Olympics, Steinkraus is the father of three boys, all of them riders, but none "addicted." Sis Steinkraus, however, became interested in dressage after seeing it in the Olympics, and went on to be a noted dressage rider, judge and show organizer. "A lot of the blood, sweat and tears that went into my riding career were really hers," Steinkraus notes. "The person who gets to ride into the ring isn't the only one who has to make sacrifices in order to fulfill an Olympic dream."

He currently works as a consulting editor for Doubleday and Company. His schedule is a busy one, with time divided between his family commitments, his career, and his involvements with the United States Equestrian Team, the American Horse Shows Association and the Federation Equestre International, of which he is a Bureau and Executive Board member and President of the World Cup Committee. He is an accomplished viola player who enjoys playing chamber music. He also likes to hunt, fish, golf and ski when time allows.

His plans for the future are "to continue doing the same as I am now for as long as I can make a contribution. My caring for what happens to the United States Equestrian Team and to equestrian sports will never cease in my lifetime."

Very different from Snowbound was Main Spring, Bill's partner for the 1972 Munich Olympics where the team took the silver medal.

Gamecock

Tish Quirk

FRANK CHAPOT

Born February 24, 1932

Frank Chapot is internationally known and highly respected for his many contributions and the longevity of his participation in equestrian events, two factors which also give him his greatest personal satisfaction. Because of his extensive knowledge of equestrian sport, when a rider's ability and judgement receives the nod of his approval, it is regarded as being of special significance.

His love of horses dates back to his childhood and began when his father bought him his first pony. Not having the advantage of today's USET junior rider programs across the United States, or an accredited trainer to learn from back in the 1930s and 1940s, Frank developed as a rider through trial and error, observation, and his own intuition. He progressed to become a leading junior rider and was a Medal Maclay winner. His strong competitive spirit

has always been one of his greatest assets and he has a reputation of rising to the occasion when under pressure.

At age 24, Frank was in the Air Force when the USET held its selection tryouts for the 1956 Stockholm Olympics. The permission he sought to try out for the team was granted and he made the team. Along with Hugh Wiley and Bill Steinkraus, Frank helped the USET jumping team place fifth in the rankings of all the best horses and riders in the world. This marked the beginning of Frank's association with the USET as a competitive rider that would last twenty years, and would include riding in six Olympic Games and producing innumerable international show jumping wins.

According to M.A. Stoneridge's book *Great Horses of Our Time*, Frank was Horseman of the Year in 1969, a top amateur steeplechase jockey, and particularly well known for his dazzling speed class exploits in the jumping arena.

At the 1972 Munich Olympics, aboard White Lightening, the "smallest gun" on that U.S. team.

Courtesy USET

1960 in Rome,
aboard Trail Guide.

Courtesy USET

Frank has been a member of the FEI World Cup Committee, a former secretary of the AHSA, a member and former chairman of both the AHSA Jumper Rules Committee and the USET Show Jumping Selection Committee, and a director of the National Horse Show. He has served as the USET's Vice-President for Jumpers, coach and Chef d'Equipe for the 1984 Olympic gold medal team, the 1986 World Championship gold medal team, the 1988 Olympic silver medal team, as well as the chef d'equipe for the 1992 and 1996 Olympic Games. He has served in this same capacity for many World Championship competitions. Frank also breeds and trains horses at his home in Neshanic Station, New Jersey and is a leading course designer, judge and jump course official.

One of the greatest dreams and satisfactions any equestrian breeder can ever hope to realize is to start a young horse from scratch, develop and train it and watch it attain Olympic status. Frank and his wife Mary did this with a beautiful grey horse named Gem Twist, who was sired by Good Twist, a horse that carried Frank to many of his international victories. At the 1988 Olympics, when Gem Twist won two silver medals, he was ridden by Greg Best and coached by Frank, who was also the USET's chef d'equipe. According to John Quirk of *Horses Magazine,* "Frank, who is not a man given to open displays of enthusiasm, jumped almost as high as Gem Twist when he witnessed this Olympic achievement."

In 1960, the Olympics took place in Rome. Hugh Wiley, Bill Steinkraus, George Morris, and Frank were the four members of the U.S. Equestrian Team. Frank rode a U.S. Cavalry veteran named Trail Guide, who was 22 years old at the time. He remembers the horse as being careful and brave. Theirs was the best American score. The team rose to the occasion and won the silver medal at this event. It was Frank's first Olympic medal and an experience to be savored for a lifetime.

Frank met his wife Mary when they were both members of the U.S. jumping team. Mary was the first woman ever to win the gold medal in jumping at the Pan-American Games. She did this in 1963 in Sao Paulo, Brazil on a horse named Tomboy. Frank and Mary's friendship grew with time as they trained and travelled with the USET. They rode as teammates in two Olympic Games. Her name was Mary Mairs when they competed in the 1964 Olympics in Tokyo, along with Kathy Kusner. Frank placed seventh in the individual competition and the team placed sixth. San Lucas was Frank's horse at that time.

Frank and Mary were married in January 1965, so went as husband and wife as well as teammates to the 1968 Olympic Games in Mexico, along with Bill Steinkraus and Kathy Kusner. They were the only husband and wife to compete in equestrian sport on the same team in the Olympics until 1996, when David and Karen O'Connor competed in the Three-Day Event on the same team. 1968 was also the year when Bill Steinkraus won the individual gold medal on Snowbound. Frank placed fourth in the individual competition riding San Lucas, a 17.3 hand Thoroughbred. They narrowly missed the bronze medal with a jump-off time of 36.80 seconds, compared to David Broome of Great Britain's time of 35.30 seconds.

At the 1968 Olympic Games, the USET also placed fourth with an even narrower margin, (a one-quarter time fault) between them and Germany's bronze medal-winning team. The competition was exciting and intense. Even though there was disappointment at having come so close, the U.S. team derived a certain amount of satisfaction from having given Germany such a close call.

The U.S. jumping team claimed another team silver medal win at the 1972 Olympics in Munich. This time, Frank's team members were Bill Steinkraus, Neal Shapiro and Kathy Kusner. Frank rode White Lightning, a horse that Mary's mother had bred. Being a small, light horse, Frank says, "She may have been the USET's smallest gun against the high, wide and very challenging German course, but in the first round she gave a very creditable performance with the next best score to Bill Steinkraus' clear round on Main Spring. Even after she injured herself, she carried on to complete the competition."

The 1976 Olympics in Montreal were the last Games in which Frank rode. He placed fifth in the individual show jumping competition. The team placed fourth, missing the bronze medal by one point. Frank rode a horse named Viscount during these Olympic Games, closing this part of his career which had spanned two decades as a USET rider.

Frank Chapot learned many things over his twenty years of riding with the team. His zeal

for wanting to win every class he entered was one of the things that was fine-tuned and changed through the years. Between jumping coach, Bert de Nemethy's counsel and instruction, and watching how Hans Gunter Winkler of Germany and his horse, Halla, always seemed to save their best for the big competitions, Frank learned to select carefully classes that would be a good preparation for the important competitions, without taking too much out of horse and rider. He learned that useful careers of both horses and riders can be unnecessarily shortened by asking a horse to peak at top level competitions too many times in too short a time frame.

Along with experience also comes the knowledge that some horses are better over long, galloping courses and others over twisty, trappy courses. Some horses take a class or two before they are ready to win; with others you can try for it in the first competition. It is always important to know what suits your horse best.

The object in show jumping in the first round is to get around the ring in the optimum time, leaving all the jumps intact. In the jump-off, speed plays a more important part. As the horse accelerates around the course, leaving the jumps standing and intact becomes more difficult. Frank relates that the well-planned jumping course should be a test of how well trained the horse is, and how well the rider can ride, think and control him. It is not just a test of how high the partnership can jump, but also of how well they have done their homework. It tests the horse's ability to extend and shorten, and his quick reaction to the rider's aids. Good judgement and knowledge of just what you can do with each individual horse is very important. A good partnership between the horse and rider evolves from the lessons they learn by making many mistakes together.

Olympic caliber horses continue to be hard to find. Through the years there has been a change in the source from which these horses are provided for USET riders, from the Army providing horses for its military riders, to horses being loaned to the team by patrons of equestrian events, to the current day system where horses may be home-bred, syndicate-owned or company-sponsored. Today, horse and rider combinations come to the team pretty much ready made.

Frank readily admits that he has been very lucky over the years to have had horses of the quality of Trail Guide, San Lucas, Main Spring, Good Twist, Manon, Viscount, and White Lightning. When I asked him what the best thing an outstanding rider can have going for him or her, he responded, "A wonderful horse."

The importance of a rider being connected with an outstanding horse is even reflected in the name of Frank and Mary's, Chado Farm. Chado was Frank's first good horse. That first good horse can mean such a turning point for a rider that it cannot be understated as a vital piece to have in place for success in equestrian sport. If a rider has a horse of Olympic caliber, his chances of making the team are much greater.

To add to his accomplishments, Frank has written an instructional book entitled, *Winning with Frank Chapot*.

GEORGE MORRIS

Born February 26, 1938

Tish Quirk

In riding circles throughout the world, when George Morris' name is mentioned or he is quoted, there is an E.F. Hutton effect. I observed this when I went to a Hunter Jumper Show connected with a one day clinic where this well-known teacher was helping students at the Stoney Ridge Farm in Chelsea, Michigan. As I waited to interview him, I wandered slowly through the crowd. Twice I heard his name mentioned, conversation in the immediate vicinity hushed, and I saw people turn their best ear toward the conversation to pick up information. Why? The same reason people have listened to E.F. Hutton -- George Morris knows what he is talking about. He has the credentials of a master to support this knowledge, and people are eager for expertise that can help them improve their own situation or abilities.

When a teacher is fortunate enough to have an understudy that has both an aptitude for riding and a good attitude, it is an answer to a prayer. Given a choice between teaching a student who has one or the other, but not both, George would pick the student with the good attitude any day of the week. The reason is that he regards this student as one who is serious about riding, and willing to work, listen, and learn, as opposed to one who thinks he knows it already.

George Morris began riding when he was eight years old. He was born into a "semi-horsey" family. His mother was from Brooklyn and her family were members of the Brooklyn Riding and Driving Club there. His father was a member of Squadron A. He describes his family as "being riders, but not serious riders." His sister rode for fun. He continued, "while we were not a horsey family, we were connected and knew a lot of people that were."

He recalls that riding was the only sport that he ever really enjoyed. It was a sport that he spent a great deal of time on and worked hard at, and he became very good for his age as he progressed through the junior ranks. To this day he still holds the record of being the youngest rider ever to win the Medal and Maclay Championship finals at the age of fourteen!

George was nineteen when he first saw the horse that he was later to ride in his Olympic competition. It was 1957, and Sinjon was at the North Shore Horse Show in Long Island. The blood bay Thoroughbred was five years old at the time and being ridden by Harry

DeLeyer. George, "just loved the horse over the outside course and thought he'd make an outstanding jumper." He shared his thoughts with Harry DeLeyer who, in his generosity and with clear knowledge of George's abilities as a rider, said he would talk to Sinjon's owner, Eileen Dineen, about loaning the horse to George for the selection trials in 1958. Mrs. Dineen was agreeable and, to this day, George Morris remains touched by the great kindness the Dineen family extended to him in allowing him to ride Sinjon.

It was Bert de Nemethy (USET trainer) and George who brought Sinjon from a very young, green six year-old to top level competency as a jumper. George recalls, "Sinjon was very precocious. He never really went green. Even as young as he was, he went like an experienced horse. He had plenty of jump. He was brave and he was careful. He had all the qualities of an Olympic horse."

It was these attributes, plus George's riding ability, that placed them fourth in the individual standings in the Prix Des Nations Jumping Competition at the 1960 Olympics in Rome, and contributed significantly to winning the team silver medal. He remembers the Olympic award ceremony as being "very, very exciting and when the American flag went up and the national anthem was being played - it was tear jerking. It was very emotional and meaningful."

"In those days," George commented, "You had to make your bed and lie in it as far as the amateur/professional rule went. There were no grey, fudging areas. I wanted to be a teacher and I had to make a living, and these were two of the main factors that helped me to decide to make a profession out of teaching and, therefore, eliminated me as an amateur participant in any future Olympics."

Gordon Wright and Bert de Nemethy are two teachers who stand out in his mind as having inspired him to want to give to others the confidence and practical application that they had given to him. From 1960 to the present day, George Morris has developed into a leading teacher both nationally and internationally. In achieving this position, he has returned the original kindness given to him by making a number of important connections for

other young aspiring riders who have shown outstanding promise. Three of the four 1984 Olympic medal winners in Grand Prix Jumping were former Morris students; Conrad Homfeld, Melanie Smith, and Leslie Burr Lenehan, plus the reserve rider, Anne Kursinski. He has taught students from Europe, Asia, Australia, Africa, Scandinavia, and Canada, many of whom now have World Cup Championships to their credit.

John Quirk, in *Horses Magazine*, described George's decision to make a comeback in the competitive arena in 1983 at the age of 45. "If people had doubts about the wisdom of his latest ambition, they were entitled, but he would not be deterred from his latest grand adventure."

"There were crushing reversals. In 1985 he was the fastest of only five clear rounds in the first round of the du Maurier Grand Prix at Spruce Meadows, but his horse, Rio, pulled up lame and had to be scratched from the second round. The look of disappointment in his normally disciplined expression spoke volumes of what it meant to him to come this far and then be thwarted by the fortunes of competition."

"When Rio returned to action after a lengthy lay-up, it was George's turn. In a freak accident while dismounting, with Rio shying, George's leg was broken, a serious fracture of the femur. He 'recovered' from this long before his advisors recommended. Returning to action, he was among the five riders who

George at age 12, winning the Medal and McClay finals
Budd Studios

The brave and careful Sinjon, George's partner on the silver medal team in Rome, 1960.   *F. Alfano*

were hurt that notorious year at Hickstead, England, when the hedge fence was permitted to grow so big that horses tried to bank it. This time George broke his neck."

"So should he have given it up at this point and been satisfied with his continuing career as a master teacher? He had no such intention. In 1988, at the age of 50, he was back at the Spruce Meadows Masters as Chef d'Equipe of the winning American Team, walking the courses with a noticeable limp. On Sunday he was competing with Rio in the first round of the $506,000 du Maurier Grand Prix, where he'd been three years ago."

"This time Rio was not lame. This time there was nothing standing between George and the goals he had set for himself in 1983. It was a memorable performance in a landmark competition, by a most remarkable rider. The ride was ideal. Rio ticked #4, but there were no other rubs. The $160,000 first prize money that he won in this one event was more than he had won in all the prior years of his long and illustrious career."

George Morris' persistence is a living example of the success that can come from tenacity of purpose. No wonder this man is so credible and has such an ability to inspire. He lives by what he teaches and victory is known to those whose determination is not discouraged by set-backs.

While George still enjoys competition, he does feel he is getting closer to a time when judging and course designing may evolve to replace competition in his interests. He also enjoys being a chef d'equipe for the USET.

When I asked him what was the highest he had ever jumped, he recalled being in a jump-off with Bill Steinkraus at the White City in London in the Puissance Class. He was on a horse named Night Owl and jumped 7'4". He commented that he "doesn't care if he ever jumps that high again, as once in a lifetime was quite enough." Sure footings and safe landings from that height aren't something a wise man on horseback would want to gamble with very often!

Regarding young riders having taken a bad

fall, George emphasizes that the immediate thing to do is to determine if medical assistance is needed and, if so, to get it. But, if the rider is not hurt, the best thing to do is to get back on the horse as soon as possible and to attack the same problem, only modified, such as making the jump lower or not so wide. George says, "It is very important for riders to understand why they have fallen, in order to prevent a reoccurrence. It depends on the level of riding whether or not the rider knows why he has fallen. Professional riders always know. Teachers have to help young riders gain insight into the reason for, more often than not, they don't know."

Twenty-five years ago, George Morris started Hunterdon Incorporated on his 100-acre farm which he manages with pride. It is an international training center and incorporates all the various aspects of his teaching and managing involvement. Located on a hill in beautiful Hunterdon County, the acreage includes two large barns, some subsidiary barns and a spacious indoor ring. The 'piece de resistance' is a Grand Prix field, of about fif-teen acres, which presents every combination of jumps known to horse and mankind. Many of the USET's three-day event riders like to train on this field as it gives them excellent preparation for the many challenging obstacles they will encounter in top level competitions. Hunterdon Inc. is about a twenty-minute ride from Gladstone, New Jersey, the headquarters for the USET.

George's book, *Hunter Seat Equitation*, is an all-time best selling book about horses and riding. In 1985 he produced *The Science of Riding*, an instructional videotape which has also been widely utilized. He has written the Jumping Clinic critique for the magazine *Practical Horseman* for twelve years. He has served in an advisory capacity innumerable times to many people seeking him as a resource regarding show jumping.

As a horseman, he feels very lucky that there are so many alternatives he can participate in, choose from and apply his abilities to. And to continue to participate and choose from these alternatives is just what he intends to do for the rest of his life.

Courtesy Michael Page

MICHAEL PAGE

Born September 23, 1938

I interviewed Michael Page when he was chef d'equipe for the United States Three-Day Event Team at the 1990 World Championships in Stockholm, Sweden. Friendly, calm and discerning, this lean, athletic man was everything you would envision a former Olympic competitor to be. While his tanned, handsome face belied his 51 years, the silver-grey hair at his temples and the knowledge he possesses gives a clue to a man well-seasoned and active in a sport he loves.

Michael Page is a visible and steadying support to the team with his experience and even disposition. In his own words he says, "I never get up too high or down too low." He was comfortable in his role as coordinator, spokesman and advisor for the team, as evidenced by the way he addressed issues and by the way he called words of encouragement to one rider and information to another. As we talked by the practice ring, I witnessed a mutual respect in his exchanges with the riders.

He is a man whose participation with the USET has included competing in three Olympic Games, three Pan-American Games, being chef d'equipe at the 1988 Olympics in Seoul and the 1992 Olympics in Barcelona, being chairman of the USET Selection Committee and chef d'equipe for the three-day event riders at the 1990 World Championships. In 1976 he was involved at the Olympics as the coach for the Canadian team. He has served as chairman of the Hunter Seat Equitation Committee for the American Horse Shows Association. You would never guess that this is a man who was not born into a horse family and who, in fact, never owned a horse of his own until after he had ridden in three Olympic Games. It was from the influence of television and the movies that Michael Page first aspired to be a rider. At the age of ten he began taking lessons at a public riding academy near his home in Pelham,

New York. He relates that "the strong magnetic feel that he had for horses as a kid is still very much a part of him today."

For 25 years he worked as vice-president of sales in the family-owned Speciality Packaging and Hat Lining Company and commuted to work daily into New York City. Several years ago the family sold the business, which then freed him to devote time to horses and to the USET, a luxury that had to be carefully balanced when he was doing both.

In his opinion, one of the best attributes of the sport is that it is something you can do for years and still enjoy in one capacity or another. Michael Page and Michael Plumb, who both started out with the USET together in 1959, are living testaments to this attribute.

When I asked him what his advice would be to a young rider who had taken a bad fall, he said, "To assess the rider's physical injury is, of course, first and foremost." Then he clarified for me, "A rider has to ride because he wants to ride. He has to make a choice. For some it will be that there are more important things in life than riding. If a rider likes what he does and wants it badly enough to get back on after the fall, the sooner he does the better."

One of the most gratifying memories that stands out in Michael's mind to this day has to do with knowing his horse's abilities and making an accurate judgement call in deciding how to ride him in the big competition. The year was 1964 and it was at the Olympics in Tokyo. He was riding Grasshopper, a sixteen year-old horse who had suffered a set-back in his training and had been unsound because of the hard going at Gladstone.

In Tokyo it had rained. The ground was soft but, about three-quarters of the way around the steeplechase course, Grasshopper became winded. Another rider might have been tempted to push the horse, but Michael knew that Grasshopper was genuine and it was his nature to give all he had, without being asked.

Michael came close to pulling him out, but somewhere between the steeplechase and the cross-country, Grasshopper got his second wind and ended up having the third fastest time on the cross-country course. This placed Michael and Grasshopper in fourth place in the individual scores, a mere 1.5 points behind the bronze medal winner, and made a strong contribution towards achieving the only Olympic medal the USET won that year - the team silver Three-Day Event medal.

It was Michael's understanding of Grasshopper and what he was capable of that allowed the horse to make such a recovery. It speaks well of both horse and rider in the partnership, when each is able to give to the other what is needed for the best performance possible on that day. When I asked Michael Page how he felt during the Olympic medal ceremonies, he said, "Both proud and relieved. Proud of the accomplishment and relieved that it was over and that I'd done the job I set out to do."

After Tokyo he retired from competition but, in 1968, the USET called him back when they found they had extra horses and not enough riders to go to the Olympics in Mexico City. It was in preparation for this Olympic competition that Michael met his wife-to-be, Georgette, who was working for the team and taking care of Foster, the horse he was to ride.

It was on Foster that he won the individual bronze medal in the Three-Day Event and helped the U.S. to win the team silver medal. His order of go placed him as one of the earlier riders, which he wasn't used to, but, in fact, it was to his advantage, as he rode before the heavy rain came. He estimates that the course was four or five times more difficult for the later riders and credits his early start order with moving him from 40th place after dressage to third in the final individual placings. He also gives credit to Georgette: "If it hadn't been for her participation with the horses and her support, I wouldn't have won the medals, and at one point I may have even stopped riding."

Today he and Georgette "still enjoy doing pretty much the same things as we did back then." They live in North Salem, New York, and board horses at a nearby farm. "We've been together twenty five years and it's been good," said Michael. In a day and age when happy lasting relationships are rare, this open appreciation of his wife increases my respect for this man.

Plans for the future include active participation in the sport he loves. He feels he has been very fortunate with his career. "I've had an opportunity to do a lot and to see a lot and, hopefully, I've contributed to the sport in a positive way."

Aboard the courageous Grasshopper, one of only three horses to have competed in three Olympic games.

Courtesy USET.

KEVIN FREEMAN

Born October 21, 1941

Wenants Brothers

Kevin Freeman's first international competition for the USET was at the 1963 Pan-American Games in Sao Paulo, Brazil. It was a brilliant beginning in top level competition, for he won the individual silver medal in the Three-Day Event and played an important part in the United States winning the team gold medal.

Next came a major sweep of wins when, for three consecutive Olympic Games, he was a member of the silver medal-winning Three-Day Event team. He is a man whose interest in both eventing and race riding has been interwoven through the years to include a number of victory gallops and trips to the winner's circle. He enjoyed major victories as a race rider in the New Jersey and Pennsylvania Hunt Cups and at the famed Iroquois Steeplechase in Tennessee.

At the 1964 Olympics in Tokyo, Kevin remembers how the other competitors joked about not wanting to be an "S.I.F." These letters stand for "Sports Illustrated Favorite" and it was regarded as unlucky to be placed in the position of having to live up to this label. Based on prior performances in eventing at the two preceding Olympic Games, the USET three-day event team of 1964 was in no danger of being called an "S.I.F." at that point. The horse Kevin rode at the 1964 Games was an Irish-bred gelding that started out as Mike Plumb's reserve horse. Kevin was placed on him when his own horse pulled up lame. He says, "Gallopade wasn't a very good mover. He was so-so in dressage, but he was a good jumper and a consistent horse." He proved to be a worthy competitor in helping capture the team silver medal.

Chalan was the name of the horse Kevin rode in the 1968 Olympics in Mexico City. "There are times when circumstances work against you to make the competition difficult," he recalls. "Such was the case at the 1968 Olympics, when there was a torrential down-

pour at the beginning of my cross-country round, causing the already poor footing on the landing side of some of the jumps to become worse and reducing the visibility from one jump to the next. Chalan landed in mud up to his shoulders at one fence and slipped in an uphill take-off to clear an oxer. The horse's confidence was badly shaken. There was no let up in the rain." In all, the horse fell three times and they were eliminated, even though they completed the course. With the top three riders' scores being the ones to count, this elimination did not stand in the way of the United States again earning the team silver medal.

At the 1972 Munich Olympics, Kevin's equine partner was a horse named Good Mixture. "He was a 16.1 hand Thoroughbred, born and raised in Oregon. He was a difficult horse on the flat: spooky, excitable, unpredictable and independent. It was a challenge to capture his mind, so he wasn't the best dressage horse, but he was just fabulous on the cross-country course."

The Munich Olympics were Good Mixture's first introduction to advanced international competition. He and Kevin had the best score of the American team, placing fifth individually and contributing significantly to the winning of the team silver medal for the United States. Good Mixture went on from the 1972 Olympics to the World Championships in 1974. There, he was ridden by the team captain, Mike Plumb, and finished an individual second to teammate, Bruce Davidson on Irish Cap, by the smallest of margins. Their combined efforts produced the first-ever team gold medal for the United States at the World Championships. Good Mixture's cross-country record throughout his career as an event horse proved exemplary. Except for this horse's final competition at Radnor before his retirement, where he stopped once at a huge drop fence onto a road crossing, he never had a jumping fault on the cross-country in his entire career.

Kevin and Good Mixture, cross-country at the 1972 Munich Games.

Milan Czerny

Kevin Freeman remembers that, for him, getting on the team was often the hardest part. It required daily preparation to remain in top form and be ready for every selection trial. Even then, it was always evident that the difference between making the team or not was often a matter of luck, good or bad, which made the margin between being a very good rider and being an Olympic rider a very slim one. Once the team was set, it was easier to focus attention on the one main competition.

He went on to talk about the "team concept" in being part of the USET. "As a member of the team, your ride can either have a positive effect, or it can jeopardize the team's standing. Very often, individual results must be secondary to what is best for the team. For instance, in eventing there is usually a plan in which horse and rider combinations perform in a certain order to produce maximum benefit for the total team performance. The first horse/rider combination to compete is usually a reliable experienced partnership but one that may not have the necessary brilliance to put them in the top placings. Being the first of the team to go around the course, they are able to provide valuable information to subsequent riders. The second horse/rider combination may be the most inexperienced or green combination. The third combination is usually experienced and capable of finishing high in the placings. The fourth combination is usually the one with the best chance of finishing in the medals individually. If the first two horses get around the course successfully, the third, and especially the fourth, combination have the green light to take some chances to improve both their own and the team's position. When things go wrong during the ride of the earlier partnerships, then the later riders must sacrifice individual success for that of the team."

Kevin Freeman has always loved both race riding and eventing. He compares the two. "There is a real exhilaration that comes from racing riding. It is fast and intense, with at least one or more horses in the field at your side bearing down on the course along with you. Your main concern is beating the other horses in the race. Keeping the proper pace for the course and the other horses in the race, getting your horse as right as possible to the jumps, and taking calculated chances over the final fences, are all part of the strategy. The race is generally over in a few minutes. It's great!"

"On the other hand, my experience with event horses is in both competing and training them. Competing an event horse and keeping it in top condition is a never-ending, time-consuming process. It takes a lot of time and patience to train an event horse to be versatile, responsive and competent in all three disciplines: dressage, cross-country, and stadium jumping. There is, however, much to be said for the satisfaction that comes in achieving a winning partnership."

Kevin went on to describe how, "in dressage the horse is required to be supple and obedient and basically under the total control of the rider. However, on cross-country you need a brave horse with initiative. He needs to be comfortable jumping at speed on uneven ground and over solid and difficult cross-country obstacles on a course he is encountering for the first time. This presents a conflicting mental outlook from the previous day's dressage performance. Most horses are better at one phase or the other, but the emphasis at the higher levels is on the good cross-country performer. A specialist in only one discipline or the other, however, is rarely a successful competitor. On the third day you ask your horse to come back from the grueling cross-country day, pass a strict veterinary inspection, re-establish his balance and mental outlook, and jump a clear, controlled stadium round. It requires a combination of good fortune to find a horse that can meet these criteria, and then a great deal of patience in training him."

A native of Portland, Oregon, Kevin spent a good deal of the summertime on his parents' farm outside the city. He started riding on home-bred horses descended from the stallion that his parents bought while on their honeymoon. Riding bareback and Western were his style until, at age fifteen, he became interested in learning to ride English. From this point, his horsemanship abilities moved him into his outstanding years as an event competitor and race rider. Then, more recently, he became interested in show jumping, with hopes of competing at the Grand Prix level. He has made a great deal of progress in this direction and won his first Grand Prix in 1993. His competitive spirit and love of horses continues to be alive and well!

His present work schedule parallels his earlier years of juggling his life's activities to participate in his race riding and three-day event competitions. Back then, he went to Cornell University, from where he eventually graduated. On weekends he commuted to Gladstone, New Jersey, the home-base for the USET, where he worked on his riding skills. He then went on to attend the University of Pennsylvania's Wharton Business School, while pursuing his race riding on weekends.

Today, he works at a fourth generation farm

machinery manufacturing business, J.A. Freeman & Son, operated by his father and two brothers. After dinner each evening, from 7:00 until 9:30 P.M., he is involved in either riding or coaching. Kevin has a small barn, with about four or five clients and usually a working student to help run the barn in exchange for training. Weekends often find him playing catch-up around his training operation, competing, or giving occasional clinics. His teaching and clinics help to defray the cost of his current Grand Prix show jumping interest. Now and then he enjoys getting away to go skiing. The bottom line is that, if you want something badly enough, you create ways to make it happen.

Participating in today's Grand Prix show jumping arena places you in a world of keen competition; it involves a sizable financial investment and requires that you have an abundance of desire and dedication. It is not uncommon for the purchase price of top show jumpers to be in the region of between $300,000 to $500,000. This is in great contrast to the Olympic Army team of the early military riders, when $160 was the top dollar paid by the Army for its horses, show jumpers included. In 1952, Mrs. Wofford paid $10,000 for the Grand Prix show jumper, Hollandia, and the Busch family bought Circus Rose for $20,000 and renamed her Miss Budweiser to compete in the same Olympic event. The exciting world of show jumping has never been the same since.

Kevin Freeman is now in his fifties and recognizes that a high percentage of competitors in the show jumping arena are half his age or younger. He also realizes that he is getting into this area of competition late in life and that he is not a full-time competitor, which is the optimum way of undertaking this effort. He has some definite pluses on his side, however. He has a wife, Barrie, who gives constant support and encouragement and he also has a Grand Prix level horse named Never Better. He is a serious man when he takes on a challenge and, while he tempers any optimism he has with realism, no one can deny that he has come a long way towards being competitive in the Grand Prix ranks.

As a writer who is very near this rider's age, and also one who believes in going for your goals, I can't help but hope that there will be some more top wins in Kevin Freeman's already illustrious and varied career in equestrian sport.

J. MICHAEL PLUMB

Born March 28, 1940

Courtesy J. Michael Plumb

When I asked J. Michael Plumb if he had another profession besides riding, he said simply and with pride, "I'm a horseman, that's my life." He elaborated on this concise, eloquent answer when he began sharing with me the many dimensions of what he does with horses. He raises and trains them, he teaches and coaches students seeking to be proficient at riding them, and he has been an international competitor since the late fifties.

John Michael Plumb was born into a horse-oriented family. His father was a famous huntsman and steeplechase rider, and his mother rode and bred horses. He doesn't remember exactly when he started to ride. "As soon as someone sat me on a horse, I suppose," he said. What we do know, however, is that his interest in competition developed early on. By the age of ten he was showing in equitation, and hunters and jumpers, and had participated in his first fox hunt. In the 1950s he became even more serious about equitation and began moving through the ranks of junior horsemen with the Medal and Maclay Championships.

In high school, Michael was involved in baseball, basketball and football, and was actually more interested in these sports than in riding at the time. In college he majored in Animal Science. Although this three-letter athlete could have chosen a career in any one of the three sports he excelled in during high school, this was the time when three-day eventing caught his attention and ended up becoming his preference. The direction his life would take was thereby chosen.

His first international competition was in 1959 at the Pan-American Games, in Chicago, on a horse named The Lark, owned by his mother. In 1960, at the age of twenty, he rode in his first Olympic Games in Rome on a horse named Markham. A quote from *The Complete*

Book of the Olympics by David Wallechinsky states that "the endurance course in Rome was unnecessarily dangerous, and only 35 of the 73 entrants completed the course." Not an easy year to make an Olympic debut, and yet Michael and Markham placed 15th in the individual placings.

In the airplane en route to Tokyo for the 1964 Olympics, Markham had to put down when he became hysterical during the flight and all measures to subdue him failed. Deeply saddened that it was necessary that his horse be destroyed, and yet both needing and wanting to compete for the team, J. Michael Plumb was put on a 'replacement horse' named Bold Minstrel. It was a good partnership, and their score helped the three-day event team to win a silver medal for the United States.

This 'catch ride' went on to become a very famous show jumper and set a record in Madison Square Garden by jumping 7'3" with Bill Steinkraus riding him. Michael Plumb spoke of Bold Minstrel with respect: "He was a very special horse -- extremely talented. It's rare to see a horse that talented in all three abilities. He was the equivalent of a 'three-letter athlete' in a horse."

The 1968 Olympics in Mexico City saw Michael paired with a horse named Plain Sailing, that he describes as "the bravest horse I ever rode." The danger element of the cross-country course was heightened by intense rains on the afternoon of the competition during Michael's ride. Jumping the fences became a matter of trust and courage for both horse and rider when "all you could really make out were the flags on either side of the jump." Once again, this man and his horse helped secure the team silver medal for the United States.

The United States Equestrian Team had a repeat performance at the 1972 Olympic Games in Munich by winning another team silver medal in eventing. This time, Michael rode a horse named Free and Easy, a Thoroughbred

Mexico City, the 1968 Games, aboard Plain Sailing, "the bravest horse I ever rode," says Michael.

Findlay Davidson

that he had bought in Maryland a year before the Munich Games. Michael says, "He was a very good cross-country horse and, in spite of a fall he took on the course, and the fact that he suffered a leg injury, he had the grit to carry on and complete the third day of stadium jumping. He was a brave horse by the fact that he gave that extra effort to finish."

In the 1976 Olympics, Michael won the individual silver medal on a seven-year-old horse named Better and Better. This brave young event horse, aided by Michael's experience, produced the second-best score in the competition, and contributed to winning the team gold medal for the United States.

Blue Stone is a horse that was donated to the USET by "Tim" Forrester Clark and who was Michael Plumb's mount for the 1984 Los Angeles Olympics. "He was a dapple-grey Irish three-quarter bred that was a sound horse, a good jumper and always dependable. You could count on him to finish and to be one of the top horses." The USET won another team gold medal at the 1984 Olympics, confirming

Michael's high rating of this reliable team hope.

Michael Plumb is a tall, lean athlete with a compelling intensity about him. When he walks a course, he makes a plan and sticks to it. He is a bold, positive rider who doesn't leave anything in his control to chance. When you consider the qualities of desire, dedication and discipline that make up a champion, this seasoned rider is a champion in every sense of that word. What makes this man's competitive

At age 12.
Budd Photos

record even more remarkable is that his achievement is in eventing, the ultimate equestrian test of versatility and durability. Eventing is not for the faint-hearted. It requires tremendous mental and physical fitness, plus a special kind of competitive bravery. For the career of an international event competitor to span some thirty years and remain so consistently competent is uniquely rare.

As a teacher, he is a man who takes much care not to let his young riders get in over their heads. "We know falls are going to happen. What we hope is that they are something that the rider can learn from, not something that is going to shake his or her confidence."

There is a story told about Mike Plumb that I confirmed to be true. In one of his competitions, the girth on his saddle broke on the fourth jump, but he was able to complete the course, keeping the saddle and himself in balance on the horse with the strength of his legs. Is it any wonder that this man has been one of the top contenders in international competitions through the years, a member of eight Olympic teams and six Olympic medals in eventing?

With Blue Stone, 1984 Los Angeles   *Cora Cushny*

Michael and the legendary Better and Better, 1972 Montreal Olympics.
Sue Maynard

HELENA "LANA" DUPONT WRIGHT

Born July 6, 1939

Alfo Baker

Lana duPont was the first woman in the world ever to compete in the Olympic three-day event. She was born into a famous family, well known in the horse racing world. The outstanding career of the horse named Kelso was part of her growing up years. Helena, who was named after her grandmother, was nicknamed 'Lana' from those early years and still goes by this name today.

Her mother was a Master of Foxhounds and it was her love of hunting and horses that set the model for young Lana to follow. The horse that became Lana's Olympic partner, Mr. Wister, was named after a good friend of her grandparents, Wister Randolph. The horse was a blood bay Thoroughbred and had been a rogue at the race track. He had an intelligent, very English-type head, but was weedy, raw-boned and skinny. Eager for activity and challenge, Lana received Mr. Wister as a four year-old, a gift to her from her mother. He proved to be a natural and courageous jumper. His natural ability, honesty and courage destined him to be a successful event horse.

Lana relates that Mr. Wister was originally not good in the dressage phase, but that she had the good fortune to secure the competent dressage instructor, Richard Wätjen, to coach her in this discipline. Dressage is the basic training which should be taught to any horse and it will ultimately improve all of his movements, making them smoother and more controlled. The discipline of dressage increases the horse and rider's coordination as a team. With the high level of competition in eventing, a poor dressage score can be disastrous to the final results.

Since she was a child, Lana knew she wanted to ride in the Olympics. It was while she was studying with Richard Wätjen that the challenge of eventing drew her interest and became clarified as something in which she wanted to become involved.

Because the sport of eventing had begun as a test for European cavalrymen and their mounts, it was a competition dominated entirely by men. As the sport evolved, the physical demands of the speed and endurance test involving roads and tracks, steeplechase and cross-country, became extremely rigorous, especially at the Olympic level. For a number of years the FEI deliberated as to whether women were physically capable of enduring the demands and dangers of this sport; in the meantime, participation in eventing was closed to them.

By 1964, women riders had demonstrated their ability to compete on even terms with men almost everywhere; three different women had won Badminton, and Sheila Willcox, winner at Badminton for three successive years, had taken the European Championship. The change in FEI policy that year finally made women's participation in the Olympic three-day event possible, and recognized the outstanding achievements of those many lady riders, whose skill and fierce determination had overcome the disadvantage of inexperience which women's late entry into eventing had created.

Before then, Lana's own persistence and desire to compete in eventing had led her and Mr. Wister to Europe. Here, she was able to gain more experience, as eventing was not as popular in the United States at that time. In 1961 she took part in three or four events before going on to Badminton, where they placed tenth.

Lana then returned to the United States, resumed dressage training with Richard Wätjen, and relocated to the USET's then newly-established training center in Gladstone, New Jersey. When the all-clear came from the

The first woman to compete in an Olympic Three Day Event, aboard her beloved Mr. Wister.   *Courtesy Lana duPont Wright*

FEI, and it opened its eventing entries to women for the 1964 Olympic Games, Lana was ready for the challenge. Her strong determination and Mr. Wister's training had all come together at the same time. Unfortunately, the screening trial came in August when Mr. Wister was recovering from a tendon injury. She rode a second horse, named Ferdinand, that she had purchased in England, and did well enough to qualify as a competitor for the Olympic three-day event team. Three of the four team members were named immediately. They were Michael Plumb, Kevin Freeman and Michael Page. Lana was one of two left to be chosen. Major Stefan von Visy, the coach and trainer, made the final choice 72 hours before the plane took off. She is still grateful to him for this decision which made it possible for her to be the first woman event rider to take part in the Olympic Games. She was proud to represent both her gender and her country as a contender.

The three-day event competition at the 1964 Tokyo Games begon on October 17. Lana's dressage ride was better than average and, although she felt there was much room for improvement, she was very grateful for the years she had spent studying with Richard Wätjen.

The night before the speed and endurance test, it began to rain and continued into the next day. In the morning it was also bitterly cold and foggy. While the course was not particularly difficult, it became extremely slippery and hazardous in the prevailing weather conditions. The cross-country course had been bulldozed through 22 miles of Karuizawa countryside. The lack of ground cover on the course inhibited traction and compounded the slippery conditions. Heavy rains plagued many of the competitors who had the misfortune of being scheduled to ride during a downpour. There were numerous falls that day, caused by the poor visibility and flooded terrain.

There were two big spreads that Lana felt she misjudged during her ride, the first being the third jump on the cross-country course. She felt that she didn't allow sufficient momentum for take-off, particularly considering the slipperiness of the ground. She and Mr. Wister took a hard fall here. The horse broke several bones in his jaw but, even though they were both badly shaken, Mr. Wister was still eager to continue. The second fall occurred over another spread near the end of the course. When they finished she described them as being "a collection of bruises, broken bones and mud." They placed 33rd in a field of 48 competitors. Talk about true grit! Both woman and horse excelled on that day. It was the day when the world saw that a woman could indeed get around an Olympic cross-country course and it was a milestone in equestrian sport history.

Lana says, "It was a great honor to have been a part of the silver medal-winning team, particularly since it opened up the avenues for many other women participants in the Olympic three-day event thereafter."

After the Olympics in 1964, Lana went on eventing for some time, while Mr. Wister dropped out of top level competition to just enjoy hunting and other less stressful endeavors after his jaw healed.

Lana then married, had two daughters, and directed her focus onto her family. About twelve years ago she competed with her children's pony in a combined driving event at Radnor, and thoroughly enjoyed it. The formula for combined driving has its counterparts in the ridden three-day event; the carriage presentation/dressage compares to the ridden dressage, the marathon to the cross-country phase, and the cones to the stadium jumping. From the single pony for fun at Radnor, Lana has developed quickly into a world-renowned pairs driver, especially noted for the brilliant dressage performances of her small Connemara/Thoroughbred crosses.

She was a member of the United States team that won the Masters Trophy at the Royal Windsor Horse Show in England in May 1989 and, that same year, competed on the American Team at the World Pairs Driving Championships in Balaton, Hungary. Lana has consistently been first after dressage, and second after the three phases at every selection trial she has competed in over the past few years. She won the Festival of Champions final selection trial in 1991, clinching her position on the U.S. team for the 1991 World Pair Championships in Zwettl, Austria.

At this 1991 World Championship event Lana duPont Wright made equestrian history for an incredible second time. In Austria, out of 60 drivers, she finished fifth in dressage and eighth overall, becoming the first woman driver ever to place in the top ten drivers of a World Driving Championship. The first team medal the United States has ever won in World Championship Driving was won by the team of Lana Wright, James Fairclough, and Tucker Johnson in 1991, the team gold!

Courtesy Jim Wofford

JAMES C. WOFFORD

Born November 3, 1944

In the horse world, the name Jim Wofford is as familiar as the sun in the sky. His dedication to the integrity and well-being of equestrian sport in America and throughout the world has stood true through many years of involvement.

As former President of the American Horse Shows Association, First Vice President of the United States Equestrian Team, and in his involvement with the Federation Equestre International, he has been instrumental in pulling together the various facets of equestrian sport. Organization and rules are vital to all sports, and it is because of dedicated individuals, like Jim Wofford, that the present high standard of protection of the athletes (both human and equine) and fairness in competition has evolved.

The first picture to record this horseman's early beginning as a rider gives the impression that he was about two years old at the time. He was born on Rimrock Farm, adjacent to Fort Riley in Kansas. It was an ideal setting for the making of a young man who always knew that horses were going to be a central part of his life. In those days Fort Riley was where the Army Horse Show Team had its base, and where the Army Olympic Team horses were stabled.

Jim's family album is full of riding competitors, including his father, two brothers, a sister-in-law, and a cousin. His father, Colonel John Wofford, was a retired cavalry officer who had been a member of the 1932 Olympic Team. His father later coached the show jumping and three-day event teams to bronze medal honors for the United States at the 1952 Olympics. Colonel Wofford was also the first President of the United States Equestrian Team and its co-founder.

Moving through the various levels of com-

petitive riding was a natural in this family. Jim went to Culver Military Academy in high school and continued his riding lessons there. He attended Rutgers University and graduated from business school at the University of Colorado. He was a national account producer for Collier Cobb Associates, a commercial insurance brokerage, from 1985 to 1988. With his strong equestrian and business background, Jim Wofford has been a resourceful and respected leader in whatever capacity he serves.

Jim's first equestrian international competition was in the 1967 Pan-American Games. The year before that, in late 1966, it was his brother who had found Kilkenny, the horse Jim was later to ride in the 1968 and 1972 Olympics. Kilkenny had been on the Irish Olympic Team in 1964 and had also competed in the 1966 World Championships. Jim's mother purchased the horse against the advice of a veterinarian who felt 'he wouldn't stay sound' and also without the horse being ridden by any member of the family. All choices in life include a risk factor and nothing is ever accomplished with-

A hint of things to come?   *Courtesy Jim Wofford*

At 1968 Games in Mexico City, aboard Kilkenny.

Courtesy Jim Wofford

out being willing to take a chance. Mrs. Wofford was willing, and her son and the USET benefited from her choice.

Kilkenny was one of only four horses whose career spanned three Olympic competitions. In 1968, Jim and Kilkenny's efforts contributed towards winning the team silver medal in eventing for the United States at the Olympics in Mexico City. Jim remembers Kilkenny as being "fast and fearless." They were the first U.S. pair to ride before the horrendous rains came. Jim remembers, "It was still raining at the award ceremonies, and it was a really memorable time. We had been training together for the past six weeks, and the top three teams had developed a good-natured competitive camaraderie that was fun to be a part of." Four years laters Jim and Kilkenny were again members of the U.S. silver medal-winning team at the 1972 Olympic Games in Munich.

At the 1980 Alternate Games, Jim won the individual silver medal in Fontainebleau, France, on a horse named Carawich. He was "a very versatile horse that had previously belonged to one of the top English event riders." The story of how Jim acquired Carawich is extraordinary.

Jim was in a large crowd at Badminton when he first became aware of the horse. As Carawich walked past, led by his rider, the horse unexpectedly stopped for a few seconds and looked right at Jim Wofford. Jim says, "It

was as though he sought me out and looked me right in the eyes. It was spooky. I inquired about the horse and was told his name, that he was a wonderful horse, but that I'd not be able to buy him as his owner was too fond of him."

Life went on, but Jim never forgot the horse. Several months later in a conversation with one of his buying contacts, the man casually mentioned, "Oh, by the way Carawich is for sale." Circumstances had changed. The horse's rider was pregnant and the decision had been made to put him up for sale. Jim gave immediate instructions to take the horse off the market and made purchase arrangements. Shortly after the horse came into Jim's possession and, like Kilkenny, he came untried beforehand. When Jim sat on the horse's back and rode him for the first time, he says, "It was like putting on a custom-made glove." The invisible bond that had begun at Badminton, when this horse touched the soul of this man, had eventually brought the two of them together. The fact that this partnership won an individual silver medal at the Alternate Olympics gives one the strong sense that, by providence, it was all meant to be.

In 1984 Jim campaigned with a horse named Castlewellan and went to the Los Angeles Olympics as an alternate. After the 1984 Olympics, Jim retired from competition, but made a brief comeback when he competed at the 1986 Rolex Kentucky Three-Day Event. At Kentucky he rode another fast horse named The

Optimist. Jim won first place and the USET Challenge Trophy at this event. With the exhilaration of a "great win," he made this his final competitive event, wanting to end this phase of his career with a good performance.

At Kentucky in 1986, Jim took some good-natured kidding about "putting on a few pounds" since his 1984 retirement. Not that he was what the general public would call overweight, but even ten pounds to athletes can be ammunition for some good teasing by fellow teammates. They even went so far as to say that the competition "wouldn't be over until the fat boy rode." And they were right, for it was him they kidded who won top honors!

Over the years Jim Wofford has accumulated an impressive collection of gold, silver and bronze medals from various national and international championship events, both for individual and team honors. The one medal that he would liked to have won, but didn't, was the individual gold medal at the Olympics which, in fact, is every top competitor's dream. Jim concedes that, for him, "It just wasn't meant to be."

Jim Wofford co-narrated Kentucky Educational Television's videotape of the 1990 Rolex Kentucky Three-Day Event, along with sports commentator Trevor Denman. Jim's respect for the other riders and his knowledge and love of the sport are apparent in his com-ments. Also noticeable is a sense of humor in describing some trying circumstances. During the grueling cross-country portion of the event, dark ominous clouds rolled in, with crashing thunder, lightning and rain. One section of the tape shows David O'Connor and his horse, Wilton Fair, competing in the heavy downpour. The horse's ears are pinned straight back, clearly registering his dislike for such unwelcome weather conditions. In Jim's narration he comments that he "suspects that David O'Connor's ears are pinned straight back too." It is a good quality when a person can add a touch of levity to an otherwise dismal situation. It goes uncontested among athletes that rain can be very unnerving in terms of what it does, both to visibility and to safe footing.

Jim Wofford's involvement with horses presents a kaleidoscope of abilities: competing, teaching, judging, being a commentator, an advisor, and an administrator. For some years he has owned and operated a three-day event training establishment in Upperville, Virginia, where many top competitors have trained. His plans for the future definitely include continued connections with horses. With tongue in cheek, he concluded, "Those who can - do, those who can't- teach, those who can do neither - administrate. I'm working my way through this progression."

Aboard Carawich on whom Jim won the individual silver medal at the 1980 Alternate Games..

Courtesy Alix Coleman

BRUCE DAVIDSON

Born December 31, 1949

Barbara Thomson

Bruce Davidson had caught my attention before I ever thought of writing this book. There is something about the way this tall, striking athlete carries himself and dresses that is very classy. It starts with the detail and sharpness of his entire riding habit, right down to the stock tie and pin. You may see him competing in the dressage competition wearing a top hat, in the cross-country in his distinctive red and yellow attire, or with a red breast strap on his horse's tack. Always eye-catching and dressed in exquisitely good taste, his warm smile, natural good looks and quiet confidence make one realize there is something special and to be admired about this man.

You cannot help but also notice that he is always in touch with the horse he is riding. I like the way he pats his horse's neck in encouragement before they come into the ring, and also afterwards in appreciation of a job well done. His communication and oneness with his horses gives me the sense that he has a very special relationship with his animals. His riding presentation is representative of someone who cares and would never give less than his best.

If ever a child was born with a predisposition to be a horseman and the ability to achieve it, it was Bruce Davidson. He remembers his early dream of wanting to learn all he could about horses. He wanted to understand them, to ride them, to take care of them and, eventually, to train them, and he didn't just want to do these things - he wanted to do them well. He remembers being four or five years-old and "being crazy for a pony." His mother had ridden, so she understood and he had his wish. This pony enabled him, as a child, to take part in Pony Club activities, junior equitation competitions and hunting.

He studies every aspect of the horses he works with - how they behave in the barn, what they are like to catch in the field - and he uses this knowledge of their individual characteristics to help train them.

He also uses a system called gridwork (which is varying combinations of cavaletti and jumps) appropriate for each horse's level of learning and designed to gymnastically teach them to use all the muscles and reactions required in competition, and to keep them fit between events. Bruce Davidson is a trainer who has the ability to bring several young horses along simultaneously. He moves them through the lower levels in a step-by-step procedure, progressively introducing them to more demanding concepts. It is not unusual to go to an event and see him competing at both intermediate and advanced levels on three or four different horses, which obviously can only be achieved by being a tremendously fit athlete.

Being a man who works with many horses, he is also a man who has had many wins, but he has a humility about this and does not take any of it for granted. He is the only rider in the world who has twice won the World Championships, once in 1974 on a horse named Irish Cap, and again in 1978 on Might Tango. At the 1990 World Championship Three-Day Event in Stockholm, he won the individual bronze medal on a young horse named Pirate Lion. He and his outstanding horse, Dr. Peaches, won the Rolex Kentucky Three-Day Event on three different occasions. By virtue of points accumulated, he has been the United States Combined Training Association's Leading Rider of the Year fifteen times, fourteen of them consecutive, and he has accumulated several gold, silver and bronze medals in innumerable events. In any one given year there are a handful of top riders in the world and this man is one of them.

Bruce Davidson has ridden in four Olympic Games. His first was in Munich, in 1972, where he rode a horse named Plain Sailing and helped secure the team silver medal in eventing. Bruce remembers Plain Sailing, a dark brown Irish-bred horse, as being "feisty, highly-strung, competitive and of great courage."

He relates that this first Olympic medal ceremony stands out as being the most memorable for him. He recalls knowing that he would always strive to see that it was the American flag that flew the highest, and he knew that it was our national anthem that he wanted to hear denoting first place, not the British or any other nation for that matter.

Irish Cap, who helped Bruce win his first gold medal at the 1974 World Championships, was his mount for the 1976 Montreal Olympics, where the U.S. won the team gold medal. A young horse when Bruce had bought and trained him, he says of this Irish Thoroughbred, "Irish Cap was a very difficult horse to work with, but once he was trained, he gave 100%. He was loyal, honest and genuine." The fact that this partnership won two major world-renowned gold medals gives strong testament to both of them for their outstanding competitive capabilities.

At the 1984 Olympic Games in Los Angeles, Bruce was again a member of the Three-Day Event gold medal-winning team, this time riding J.J. Babu, with whom he also won the Chesterland Three-Day Event in 1981, the Rolex Kentucky Three-Day Event in 1983, and placed second at Badminton in 1982. Four years later, in 1988, he placed 18th out of 50 competitors at the second Olympics riding Dr. Peaches, a horse that Bruce had won Kentucky with on three different occasions - in 1984, 1988, and 1989.

In 1995 Bruce Davidson also had one of the most significant victories of his career when he captured the first place title at the Mitsubishi Motors Badminton Horse Trials in Badminton, England. His history-making performance there on Mr. and Mrs. George Strawbridge's 10 year-old Thoroughbred, Eagle Lion, was the first time an American had ever won this competition, regarded as the most difficult and prestigious three-day event in the world. Bruce and Eagle Lion achieved this win with fault-free efforts in both the cross-country and show jumping portions of the competition.

No greater example of "equestrian excellence" can be stated that would equal this exceptional horseman claiming the top individual positions at the World Championships, the Pan-American Games and at Badminton, as well as two Olympic team gold medals. All of these awards were in three-day eventing, regarded as the most demanding and diverse discipline among all the equestrian sports.

At the 1996 Rolex, a key qualifying event for Bruce's attempt to be on his sixth Olympic team,

Bruce at six, with his first horse Mickey.
Courtesy Mrs. F.W. Davidson

he took a fall while competing on the nine year-old bay Thoroughbred Heyday, and sustained a broken shoulder. In addition to the fracture, another unfortunate outcome was that it prevented him from riding Eagle Lion to Olympic qualification. Bruce is quick to comment that anyone who has Heyday in his barn is a lucky person, but it was on Eagle Lion that he won the gold at Badminton. As his more experienced horse, Eagle Lion presented a better chance to win gold at the 1996 Olympics. He appealed the ruling but it remained unchanged; no exceptions are allowed.

In keeping with his unswerving faithfulness to the sport he loves, it came as no surprise to anyone that he proceeded with the nervous but brave Heyday with a plan to give the best ride he and the young horse were capable of.

In Atlanta, the U.S. was in the lead after dressage. All of the U.S. riders achieved personal best dressage scores. On the cross-country portion, the U.S. encountered some serious problems when Karen O'Connor's horse Biko had a refusal, and Jill Henneberg's horse was eliminated. There was additional pressure on the final day to hold a medal position, since only three of them were qualified to compete in the show jumping portion of the test. Karen and David O'Connor had spectacular clear rounds much to the delight of the "home court" audience. Heyday and Bruce gave it their best effort, but dropped three rails. The U.S. claimed the silver Three-Day medal.

The 1996 Olympics was the first time that separate competitions were held for individual and team medals in the three-day event. The reason for the change was the International Olympics Committee's (IOC) policy that two

At his first Olympics, Munich 1972, aboard Plain Sailing. The team took the silver

Gamecock

medals cannot be won for one effort. In accordance with the new policy, course designer Roger Haller had to create two courses in one. Many of the obstacles were jumped in both competitions, while some were for individual or team competition only. Other fences were jumped in a different sequence to avoid giving riders competing in both events an unfair advantage.

Some people liked the idea of having two separate competitions because in the individual competition the rider has the freedom to go "all out," without having to be conservative in any way to preserve the team score. Bruce favors having just one competition. He also feels that each nation should send six riders to compete in the same competition, believing that would determine which nations are the strongest.

Bruce relates that his greatest satisfaction comes from realizing that all of the horses he has ridden to success are horses that he helped make

Aboard Irish Cap, 1976 Montreal Games.

Courtesy USET

into champions. He is especially fond of working with young horses and bringing them along.

On the other side of training and competing horses is retiring them. I had been to the Rolex Kentucky Three-Day Event in 1990, where Bruce Davidson's fourteen year-old championship horse, Dr. Peaches, had been honored at a retirement ceremony. I asked him what goes into the decision to retire a horse, besides the obvious factors of age and soundness. He said that Dr. Peaches had given so much that he wanted to retire him after he had won a major competition, not to push him another year where he might have ranked thirteenth, but to retire him when he was "at the top." This consideration for the spirit of the horse, and the love and respect of the rider for the animal is one more example of this gifted horseman's relationship with his horses.

When questioned about advice he would give a rider that had taken a bad fall, beyond assessing medical care, he said that, "it is important that they understand why it happened so they don't put themselves in the same situation again, and to determine what could have or should have been done to save the situation." He also feels that, "a rider must be competitive by nature and if there is a lot of mental warfare and worries about falling, then that person is not in the right game."

Plans for the future? Bruce Davidson replied, "I'd like to be a racehorse trainer." For a horseman who openly admits that he "particularly loves working with young horses, bringing them along, teaching them and making them into winners," it is easy to see why this would be his choice for the future. His long relationship with horses over the years shows that he truly cares for them and takes time to understand them.

NEAL SHAPIRO

Freuly Photos

Born July 22, 1945

Neal Shapiro's first acquaintance with horses came at age five when he accompanied his parents on weekend outings which included hiring and riding horses by the hour. His attraction to the animals was immediate and enduring. When his family moved to Brookville, Long Island, they unanimously chose to begin acquiring their own stock of horses. Along with his brother, sister and parents, riding continued to be a family event they all enjoyed, now in their own backyard.

Neal's parents saw that his interest in horses was passionate and sought to improve his riding ability by enrolling him in a local stable that gave lessons in horsemanship. The owners apparently felt he had no talent to develop, for they rejected him. Little did they know that this young boy would continue to fend for himself, eventually developing into an Olympic medal winner. Little did they know that this young lad's spirit would not be crushed by their negative opinion, as it had the potential so to do. Their opinion was countered by a tenacious belief in self and a love of horses that wouldn't be stopped.

Neal spent the next few years riding his backyard horses. As frequently happens when you own horses and enjoy riding, you fall into the horse show routine, and the Shapiros were no exception. At the horse shows, Neal listened and took care to observe everything he could about riding, and he soon began winning ribbons in the hunter/jumper divisions.

On the weekend of July 1961, an event took place that was instrumental in causing Neal to seriously consider riding as a career. Completely unannounced, a horse trailer pulled into the Shapiro driveway with a big grey, former rodeo horse named Charlie Grey standing inside. He had been sent by Jack Amon, a man whose knowledge of horses had helped the Shapiros in many ways with the care, buying and selling of their animals. Jack's intuition and keen eye for

horses had recognized this horse's potential. After talking with Jack, the Shapiros added Charlie Grey to their small collection of horses and promptly renamed him Uncle Max.

It didn't take long to discover that Max had some serious quirks. When the horse knew he was going to be mounted, he would take off running. Neal reciprocated by launching surprise attacks of leaping into the saddle from various locations, including the hood of a car, a bale of hay and even from a rooftop. When Max got wise to the surprise attacks, Neal's resourcefulness even reverted to the rodeo method of dropping a rider onto the saddle from above the stalls. With time and patience, Max eventually allowed Neal to mount him with the assistance of just one person and the two of them developed into a successful partnership.

Later the same year, Neal became the youngest rider, at age fifteen, to win the American Horse Shows Association's Green Jumper title with Uncle Max. The following years proved to be some of the most outstanding in Neal's riding accomplishments, accomplishments which he continues to speak of with pride today.

In 1962, Max was the Professional Horseman Association's Reserve Champion, with Ben O'Meara's Jacks or Better being the Champion. In 1963 these same two horses reversed the honors, with Max winning the championship title. At the end of the year, the Shapiros purchased Jacks from O'Meara to combine forces with Uncle Max. In 1964, Uncle Max and Jacks or Better once again claimed the champion and reserve titles, exactly as they had in 1963, only this time both horses were from the same stable and were ridden by the same rider, making this accomplishment a first at the PHA Championships.

Acquiring two top horses and accruing top honors were the catalysts that changed Neal's original goal of just doing well at horse shows to now aspiring to be a member of the USET and to compete in the Olympics. The first part

day of the Derby and never rubbed a fence the entire way around. It was at the big Hickstead Bank, which is 10′6″ high, that he chose to try a "Pegasus" move. Although he went up the front side of the bank without any problems and neatly jumped the fence at the top, instead of sliding down the other side, as he was supposed to do, he took a flying leap from the top and landed in a heap at the bottom of the bank. Neal compares the sensation to "stepping into an empty elevator shaft." He was on the ground before he even realized what had happened. They recovered and completed the course with no further faults, but, unfortunately, the fall dropped them back to sixth place.

It was autumn of 1969 when a horse came along that Neal thought might be the one every rider hopes for. Patrick Butler had purchased a horse named Sloopy for the USET, with some input from Neal's father and also with Neal in mind to be the rider. The partnership proved to be a good match, culminating in a medal at the Olympics, but they didn't get there without a good bit of work and some trials to boot.

Sloopy was not a push-button horse, but then neither was Neal used to dealing with a push-button horse. All of his work with Max proved to be a good preparation for the challenge that Sloopy gave him. While the horse was a clean jumper, and definitely not a stopper, he had a mind of his own. He wanted his work to be over quickly and, if it wasn't, he'd let Neal know that he'd had enough by stopping in a corner and repeatedly rearing up and down or trying to spin his rider off. When Sloopy realized

of this dream became a reality in 1964 when, at the age of nineteen, he was chosen to represent the USET as an alternate rider. Neal's international debut was so successful with Max and Jacks that he also earned the privilege of competing in New York that year at Madison Square Garden.

The winters of 1965 and 1966 were spent at the USET training center in Gladstone, New Jersey, working with Bert de Nemethy, who helped Neal to revamp his self-taught riding style. With much work on the part of both trainer and rider, a gradual transition occurred which produced a more polished style but which, at the same time, enabled him to retain what he had learned through natural feel and instinct.

The summer of 1968 stands out for Neal as a memorable time. The team was in Europe as part of their Olympic preparation. Things had improved for Neal and Max, who were working well together in their partnership. The element of unpredictability continued to be part of Max's makeup. On occasion, he would jump every fence on the course clean and then stop at the last one. Overall, the two were doing well and feeling much more comfortable on the long European courses. It was at the Hickstead Derby, in England, that Max's reputation for finding "something different" to do on course reached its all-time high point.

Max was jumping exceptionally well on the

that Neal wasn't giving up his position, he would lunge into the air again and again, getting madder and madder.

On about the fifth day of repeating this scenario, Neal and Sloopy had a battle of wills. When Neal would discipline the horse for his bad behavior, Sloopy would get more and more irritated and launch himself higher and higher - until finally he got tired of the whole ordeal, and gave a low sigh as if to say, "You've won this one, Buddy, but I'll get even with you some day."

Payback day came at the airport, when sixteen of the USET's horses were preparing to board the plane to go to Europe to gain more experience on the courses there. Sloopy had loaded into his shipping box without any trouble but, when the aircraft required some necessary adjustments to meet the safety code, his tranquilizer began to wear off during the delay and he decided he wanted out of his box. Neal watched in horror, along with the other team members, as the dark brown horse's front legs came out over the box and he began to thrash in an effort to free his hindquarters. To add to the horror of the moment, planes were now coming in for a landing and the noise terrified him. To administer more tranquilizer when a horse is in this state of anxiety would not have been a good choice, because it could have had a reverse effect. With this consideration, as well as that of endangering the lives of others on board the airplane, the reluctant decision was made that Sloopy be left at home. The summer of 1970 was a long and lonesome one for Neal.

Sloopy's need to get experience on the big European courses was essential in his preparation for the Olympic Games in 1972, so in the spring of 1971 Bert de Nemethy booked passage by ship for Neal and Sloopy. Neal remembers the exact day, May 5. It had seemed like a good plan to bypass the airplane route but, after pulling out of the calm New York harbor aboard the ship, he soon came to believe that May 5 was going to be his last day on earth. He regards the *Poseidon Adventure* as a joyride compared to his ocean journey. For seven of the most nauseating days of Neal's life, he recalls that the ship did not stop rolling from New York to the harbor in Le Havre, France. He describes his 168 hours on board in the following way: 100 of those hours he was flat on his back in bed, 32 hours were spent hanging over the deck's railing, and the other 36 hours he was staggering either to or from the bathroom.

Meanwhile, Sloopy had eaten the whole time he was on board and was as fat as a pig when he got off the ship. Neal had lost fifteen pounds and was never so glad to see dry land in his life. After Neal recovered from the trip and Sloopy had gotten back into condition, they met up with the team and proceeded to have a very successful competition tour.

It was at Aachen that Sloopy showed everybody what he was made of and charmed the European crowds. The big course captured Sloopy's full attention and respect, and the new environment stimulated him to jump everything with inches to spare. Once he was on course he was all business and neither the height nor width of the jumps presented any problems to him. He jumped three clear rounds in the Nations Cup to help the United States beat the British team. On the last day of the show he hit only one fence - a wall set at seven feet in the fifth round of the Grand Prix. The jury decided to end the class there and tied Neal and Sloopy for first place, along with Sans Souci of France ridden by Marcel Rozier.

The old expression, "One day you're up and the next you're down," certainly applies to show jumping riders. In 1972 Sloopy flew to Europe beautifully on the same plane as the other horses but, on Grand Prix day at Aachen, Neal was watching the competition from the stands instead of riding. Back at the barn, Sloopy had an undiagnosed fever and concern was justified as to whether he would recover in time for the Games, which were only eight weeks away. When they were unable to determine the cause of Sloopy's lingering illness, after two weeks of varying veterinary opinions, Bert de Nemethy and Sloopy's owner, Patrick Butler, sent for Dr. Danny Marks from the States to join them to see if he could find the answer. Danny met them at La Baule, France, even though the luggage and the medicines he had packed did not. His veterinary skills were called upon that very day to stitch up a gash in Snowbound's head from a freak accident, in addition to examining Sloopy. The Games were too close for comfort and there were some major things going wrong. A "what next" feeling, interwoven with watching the other teams putting the final touches on their horses, while the Americans felt they were just patching and hoping, gave way to some thoughts that all their efforts were futile. Even if they made the competition, would they be prepared to go two, or maybe even three, rounds against horses who were fit, healthy and prepared to do their best?

The new medicines Danny sent for finally came and soon Sloopy's temperature went down. Now he had to be strengthened for the big job ahead of him. Neal's attitude was that he had waited ten years to get to this point; they had a job to do and he most certainly did not want to wait for another chance. Fortunately, Sloopy began to improve to the point that he looked and acted like his usual self. Neal felt encouraged when Peter Zeitler, Sloopy's caretaker and the man who knew him best, said he would make it.

One month before the Olympics, Neal was finally able to ride Sloopy. They had to cram into four weeks what you would like to take four months to do; and the cliff-hanger wasn't over yet. At a schooling session in Munich during the final week of that intensive month, Sloopy sliced his left hind leg when he took off long at the water jump and his hind legs went in the water. This injury required thirty of Danny Marks' neat little stitches to close. The team could not believe they were meant to have all this bad luck.

To the amazement of all, Sloopy came out sound the next morning - just five days away from the individual competition. His wound continued to heal well, with Neal and Danny making middle-of-the-night bandage changes and wound checks.

September 3 finally came and they all knew Sloopy felt fine when he lifted his groom, Peter Zeitler, off the ground by the lead rope.

As Neal walked the course, the fact that the jumps were huge impressed him and he wished that he and Sloopy had been luckier in their preparation. The course consisted of fourteen obstacles with seventeen jumping efforts and no major traps, except for several turns which

required great precision. Neal felt that the designer of the course had not built anything that Sloopy couldn't jump. Fifty-four riders from twenty-one countries were to start, with the top twenty competitors returning for a second round and a jump-off if necessary.

The first round presented no great difficulty for Sloopy, although it was not "play" for him as many of the other competitions had been. The combinations and the big oxers required his full attention and effort. The only problem arose at the water jump, which was situated at the end of the stadium after a sharp left-hand turn from a vertical. It required you to make your move at the water as soon as you landed from the vertical. Sloopy met it well but, upon landing, his hind foot landed on the tape, thus incurring a four-fault penalty. This was his only penalty in the first round.

The course was raised for the second round and shortened to ten obstacles with thirteen jumping efforts. Neal and Sloopy had an oxer down in this round, giving them a total of eight faults for both rounds. At first, Neal's eight faults did not look very good compared with three horses that still had clear rounds and three more with four faults. But the truth in competition is that it's never over until it's over.

One of the clear horses finished the second round with 16 faults, and all three of the four-fault horses from Germany faulted out of the competition. Anne Moore from Great Britain

At the 1972 Munich Games, with the challenging Sloopy.

Gamecock

86

and Graziano Mancinelli from Italy both ended up the second round with eight faults, which made Neal's score tied with them. These three riders went into the third round in a jump-off against the clock. This was the first time since 1952 in Helsinki, that a jump-off was needed to determine the individual gold medal winner.

Neal and Sloopy were the first to go in the jump-off. By this time Sloopy was beginning to show some signs of being tired. Neal knew he had to be clean and fast in order to put the pressure on the other two riders. He started on his way and made some good sharp turns getting over the fences where he was cutting his corners. In the middle of the combinations, however, fatigue took its toll on the horse who had suffered two setbacks and made two recoveries in his preparation to be there. Sloopy rolled a rail off the middle element of the combination and another at one of the two final oxers on the course, giving him a total of eight faults in the jump-off. The rest of what happened was out of Neal's hands.

With only Anne behind him, Graziano took his time and jumped a cautious but clear round. Anne pulled out all the stops and went for the gold. When her horse came to the combination in the jump-off that it had crashed into during the second round, it said "no go" this time and ran past it. She whipped around, took him over the jump, and finished with only the three faults for the refusal, giving her the silver medal, Neal the bronze and Mancinelli the gold.

During the medal presentation, Neal felt honored to have the bronze medal presented to him by Prince Philip. Sloopy must have taken a shine for the gold, however, for he took a mouthful of the Prince's jacket and gave it a healthy jerk.

As Neal and Sloopy made their victory gallop around the stadium that day, Neal breathed a sigh of relief that they had made it through this part of the competition and that it was over. He felt that a lot of people had earned a piece of the medal that was hanging around his neck - Bert de Nemethy, Patrick Butler, Peter Zeitler and Danny Marks - and he knew he would be forever grateful to them for their contributions. Neal felt that a portion of his life's ambition had been fulfilled on that day and, without their help and dedication, it never would have been possible.

They still had one more competition to go. The team event was one week away, and it was that day that the riders had to focus on. The Nations Cup took place in the main stadium and was the final closing event for the Olympic Games. It was also "curtains" for many of the top riders. Neal describes the course with three letters, B-I-G, and the scores showed it. All of the fences produced knock-downs, and the double and the triple produced several refusals. The light but constant drizzle of rain added one more dimension of risk to an already difficult course.

Neal and Sloopy were the eighth combination to go and the first for the USET. As they jumped the first fence, Sloopy slipped a little and it was obvious that the footing was slick. He jumped the second fence without any problem. At the third obstacle, an oxer 5'3" by 6'6", he threw a shoe and had one rail down. At the fourth fence, the "trouble double," he lost his footing as he began to leave the ground, and slid through the first part of the combination. He almost went down, but managed to scramble to his feet. Neal got him back into position as they reset the fence.

As they stood there waiting for the fence to be rebuilt, all Neal could think about was that he wasn't going to let this set-back get out of control. He had to finish and finish in the allotted time. He knew his three teammates were counting on him and he was not about to let them down. The horn blew to signal Neal to continue and the pressure was on. Neal quickened Sloopy's pace in an attempt to stay within the time allowed and also to communicate to him that his rider meant business. Sloopy completed the rest of the course with no further faults and within the time required; even with the six seconds added to their score that FEI rules require whenever a fence is dislodged by a refusal.

The USET ended up second to the heavily-favored Germans with only a quarter-fault difference away from the gold medal. It was disappointing to be so close (two seconds would have made the difference), and yet so far away from first place; but it had indeed been a thrill to have given them such a close run, in spite of all the difficulties the U.S. team had encountered. There was pride in claiming the first medal for the Jumping Team since 1960.

Neal has been associated with training trotters in one way or another since 1969. He gave up showing horses in 1978 and turned full-time to the breaking and training of harness race horses at Saratoga. In addition, he is a skillful licensed pilot, which has proven to be a very practical asset in his travels up and down the East Coast. Recently, he took up tennis and continues to enjoy time on the court whenever his busy schedule permits.

Due to the interest that his two daughters take in horses, history repeated itself by placing Neal back into the hunter/jumper competition routine again. He has even done some informal competing recently because of this reconnection.

The name of his farm is Hay Fever Farm. This name won out over Asthma Acres, which brings out another piece of information about Neal and his Olympic medal winning accomplishment. Even a young lad who has asthma, who is told by the managers of a riding school that he has no talent, who owns horses with some serious quirks to reckon with, and who has one set-back after another—can with persistence, love, and dedication achieve Olympic honors.

His plans for the future are to keep the harness racing business competitive by continuing to contribute in his capacity as a trainer. He attributes success with horses to their natural ability, luck, and to keeping them sound and healthy. His Olympic experience testifies to the precarious balance of these three elements and how, even when the odds seem to be against you and victory an elusive goal, it is still possible.

KATHY KUSNER

Born March 21, 1940

Courtesy Kathy Kusner

When I first spoke with Kathy Kusner on the telephone, knowing that her multiple achievements included scuba diving, being a pilot, skydiving and being a competitive runner, as well as an accomplished rider, I told her I felt as though I was talking to the female counter-part of the movie character, Indiana Jones. Having great determination, and travelling to the far corners of the globe to meet the challenge of new frontiers, certainly describes both of them. Also, following their instincts in a search for knowledge and the actualization of daring accomplishments, links them still further.

Kathy grew up in Arlington, Virginia. Her first memories of riding are of pony rings where she would lead in order to get more rides. She remembers repeatedly nagging her parents to buy her a pony. She was twelve when she finally wore them down. A $150 Western pony named Champ was the result. He became self-supporting because she sold pony rides on him when she wasn't zooming around the neighborhood on him herself. She can still see the neighbors shaking their fists and threatening to call her mother when she thinks back to those early days.

Unable to afford a saddle, she taught herself to ride bareback. With little more than an intense passion for horses and an unshakable ambition to pursue a skill with them, she began taking lessons from Jane Dillon, for whom she worked on weekends, taking care of the riding school horses. As she became a better rider, the local horse dealers started to ask her to do some riding for them. With these prospects she gradually moved up through the riding circuit, progressing to better horses and better shows.

Over the years, Kathy made the transition in style from unpolished and rough around the edges to great technical elegance and poise. Hers is the story of the diamond that held all the qualities of brilliance but required the processing to achieve its full potential. She went from a horsewoman of unknown status to one of international recognition; a rider whose

Kathy and Fleet Apple,
1972 Olympics.

Gamecock

expertise in show jumping is sought today for clinics and lectures on riding, training and showing horses. She travels throughout the United States and to other countries, including France, Italy, Japan, Canada, New Zealand, Australia, Guatemala, the Philippines, Argentina, Brazil, Iran, Paraguay, Peru and Spain.

At age sixteen she went as a groom to help a friend of hers who was showing a horse at the Pennsylvania National Horse Show in Harrisburg. It was the first time Kathy had seen the USET compete. She was so impressed with their performances and the manner in which the horses were cared for and turned out, that she knew right then that someday she wanted to be a part of the team. How she was going to attain this goal was very unclear at that time, but she refused to compromise her dream once her focus was set.

It was Mrs. A.C. Randolph, one of the owners Kathy did a lot of riding for, who enabled her to go to the next USET selection trials. When Kathy shared her dream of being on the team with this woman, it was she who secured the palomino High Noon especially for this purpose, a horse that Kathy had been riding for a dealer named Tommy Jones.

While she felt that she and her horse generally looked a "little country," her potential was recognized and she was invited to come and train with the team. Her dream began to become a reality. Through the knowledge and insights of coach Bert de Nemethy, she gradually learned the whys and wherefores of what she was doing and also a more accomplished way of doing it. The transition from her very practical but unpolished training up to that point began to change and take new form and depth.

This transition did not come easily. Probably as a result of over-trying and wanting to do everything perfectly, Kathy temporarily lost the use of her natural ability and became stiff and ineffective. She had such a desire to do everything exactly Bert's way, wanting desperately to produce a flawless performance. For a while it seemed to her that the harder she tried, the worse things became.

When Kathy first rode for the USET in 1961, she inherited George Morris' horse, Sinjon, after George dropped out of the circuit to study acting for a brief period. She was understandably excited about riding Sinjon, as he was a personal favorite of hers, and she looked upon him as her hero. The opportunity to ride him was beyond her wildest dreams. But she was, at this time, still so wrapped up in the classical correctness of her performance, that both she and the horse went into a temporary slump.

It was not until Kathy was back home during a break in the USET training session that things began to work out for her. It was here, with some time of her own, that she began to absorb what Bert de Nemethy had taught her and to integrate it with her natural abilities.

She then had the good fortune to have friends who secured two outstanding jumpers that helped to bring her along. The first was a horse named Unusual, who was bred from the same mare as two Olympic jumpers, Miss Budweiser and Riviera Wonder. Mrs. Francis Rowe was the person responsible for connecting Kathy with Unusual. During a brilliant fall circuit on Unusual, Kathy established herself as an outstanding rider. Her self-confidence and ability grew much stronger, as she was now using her natural feeling and talent along with Bert de Nemethy's education.

In the fall of 1962, Kathy was abroad with the team when her friend, Ben O'Meara, the owner of Colony Farms where she frequently rode, found a horse they named Untouchable. He was ten-years-old at the time, rather weedy-looking and somewhat erratic in his behavior, but Benny's intuition told him that the horse had Olympic potential. Benny turned the horse over to Kathy when she returned home. Untouchable became virtually unbeatable in the United States and established himself internationally as one of the best in the world.

A chestnut horse with a white stripe down his face, Untouchable, says Kathy "was a horse with a very hot temperament. Though his disposition would get us into a lot of problems while approaching fences, his talent and class would jump us out. His versatility was extraordinary. He had a natural instinct to avoid touching a jump, folding his legs up tightly as he cleared his fences, with a beautiful bascule (the rounding of his back that is one of the jumper trainer's schooling aims) and extraordinary use of his head and neck."

Kathy credits Ben O'Meara as the single most influential person to her as a rider. In *Great Horses of Our Time*, Ben O'Meara is described as "one of the most colorful, popular, enterprising and successful professional horse-man in the United States. He had an extraordinary gift as a talent scout, trainer and horse show rider." Kathy says he revolutionized the art of schooling and riding jumpers and that what she learned from him is still a major factor in what she does with horses. Very tragically, this special man was killed in an airplane accident.

Kathy feels that Untouchable was the horse she learned the most from and that he prepared her for several other high-class horses she had the opportunity to ride. Aberali, owned by Mr. and Mrs. Patrick Butler, was certainly another special horse and, "if ever a horse jumped and moved more like a deer than a horse, it was him," says Kathy. It was on Aberali that she did the riding for the long shots in the Disney movie "The Horse in the Grey Flannel Suit."

At the Pan-American Games in 1963 at Sao Paulo, Brazil, Kathy rode Unusual and helped to win the team gold medal. At the 1967 Pan-American Games in Winnepeg, it was Untouchable who was Kathy's partner when the team won the silver medal that year. With Untouchable at the 1964 Olympics in Tokyo, Kathy's responsibility was increased when Bill Steinkraus' horse, Sinjon, (the same Sinjon that George Morris and Kathy had ridden) went lame two days before the team event, depriving the U.S. team of its most dependable combination. Kathy and Untouchable rose to the occasion. The United States finished sixth as a team, with Kathy ranking thirteenth among the 42 individual scores, and first among the women riders.

Untouchable and Kathy also went to the 1968 Olympics, where the U.S. team ranked fourth after Snowbound pulled up lame after Bill Steinkraus' brilliant individual gold medal victory on him. The American team lost the bronze medal to the German team by a mere quarter of a point, representing a one-second time fault.

Kathy rode in three Olympic Games in all. By the 1972 Munich Games, Untouchable was past his peak. When the horse Kathy was scheduled to ride, Old English, pulled up lame two weeks before the Olympics, she was placed on Fleet Apple, Bill Steinkraus' second-string horse. She describes Fleet Apple as "a tall bay horse with a lot of talent. He was a very sensitive and nervous horse who had to have cotton put in his ears so that he wouldn't be frightened by the crowd. He was a lovely horse who tried hard to jump clean." Kathy and Fleet Apple placed tenth in the individual scores, competing against 56 other riders. The United States Jumping Team comprised of Kathy, Neal Shapiro, Bill Steinkraus and Frank Chapot, won the team silver medal.

Through the years, Kathy has developed a sophisticated riding technique that is universally admired for its elegance and effectiveness. She is described in *Great Horses of Our Time* as being "petite and pretty, looking more like a fashion model than an intrepid horsewoman." M.A. Stoneridge goes on to say, "her charm and slender figure are, however, accompanied by a strong riding seat, nerves of steel and an indomitable competitive spirit." Kathy has been known to admit, "the tougher the competition, the more fun it is."

When I asked her if it was difficult to memorize the different courses, and particularly the changes from the first to the second round, she replied, "You develop your concentration abilities over time to help you remember the courses." It's never just a matter of memorizing the sequence of the course. It involves knowing a number of other details also, such as how many and what kind of strides there are between the jumps, incorporating your knowledge of your horse's capabilities into your plan of how you will ride the course, and organizing at what angles you can approach the jumps when you go against the clock."

In addition to her show-jumping successes, Kathy has been a consistent winner in a number of flat and timber races in Maryland and Virginia since the age of sixteen. In 1968, after mounting a successful legal challenge, she became the first licensed woman jockey in the United States, riding races up and down the Eastern Seaboard and in Canada. She went on to ride in flat races in many countries, including Mexico, Germany, Columbia, Chile, Peru,

Panama, and South Africa. She was also the first woman to ride in the Maryland Hunt Cup, the toughest timber race in the world.

Beyond her riding achievements, Kathy is a skilled pilot with a commercial, multi-engine, instrument and seaplane rating. She also has a commercial glider rating and has acrobatic skills. She obtained a Lear Jet type rating and became the first woman to work as a Lear Jet Pilot for Executive Jet Aviation, which was the largest jet charter company in the world.

As an experienced scuba diver, she had the opportunity of diving in most of the best waters in the world, including the Red Sea, the Great Barrier Reef, the South China Sea and the Bohol Sea, in addition to areas off the coasts of Grand Cayman.

Kathy is also an enthusiastic and competitive runner, winning her division in track and field events and road races. At the end of 1994, she had completed 54 marathons and 16 ultra-marathons, winning several including the Pike's Peak Ultra-Marathon in Colorado an amazing three times. She has also won her division in almost every 10,000 meter road race in the Los Angeles area.

In addition, Kathy works as an expert witness and appraiser in connection with horse-related legal matters and has experience as a course designer and television commentator for Grand Prix show jumping events. She has also written articles published in several well-known journals. In 1990 she was inducted into the Show Jumping Hall of Fame.

She continues to this day to be a multi-talented individual who loves a challenge and embraces life in an attempt to gain a clear knowledge and true respect for all things she undertakes.

Indiana Jones, eat your heart out. Paramount Studios will have to make several more sequels for you to catch up with this woman!

HILDA GURNEY

Susan Sexton

Born September 10, 1943

At the 1976 Grand Prix Olympic dressage competition in Montreal, Hilda Gurney was one of three women from the United States to have achieved scores which placed the U.S. dressage team as the bronze medal winners. For the U.S. it was the fourth dressage Olympic team medal in history. The previous medals had, however, been won by teams of men.

In 1976 it was a trio of women who rode proudly on their prancing dressage horses into the arena at the medal ceremony to claim their reward. When I asked Hilda Gurney what thoughts were running through her mind during the medal awards, she surprised me when she said, "My full attention was on keeping the explosive energy of my horse, Keen, under control. I just wanted to survive this ceremony. As it was, the ribbon on my bronze medal broke because of all his antics and we had to go back to the grounds later with a metal detector to find it. Actually it was great fun and I thoroughly enjoyed it."

Hilda Gurney's mother tells her that she had already "flipped out for horses" at age three. Being born into an aviation family, her interests differed from the rest of them. She modestly says, "I guess I was the weirdo in the family." It was through her own personal determination that she became a horsewoman. She began saving money for her own horse by taking on the job of feeding horses at a neighbor's stable. Her neighbor was the master of a local foxhunt and she began an association with this hunt, gradually working her way into getting riding lessons.

At age fourteen she finally had enough money to buy her first horse, a Thoroughbred off the track, which led her first into hunt seat, then eventing and eventually into dressage. She fenced in her own paddock on the land owned by her family.

Hilda bought her second horse, Keen, in the fall of 1969, not long after she had won a national horse trials competition. She now owned two horses and her interest was leaning towards dressage. It seemed to her that eventing horses were frequently laid up. And, at age 26, she had the obligation of her job as a special education teacher. In the end, dressage seemed to be the most viable choice. She liked the challenge of it and felt she had the patience and dedication, coupled with her unswerving love of horses, to do well in this discipline.

Before finding Keen at the Alperson Thoroughbred Farm, she had been to the 1968 Olympics in Mexico City and had the chance to see the big, powerful horses that were being shown there in the Grand Prix dressage competition. When she first saw Keen, he was a three-year-old. He stood 17.2 hands, and was a beautiful chestnut color with a white blaze down his face. He was obviously a big mover and had the energy and size that reminded Hilda of the top level dressage horses she had seen in Mexico.

Hilda bought Keen for $1,000. She says of him, "He was hot-spirited and always willing to work. He was elastic, free, and always full of vim and vigor - a super athlete. I never had a problem getting him active. My problem was always to keep him from exploding with energy." She spoke also about the charisma Keen had and of the special rapport that developed in their partnership. She went on to describe his indomitable will. While she regarded herself as a good rider, she was never his master. She took the time to learn his ways and to work with full knowledge of them.

After fourteen years as a special education teacher, Hilda retired from that career and went full-time with her first love—horses. She began teaching, riding, and training horses and doing some breeding of dressage horses. She progressed to being a world-class contender when she won the individual silver medal and the

team gold medal at the Pan-American Games in Mexico City in 1975. Her skill as a dressage rider was reaffirmed at the 1976 Olympics when the USET claimed the team bronze medal, and again in 1979 at the Pan-American Games in San Juan when she and Keen won the individual gold medal and their efforts helped win the team gold medal. In 1983, on a horse named Chrysos, she went on to win another individual silver medal and a team gold medal at the Pan-American Games in Caracus, Venezuela.

In 1980, Hilda bought the farm where she currently lives and named it Keenridge after her champion dressage horse. Keen continued in competition until he was nineteen years old. Even in his final year of competition he was still performing brilliantly, although he was beginning to experience some soundness problems. At the 1984 Olympic Games in Los Angeles, Keen placed fourteenth out of 43 dressage competitors. Hilda had the top American score. In 1985, Keen placed second and was on the gold medal-winning team at the North American Championships at Old Salem Farm in North Salem, New York. His energy always abounded. He was retired to become a young rider's horse so that he wouldn't need to be worked as hard. He was always a willing and worthy mentor.

Keen still enjoyed working, even at age 23 when he began to suffer from health problems. After he had several strokes, Hilda made the difficult but correct decision to have him put to sleep. He enjoyed some mild exercise even on the day he was put down. Hilda never allowed him to suffer. He was buried in her backyard as a vital part of Keenridge.

Today Hilda continues to be an active competitor. She relates that three is a good age at which to begin training dressage horses. Then, if they are very talented, by around eight years old, you might just be lucky enough to have a Grand Prix competitor on your hands.

On any given day, Hilda may work as many as fifteen to twenty dressage horses. She states

that it is far easier for a rider to ride a trained dressage horse than it is to have to start one from scratch. She also trains a select number of Grand Prix dressage students and takes genuine pride in seeing them do well. Hilda relates that the hardest thing she sees for a dressage rider to develop is an excellent seat and clear and effective aids for the horse. These aids consist of weight changes in the seat, leg pressure and rein cues. Developing an outstanding work rapport with the horse is also essential in being able to perform as a free, flowing unit. Hilda says, "Dressage is a matter of the rider's knowledge and the horse's body that, with time, fuse into a performance that reflects a mutual respect and understanding of one another."

Her video *Selecting your Dressage Horse* provides valuable information to riders of all levels in their search for just the right horse. Her outstanding knowledge of equine temperament and natural ability serve as the basis for evaluating the desirable qualities essential in the discipline of a dressage partnership.

Hilda Gurney looks forward to many more active years working with horses in her continuing role as competitor, teacher and trainer. It is obvious from the way she speaks about her horses and her students, that she is doing what she loves to do most. She has a winsome smile and an innate kindness and patience with horses. She has learned to trust her own intuition as to what is right for her horses. She likes a challenge and she has never shied away from the hard work and persistence that is required for achievement in her chosen discipline. She continues to strive for that special brilliance she knows is possible in dressage, thanks to her former superstar, Keen.

DOROTHY MORKIS

Born December 29, 1942

Terri Miller

Dorothy Morkis began riding at summer camp when she was eight or nine years old. She was "just crazy about horses" and spent as much free time as possible at a nearby hack stable - just to be around them. She started out pretty much as a self-taught rider who acquired her first horse as a high school student and began showing it as a hunter jumper in local horse shows.

By the time she was in college, her first horse was retired and she needed a younger one. She found a Thoroughbred off the track to begin working with. "While he was a good mover, he was a little bit of a chicken and definitely not a jumper. Up until this time I had ridden pretty much just for the fun of it. It was during my college years that Richard Ulrich, a dressage enthusiast and teacher, sparked my interest in this discipline. Over the next three or four years he helped to bring me up through the third level of dressage. It was during this time that my concentration and direction as a horsewoman became more focused."

After she got married, Dorothy remained involved with riding. In 1964, when the Lipizzan horses toured America, she befriended one of their top riders and trainers, Ernst Bachinger, through their mutual interest in dressage. Years later he was the person who was instrumental in helping her find Monaco, when she was looking for a horse that could do the flying changes.

In September of 1971, Monaco arrived at her boarding stables in Raynham, Massachusetts. Dorothy says of him, "He was the kindest, sweetest animal. He was a wonderful big, grey Hanoverian horse. He was consistent in all of his performances and in every transition. It was my good fate that he came to be my horse."

I asked Dorothy about the sequence of dressage tests, which remain the same for four years. I wondered if, after so many repetitions of the test, the horse would begin to anticipate the next move and by so doing, might either break into a different gait early, or move into a wrong sequence if the test were then changed. Her answer was, "The horse knowing the test can work for you or against you, but the goal of the rider should always be to have the horse's attention by giving clear and consistent aids throughout the test so that there is no uncertainty between the partnership regarding what part of the test is being executed at any given time."

Dressage has very practical applications for any horse, not just the Grand Prix competitor. It is at the Grand Prix level, however, that dressage is elevated to its highest form. There the movements can be seen perfected to an artistic balance that rates such descriptions as "magnificent" and "sheer elegance."

Dorothy's first international competition as a member of the United States Equestrian Team was in 1975 at the Pan-American Games in Mexico City, riding Monaco. At this event she won the individual bronze medal and was a strong contributor to the team's gold medal.

She recalls the tension and pressure, a good amount of which she admits was self-imposed, before she was named to ride in the 1976 Olympics in Montreal. The names of the final team members were not announced until the day before the event. Once into the competition she recalls tension creeping in with such intimidating thoughts as, "If I make a mistake, the whole world will be witness." In spite of these anxieties, the familiar routine of concentration and discipline tend, more often than not, to take over once the rider is in the ring.

In the individual Grand Prix dressage competition, Monaco and Dorothy produced what was for many years the highest American score. They placed fifth individually out of a field of 27 competitors from around the world. In the team dressage competition Dorothy, along with teammates Hilda Gurney and Edith Master, won the bronze medal. It was a proud day! Dorothy remembers being the last competitor to ride. When the test was finished, she had no idea how she and Monaco had placed. "When the scores went up on the board and we realized we had won the bronze medal, there were tears and we were in shock. At first it's difficult to comprehend what you've done."

Dorothy and Monaco also represented the United States Equestrian Team at the World Championships in Goodwood, England. They placed eleventh individually and fourth as a team. She was proud of her horse. He was eighteen years old at the time and was retired shortly after this event. He lived to be 23 years old.

From 1978 to 1988, Dorothy was a representative on the Athletes' Advisory Council for the Olympic Games. This is a committee which is composed of one athlete from each of the sports in both the summer and winter Games. In 1985 she was given the chairmanship of the Apparal Committee which includes the responsibility of selecting the parade outfits and award suits worn by the athletes at the Olympics. "It's been an interesting experience, looking at clothing, including designer lines, in addition to reviewing and choosing luggage and various other gifts for the athletes."

My final question for Dorothy was about the growth and development of breeding farms for dressage horses in the United States. "Dressage breeding has grown immensely in

On Monaco, helping to win the dressage bronze medal at the 1976 Montreal Games.   *Gamecock*

the United States and we are producing some really top quality horses," she said, "and I expect this trend to continue to an even greater degree in future years."

Dorothy was a contender for the 1992 Olympics in Barcelona. She continues to be one of America's leading dressage riders and instructors. She enjoys teaching students at her stable, ranging from novice to the more serious, advanced riders who have their sights set on being Olympic Grand Prix dressage competitors just like their teacher.

EDITH MASTER

Born August 25, 1932

Gamecock

Edith Master's voice warms when she talks about the horses she has ridden in Grand Prix dressage competitions. She and her little grey horse, Helios, made remarkable progress together. In only her third Grand Prix competition, she represented the United States Equestrian Team at the 1968 Olympics in Mexico City. Helios was also her partner when she rode for the USET at her first World Championship competition in Aachen, Germany, in 1970.

Dalhwitz, affectionately called 'Witzy,' was the next horse Edith spoke about. "He was a beautiful chestnut Hanoverian with a white star and snip on his face. He was big boned, a real mover and quite frankly, a difficult horse to ride." It is her observation that some of the best horses are difficult to ride.

Edith and Dahlwitz were a successful combination, competing against the top riders in the world at the 1972 Olympics in Munich, the 1974 World Championships in Copenhagen, the 1976 Olympics in Montreal and the 1978 World Championships in Goodwood, England. They

In 1976, helping achieve the bronze with "Witzy."

were also slated for the USET 1975 Pan-American team but, due to an injury to her horse, she was unable to compete.

It was at the 1976 Olympics in Montreal that Edith's individual score, together with those of her teammates, Dorothy Morkis and Hilda Gurney, placed them in the honor spot of winning the team bronze medal in dressage. It was indeed a sight to behold when these three women and their horses came into the arena to claim their prize. For Edith it was an exciting highlight to her outstanding career, encompassing three Olympic Games, one Pan-American Games and three World Championships. Her great accomplishments were backed by desire, dedication and determination.

Edith began her love of horses as an eight year-old riding bareback at a farm across from her parents' summer place in Cape Cod. These first riding experiences led to lessons when the family returned to their home in Manhattan. As a young girl, Edith was introduced to dressage through films of the Spanish Riding School. The beauty, elegance and artistry of the sport thoroughly captured her imagination.

Edith studied and rode with a number of dressage instructors through the years, including Richard Wätjen, Robert Hall, Reiner Klimke, Fritz Templemann, Harry Boldt, and Heinz

Lammers. She absorbed valuable methods and techniques from each of them, but there were a number of times along the way when she needed a fair share of perseverance.

At one point, she encountered a trainer who told her she had no talent. Being young and not overly self-confident at that time in her life, his words hurt and she began to doubt herself. She even dropped out of riding for a couple of months until she discovered how much she truly missed it. Realizing the mistake of allowing someone else to control her life decisions for her, she returned to her riding with renewed determination and more drive than ever. Her multiple riding accomplishments over the span of her riding career have proved that her decision to persevere was right on the mark.

In reminiscing about her Olympic participation, Edith remembers her first competition at the 1968 Games in Mexico City as "no piece of cake," due to an accident that happened on one of her first days there. The athletes' living quarters were set up on hills with multiple irregular steps leading down to the road. She and her fellow teammates were on their way down the steps to catch the bus to the stables when she took a fall, which broke a bone in her hand and required stitches in her knees and on her shin bone.

Questions began to fly. "Are you going to be able to ride?" "Should we put someone else on your horse to work him?" Edith was firm in her resolve to ride the horse herself. So, before the competition, she worked Helios without the use of stirrups and without wearing boots. Novocaine helped, but it was not until just two days before the Grand Prix that she was able to put on her boots. She praised Helios as being "an absolute gem. He was totally honest and did the best he could."

Edith also recalls the unforgettable experience of marching in the opening ceremonies of the Olympics as a member of the USET. Getting acquainted with other competitors from around the world was something she especially enjoyed, since the wide variety of people and their interests was fascinating. One of her favorite acquaintances was an athlete on the shooting team from Kenya.

In 1978 Edith won the U.S. National Grand Prix Dressage Championship with a horse named La Paloma (which in Spanish means 'the dove'). Since Edith had purchased La Paloma as a three year-old and trained the mare herself, this win was particularly satisfying.

Edith is admittedly outspoken and she continues to retain her individuality in this respect. Some of her opinions have not always endeared her to others, but she has often proved to be 'on target' from start to finish.

Edith has a special ability to dedicate time and patience developing the full potential of her dressage horses - not to mention her orchids, her exotic birds and the beautiful Japanese lace maples, all of which require the same dedication. Aracorn, her farm, is named after two of her favorite things: the aralia plant and the unicorn. She also likes photography, enjoys all six of her dogs (when they are getting along) and is involved in working with the Humane Society to prevent animal abuse. Her farm has a number of orchards, and plenty of deer which she protects from hunters.

Her equestrian skills have involved her as a prominent dressage competitor, trainer, instructor and judge. When she has an outstanding dressage ride, she exhilarates in the feeling and thoughts of her Olympic past. She remains open to future possibilities of Grand Prix dressage competition.

EDMUND "TAD" COFFIN

Born May 9, 1955

Courtesy Tad Coffin

Tad Coffin and theThoroughbred mare, Bally Cor, were a winning partnership. Within two years of competition, they achieved four of the most sought after gold medals in international equestrian sport. At the 1975 Pan-American Games in Mexico City, they captured the individual gold medal and, along with their U.S. teammates, won the team gold medal also. At the 1976 Montreal Olympics they did a repeat performance and were presented with both the individual and team gold medals at the awards ceremony. Tad Coffin was the first American to win the individual gold medal in eventing and continues to be the only individual American gold medalist in this discipline to this day.

While Tad recognizes the outstanding individual accomplishment in winning these gold medals, he is the first to point out that individual honors are the result of a team effort. USET coach, Jack Le Goff, was the orchestrator of this effort and was assisted by Bally Cor's groom, the team vet, blacksmith, and encouraging supporters. Tad feels that, rightfully, they should all have shared the podium with him at the medal presentations. He feels fortunate that, on those particular days at those particular moments, he and Bally Cor produced some great performances.

He is not deceived into thinking that he was the best rider in the world on the best horse, or that the same results would have reoccurred on any other given day. He is both grateful and

Aboard the wonderful mare Bally Cor, 1976 Montreal, the individual and team gold medal winners — a remarkable achievement!

Gamecock

humbled by what happened to him. He also recalls, at the medal ceremony, how very proud he felt to represent his country and to be an American.

Love of horses and an aptitude for riding emerged early in Tad Coffin's life. Both his mother and his grandmother had been riders and his contact with horses began at a very early age, with access to his grandmother's horses. By age five his family moved to Long Island where they established themselves on an acreage, with a barn that stabled 40 horses. By age twelve, he was successfully showing in equitation and dressage. Tad began combined training (horse trials and three-day events) as a young teenager when his family went to Vermont for the summer and he had the good fortune to enroll in the summer teaching program of the Green Mountain Pony Club.

Raul de Leon was an inspiring and influential teacher with whom Tad rode for all of his junior years. Raul was a Cuban immigrant who came to the United States in the early 1960s. He had an international show jumping background and was an avid follower of the teachings of USET coach Bertalan de Nemethy. With Raul de Leon's help, Tad developed the riding skills which helped him to be selected for the USET's resident riding program. Tad Coffin feels that being in this program in 1973 was the best thing that could have happened to him. He is indebted to the USET for the

knowledge in horsemanship he acquired through this experience. He paid close attention to the theories of riding and training that he was being taught. He learned the highest standards of every aspect of being a rider and of taking care of horses. He learned what a fully-rounded program of stable management entailed in terms of cleanliness, feeding and grooming. He was taught the maintenance of equipment. He learned the wisdom of choosing competitions that were in the best interest in the development of the horses.

Tad recalls that Jack Le Goff, a former Olympic rider with the French team, had been hired by the USET in the early 1970s. It was Jack's plan to develop the USET into a three-day eventing power and to develop a young riders' program to complement this goal. Bally Cor had been donated to the USET during this same time frame. It was Jack's responsibility to match the horses with the riders and it was, therefore, his decision to team up Tad Coffin with Bally Cor in 1973.

Tad describes Bally Cor. "She was 16.1 hands high, well-proportioned and reasonably solid. She was dark brown and her coat was beautiful in the summer, when the sun reflected even darker dapples of brown beneath. She was sensitive, but not flighty or nervous. She was very intelligent, very courageous, eager, aggressive, and versatile. At face value she did not measure up to the qualifications required of an international three-day event horse, as she did not possess the kind of physical scope of moving or the jumping ability to place her at the top. However, as is always true, the proof is in the performance, and she gave of her best."

Tad Coffin feels that Bally Cor was able to accomplish what she did because of the total coordination of her training and care program under the coaching of Jack Le Goff. It encompassed the way she was ridden and trained, the high standards of her stable management and the deliberate choice of competitions that were selected to bring her along carefully and systematically.

Tad Coffin also credits Jack Le Goff with the development of his own sense of discipline as a rider. "Jack knew the horses and the riders very well. He knew if you weren't riding up to expectations. He helped you to identify corrective action and he didn't tolerate anything short of your best effort. He taught us how to practice and how to maximize the value of many simple training exercises. I knew that, if I wanted to be successful, I had to live up to my part. Jack also taught us to focus our concentration on the effort in hand and to block out peripheral thoughts. He taught us not to be overly impressed with our appointment to the Olympic team, but rather to keep focused on our goal. He had a way of helping us to develop the exact degree of concentration necessary to deal with the pressure at hand. I'm indebted to him for all I learned."

Tad Coffin acknowledges Jack Le Goff, Raul de Leon and Bert de Nemethy as sources of his past and present successes. The knowledge he acquired from them gave him the foundation to establish his ongoing life's work as a trainer and teacher in all disciplines.

One of Tad's first good memories of coaching came not long after he left the USET. It was with his junior team at the North American Young Riders' Championships in the New England area. His team won the individual and team gold medals three times in a row - an unprecedented record. It gave him genuine pleasure to give back to others what he had cumulatively learned from those who had taught him. For several years he was head instructor and managed the Flying Horse Stables in South Hamilton, Massachusetts, well known for its superb training facilities. Both the USET Three-Day Event Training Center and the USCTA offices were also located in South Hamilton at that time.

In 1984 Tad was offered an opportunity to team up with his former coach, Raul de Leon, in a joint endeavor and his decision to do so led him into a co-directorship of the residential program for riders and instructors at the Westmoreland Davis Equestrian Institute in Leesburg, Virginia. He served in this capacity for five years.

Today he is self-employed and works at a private farm in Haymarket, Virginia, where he channels his energy and horsemanship expertise into selecting and training top level horses. He also teaches a few talented students in preparation for international competition. His plans for the future comprise of "more of the same."

MARY ANNE TAUSKEY

Courtesy Mary Anne Tauskey

Born December 3, 1955

Mary Anne Tauskey remembers, as a young girl, running to the garage of her New York suburb home on Christmas Day to see if Santa had left the pony she had been pleading for, and being utterly disappointed to find that her father's car remained the only occupant. Her avid love of horses and burning desire to learn to ride only became stronger as time passed. At the age of nine, and blessed with totally supportive parents, she was given her first pony which she named "Tally Beau."

Her family moved to Texas when she was nearly eleven years old. This is where she began taking lessons from a Hungarian couple, Major and Mrs. Charles T. Valki, who managed a large stable in the area. It was the Valkis, more than any other instructors, who directed and inspired Mary Anne to want to strive to attain the upper levels of horsemanship. She was in a group of young girls that this couple took to Europe one summer. It was there that she was exposed to world-class horses as they watched the Grand Prix dressage and show jumping competitions at the World Championships in Aachen, West Germany. Their European exposure also included a tour of the Spanish Riding School in Vienna, Austria.

Before her family moved to England when Mary Anne was fourteen, it was the Valkis who recommended that, once she was settled there, she should contact Lars Sederholm at his training facility, Waterstock House, near Oxford, in order to obtain a position as a working student with him. This she did. It was here that she had her first contact with world-class riders who were training with Lars, and also with the Badminton Three-Day Event and its "top-of-the-line" cross-country course.

Although Mary Anne's father was not a horsey person, he was sensitive to his daughter's interests and he arranged for the family to move to Kent, just south of London, so that she

could have a horse. As a businessman, this choice meant that he had a daily commute to London where he worked as a chemical engineer.

By the time Mary Anne had finished high school, her interest in eventing was firmly established. It was time to get serious about finding a suitable event horse for her. It became a ritual for her father to pick up the latest issue of *Horse and Hound* from a newsstand in London each Friday. By the time he arrived home, he had pretty much circled all the advertisements that looked worth investigating further.

Horse hunting took them to Lord and Lady Hugh Russell's training facility at Wylye in Wiltshire. Although she never ended up getting the horse she went to see, because he didn't pass the veterinary examination, she was greatly impressed with their establishment and knew that someday she would like to return.

One week later, after a long trip first by train and then by car, she was face-to-face with Marcus Aurelius, the horse who was to become her eventing partner. Mary Anne recalls being tired and disappointed when she first saw him. "At 15.1 hands he was too small but," she continued, "we had come so far and I decided I'd at least try him out." Much to her surprise, when she rode him he felt solid and he had a huge stride. "He rode like a big horse and there was something sensitive and responsive about him that I really liked." After riding him, Mary Anne had a good feeling about his potential and the purchase was made.

Arrangements were next made to take Marcus Aurelius to Lord and Lady Hugh Russell's training facility at Wylye and for her to become a working student there. Mary Anne sought out Lady Russell's opinion of her recent purchase and was told that she had found a good cross-country horse. To help meet expenses, and in order to have some extra spending money, Mary Anne took a job as a waitress at the local pub just down the road from Lord and Lady Hugh Russell's home, Bathampton House, in addition to her duties as a working student.

As fate would have it, she was in the very place where the U.S. three-day event team had set up summer headquarters before the 1974 World Championships at Burghley. Not only did they stable and train at Bathampton House, but they lived at the Inn where she worked as a waitress. She talked with them, she watched their schooling methods and she gleaned everything she could from these contacts. It was about as ideal a place for an aspiring young rider to be as any in the world. In her own words, "It was a fabulous summer."

Six months later, Mary Anne's family moved back to the United States and located in New Vernon, New Jersey, not far from the USET headquarters in Gladstone. She stabled Marcus Aurelius at the McLarty's, having known their son, Ritchie, from a brief affiliation with the Pony Club as a young girl. Ritchie, at this time, had plans to try out for the USET Pan-American Three-Day Event Team. He was helpful and encouraging to Mary Anne and she went along to the selection trials at Ledyard with him to compete on Marcus Aurelius in the Open Intermediate division there. At the last minute, through a combination of encouragement and a "dare" from Ritchie, she filled out a form to declare herself as a candidate for the team. Much to her surprise and delight, she made the long list, but never in her wildest dreams did she ever imagine she would make the short list.

When the final selection was made, Mary Anne was one of the chosen names. In her mind she felt that better riders than she had not been included, but she also realized that she had indeed done well and that she had a sound horse who could be counted on to get around the course. They had definitely held their own at the selection trials, placing consistently. In addition, Marcus Aurelius' compact frame, short cannon bones, and good feet served him well soundness-wise. He was a tough little horse, well able to withstand the demands of the sport, both in training and in competition.

At the 1975 Pan-American Games, their debut at an international team competition, she and Marcus Aurelius placed seventh individually and the U.S. team took the gold medal.

In the development of their partnership, Mary Anne describes a remarkable rapport that existed between her and Marcus Aurelius. Their bond was so special that she has never encountered a duplicate for it and does not believe she ever will. "He was a very talented horse, but he was also very insecure. He hated to be alone. He shied away from water and would just as soon run the other way if we encountered a puddle." Mary Anne worked patiently and consistently with him. They both grew to know what to expect from each other. At the end of the work day she would fill her pockets with sugar cubes and ride Marcus Aurelius down to a pond, where they would spend leisure time together. He would enjoy grazing near the water and then walking in and out of it with Mary Anne on his back. Always being generously rewarded with sugar cubes, he gradually overcame his fear of water. A unique trust developed, and Mary Anne was so in tune with him that she seemed able to read the little horse's mind. He became one of the most fearless horses when it came to negotiating water obstacles on the cross-country course.

This bonding also resulted in her sticking up for her little horse when key people, such as coach Jack Le Goff, referred to him as "the pony." It was during this period that the television show "The Bionic Man" was running. Mary Anne started attributing Marcus Aurelius' good efforts to the fact that he was her bionic pony. "By golly, if I can't get people to stop referring to him as a pony, then I am at least going to elevate that status to something more special." The term caught on and Marcus Aurelius became the USET's Bionic Pony.

In the Three-Day Event at the 1976 Montreal Olympics, Mary Anne was the second woman from the United States in the history of the sport to represent her country. She cites Lucinda Green, another three-day event competitor, as having been one of her greatest inspirations in terms of both her positive attitude and her compassionate approach to her horses. Marcus Aurelius proved himself to be the sound anchor horse that the selection committee had felt he would be. He jumped around the course, in fine order, placing 21st in a field of 49 competitors. The U.S. won the Three-Day Event team gold medal at this Olympics. Mary Anne recalled that a portion of the cross-country course went across a section of a golf course - the kind of terrain many eventers dream of riding over. However, the night before the speed and endurance test, torrential rain pelted the area and the joy of riding across the golf course was

On the cross country course at the 1976 Montreal Games, with the 15.1 hand Marcus Aurelius.

Gamecock

definitely lost when they hit this boggy portion where the grass had held the excess water.

At the awards ceremony, Mary Anne remembers feeling the "lesser of the greats" as she stood with Mike Plumb, Bruce Davidson and Tad Coffin to receive the team gold medal. She was touched when Bruce Davidson nudged her to receive the medal on behalf of the team. She openly admits getting choked up when the national anthem began to play. During the victory gallop her "Bionic Pony" kept her busy when he all but ran away with her.

In 1978 Mary Anne was selected to compete as an individual at the World Championships after having not made the team. She placed twelfth among all the competitors. Had she been on the team, the U.S. would have won the gold, rather than the bronze team medal. Such is the fate and irony of choices and team competitions.

Mary Anne recalls the 1978 World Championship course at Lexington, Kentucky. "It was the biggest course anyone had ever seen. Size-wise the fences were formidable but jumpable. It was hot and humid and, on the day of the cross-country competition, the weather was almost unbearable. Marcus Aurelius was in top form. I felt he had never been more fit. Since the air was so heavy and a threat to our horses' respiration, Jack Le Goff cautioned us not to apply too much speed too soon.

"Three-quarters of the way round the cross-country course, as fit as he was, Marcus Aurelius was noticeably tired. There was a point when I actually wondered whether or not I had enough horse left to jump the remaining fences. He never got the second wind that I hoped would come by taking it easy between the fences. Each jump became more and more of an effort. I had the sensation that his strides were no longer free, but labored. The challenge was no longer how boldly we could negotiate those obstacles, but whether or not we could finish this marathon at all." However, Marcus gave his "all" and completed the course in better physical condition than many of the other horses.

As fate would have it, the Kentucky World Championship would be the last event for Marcus. In just four years he had gone from the novice level to the very top of the eventing ladder.

The following spring, Marcus Aurelius pulled a suspensory ligament and, for the first time in his life, he was lame. He was then retired, since he had done "it all" and there was no point to push him further.

Riding a new horse called Augustus, Mary Anne found his talents to lie in the show jumping arena. She then migrated to the exacting and technical realm of show jumping with the masterful help of Bert de Nemethy. She feels this time spent show jumping was a natural progression and "graduation" from eventing. What she learned there was as invaluable as it was exciting. Also, it gave her a more refined approach to "schooling over fences" that today she is anxious to pass on to others.

Mary Anne Tauskey is a woman who has trusted her own intuition, and she continues today to live true to her values and priorities. She has three young children and feels that to be an active competitor would take too much time away from them during their developmental years. Living in the Radnor Hunt area, she does find time to teach and to school horses for other people, training jumpers and working with horses on the flat. She would like to "give back" to the sport some of the wonderful knowledge and experience it has given her. She has introduced her children to horses as an option to enjoy and, only if there is some inner drive on the part of any one of them, will competition be a part of their lives.

She is also involved in riding for the disabled, which she finds rewarding. Recently she drove up to the farm of one of her good friends in Maryland where Marcus Aurelius is stabled. He is now 27 years old. She put a lead rope and shank on him, jumped on him bareback and went for a ride, "just like old times." Her ongoing love of horses continues to weave itself through her active life.

TORRANCE WATKINS

Born July 30, 1949

Courtesy Torrance Watkins

On the final day of the 1984 Olympic Three-Day Event in Los Angeles, Torrance Watkins Fleischmann was the only American rider to have a clear round in the stadium jumping phase of the competition. Along with the outstanding performances of her teammates, it was Torrance's clear round that gave the American team the edge in claiming the team gold medal. In a field of 48 individual competitors from around the world, she and her horse, Finvarra, achieved a fourth place ranking.

Torrance stood on the awards ceremony platform with her equestrian hero through the years, Mike Plumb, and with another petite horsewoman, Karen Stives, who had placed second individually. It was a proud moment. Torrance reflects, "It's not always easy to realize, when you walk a path, just where it will take you, or that your life will never be the same for you again." She recalls being very impressed with the wonderful, supportive crowds. She also remembers, at one point, turning around and seeing Finvarra looking right at her and realizing how far all the hard work and dedication had brought them. She came away from her Olympic honor more determined than ever to improve. "It made me want to strive to be the very best I can possibly be."

How did this dedicated horsewoman work her way up to Olympic status? Her acquaintance with horses goes back to age four, and she credits her mother "who was and is a fine horsewoman" with having taught her correctly about horsemanship. She worked with ponies before horses, and had to earn the right to have her own saddle. Torrance feels a tremendous respect is learned when you have to pay for your own way. "We had to earn the privilege of riding by working for it. There was no limit to the chores my parents would dream up for us to do to accomplish this purpose."

Torrance's father was an airline pilot who flew out of J.F. Kennedy Airport. Never having a keen interest in horses to begin with, he was also often physically absent because of his job during her developing years as a young horse-

1984 Los Angeles, cross country with Finvarra.
Patty Mack Newton

woman. The family's friends did, however, include Charles Plumb, Mike Plumb's father, who trained racehorses and hunted with the Meadow Brook Hounds. Charles Plumb gave Torrance her first lessons beyond her mother's instruction. By the age of twelve, the makings of a serious horsewoman had taken root and she knew then that someday she wanted to be on the United States Olympic Team.

During her teen years, Torrance's family went through a crisis requiring some difficult decisions that, in the long run, ended up keeping the family together. But, during a three-year interim, she was sent to live with her grandfather in South America who was, at the time, with the State Department in Lima, Peru. Torrance began show jumping there and also began to learn more about dressage. Occasionally, when her grandfather's duties would prevent him from being at one of her horse shows, he would send someone from his office to be there to cheer for her. His message was always, "You are important. You count. I love you."

In South America, because of her grandfather's tremendous foresight, Torrance learned about arts and culture. She learned a respect for herself and for others. However, it was not until

months after she returned to the United States that she competed in her first event.

At the age of fifteen she was back in the United States studying international relations at the University of Denver. All the spare time she could find was spent looking for horses to ride. It was during this time that an arrangement was made with Michael Ann Walters. Michael Ann would send kids to the Pony Club to be taught horsemanship and jumping skills by Torrance and, in return, Torrance began riding an Appaloosa for Michael Ann, with the goal of showing it at the Denver Stock Show. It was during this time that Torrance learned how to ride and show Western and developed a knowledge and respect for this style of riding.

The next landmark in her life came with a strong message from her father to return home to New York so that her family could be together again. Once there, she began working as a fashion model and photographers' model, still seeking horses to ride in her spare time. Her skill as a rider, trainer and teacher became established during this period and, through a network of family friends who were horse oriented, she was given the opportunity to bring several horses along in their training and to compete them in horse trials and three-day events. Bonanza's Little Dandy, Red's Door, Shore Shot and Poltroon were just a few. This was the time when her interest and participation in eventing became firmly established.

It was on Red's Door, owned by a family friend, Iris Freeman, that she got the opportunity to ride for her country as an individual in the 1978 World Championships at Lexington, Kentucky. Although the high humidity and temperature at this competition made it a gruelling event, plus the fact that she had a spectacular fall and was briefly pinned under water at 'the Serpent' fence, she and Red's Door placed fifteenth overall. The U.S. won the team bronze medal at this championship.

Poltroon, owned by a good friend, Kim Marra, was the horse Torrance rode in the Three-Day Event at the 1980 "Alternate Olympic Games" in Fontainebleau, France, and on whom she won the individual bronze medal. "Poltroon was a little mare, 15.1 hands high," says Torrance. "She taught me so much. I had to have tremendous self-discipline to ride her. She was very independent and, while she wasn't a big horse, she was big in mind and spirit and in the way she moved. She gave so much of herself. She had such incentive and heart. She was always a favorite of the young kids and crowds in general and was affectionately known as 'the pony'." After Fontainebleau, Poltroon came down with a temperature and developed pleurisy. She was retired and turned out as a brood mare and has had several foals. "I miss her to this day. She was such an individualist and a soul like hers is something that can just never be duplicated."

In 1982, Torrance went international again as a member of the United States World Championship Three-Day Event Team in Luhmuhlen, West Germany. Here she rode a horse named Southern Comfort that she had purchased from New Zealand's Mark Todd. They placed twenty-first and helped to win the team bronze medal. "Southern Comfort was a powerful cross-country horse but was weak in the dressage phase when I first acquired him. He was very shy, but such a gentleman - he still is to this day! At that time he gave my two good young horses, Finvarra and Arctic Leaf, a chance to grow and become more experienced without pressure."

When I asked her how she came into contact with Finvarra, the horse she rode in the 1984 Olympics, she related, "I was hunting when I encountered Charlie Fleischmann on Finvarra. He was having trouble keeping the horse on the ground; Finvarra kept trying to rear. We talked a little bit and decided to switch horses. When I got on Finvarra I had a strong feeling that there was something very special about him. I think I got along with "Andy" (Finvarra) better than Charlie did and when Charlie and I were married, he very kindly gave me Finvarra as a wedding present." When Torrance got back from her honeymoon, she went straight to Jack Le Goff for help in training her new horse.

Although Finvarra had never evented before, Torrance found the horse eager for the challenge it required. He progressed rapidly and in his third preliminary level competition at the three-day event in Chesterland, he finished in first place. Finvarra was a chestnut with a crooked blaze down his face. He stood 15.3 hands high and was a difficult horse to teach in some respects. "His temper kept getting in the way," as Torrance puts it, "and he had so much knowledge about his own ability." Their fourth-place standing at the 1984 Olympics and their clear round on the final day of stadium jumping attest

to the strong working partnership that developed between this feisty horse and the fine-boned woman who rode him.

Not quite a year later, in the spring of 1985, Torrance and Finvarra travelled to England to compete at Badminton, the most prestigious three-day event in the world. At Badminton, Torrance had the most thrilling and memorable cross-country ride of her career and she and Finvarra finished in an exciting fourth place.

Torrance and Finvarra were also members of the U.S. team at the 1986 World Championships in Gawler, South Australia. Within this same time period she was also working on bringing along several other young horses.

When she talks, she radiates a positive energy. She is an insightful and reflective person. She knows where she's been and she knows where she's going. She has retained a good perspective on life and the ability to laugh easily in spite of enduring some devastating hardships. A barn fire in 1988 destroyed four of her international horses. Curragh was one of these horses. At the time of the fire he was already long-listed for the 1988 Olympic Games in Seoul, Korea, having won the first of the Olympic selection trials. The other horses - Arctic Leaf, Pigale and Calliope - were all scheduled to go to other international competitions that year. It took Torrance quite a long time to get her feet on firm ground again and her goals refocused. She credits her working students, who still looked to her for direction, with helping her begin to move forward again after this tragedy. Without her students, some very special friends and, of course, her parents, she feels that the immobilizing numbness that followed the grief she had over losing these horses would have taken even longer to overcome. While a loss like this can be calculated financially, there is no price that can put on all the time and energy that goes into training top international horses, or the hopes and goals that they represent for the future. And, of course, also unmeasurable is the grief that comes from the attachment and love you had for them. To rebuild from these depths takes a survivor. Torrance Watkins is just such a person.

The neat thing about survivors is that, once they get their feet on firm ground again, they are stronger than ever. For the past several years she has had her horses at Quail Run Farm, just outside Middleburg, Virginia, and is very active competing and training her horses and helping other event riders.

MELANIE SMITH TAYLOR

Born September 23, 1949

Courtesy Melanie Smith Taylor

Melanie Smith Taylor learned to ride before the age of three on her parents' farm in Germantown, Tennessee. Her grandfather, who raised Shetland ponies at his Sunny Crest Farm near Fort Dodge, Iowa, gave Melanie and her sister their first ponies. Both of these ponies produced foals, so they were then off and running in their own pony business in Tennessee. This opportunity eventually developed into a riding school, run by her mother. Melanie, her sister, and her mother became involved also in buying, training and selling horses and ponies.

Melanie had a natural talent. As the years progressed, if a horse needed re-schooling, she was the one delegated to working with it. Her learning came from riding, leading her mother's lessons, and reading books. The closest thing she had to formal lessons was her membership in the West Tennessee Pony Club.

At age eighteen, she drove 800 miles to attend a riding clinic given by George Morris in Knoxville, Tennessee, because she wanted to acquire more technical insight. Up to this time, she had ridden primarily by "sight" and "feel" and was unfamiliar with such modern techniques as counting strides. When she asked George Morris if she could come and study with him out on the East Coast, he was honest with her. Her age was wrong. She was just out of the Junior Division and her horse wasn't good enough. There was no division for her and he felt it would be a waste of her time and money.

Armed with determination, she went back to the clinic the following year, and informed him that she was coming to Florida, anyway. She drove there in a purple station wagon, pulling a purple horse trailer. She groomed, braided and worked in exchange for lessons and to help pay expenses. With this kind of determination, and a burning desire to become good enough to ride on the Olympic team someday, things sometimes

have a way of working out. The Irishman, her horse that wasn't thought to be good enough, rose to the occasion and was the Amateur Jumper Champion of the Florida circuit. He eventually won the National Amateur Jumping Championship in 1970, in addition to winning the championship or reserve at every show but one that same year.

When Melanie started riding with George, she could not believe there were so many things to think about. She later came to realize that she was doing many things correctly, but just didn't know the technical terms for them. To have natural ability, coupled with technical knowledge, is the best combination of all for the horse-rider partnership.

After a few years, Melanie had made enough of a name for herself as a rider to have acquired a sponsor and she was seriously looking for a world-class horse. The search ended in Holland. After getting lost and travelling through a severe thunderstorm, they were finally at the farm they were looking for. When Melanie saw Calypso for the first time, her immediate thoughts were that he was "tiny and fat and strapped down in a martingale that was too tight." To her surprise, when she got on him and rode him, she felt something special about the way he responded. When she took him over a few fences, she also "felt the power." Being under sixteen hands classified him in the jumping world as being a small horse, but apparently no one had informed him, for he moved in a way that denied his size. Melanie knew that several other top professionals had tried him, but thought he was too small and a big risk for a four-year-old. Her intuition told her he would be worth it.

Perhaps the horse sensed that someone believed in him for the first time. What is known is that the partnership developed in a steady and progressive fashion. In the fall of the following year, Melanie and Calypso won their first Grand Prix. It was 1979 and, with Calypso doing so well, he was delegated to be her back-up for the 1980 Olympics if she made the team.

Calypso and Melanie at the 1984 Los Angeles Games.

Another great partnership that Melanie had in the late 1970's was with a horse named Val de Loire, who was the Grand Prix Horse of the Year in 1978, when Melanie was Leading Lady Rider, Grand Prix Rider of the Year, and Horsewoman of the Year.

At the Alternate Olympics in 1980, Melanie ended up riding Calypso again. Before the competition, a stall accident gave Calypso the disadvantage of an injury going into the competition. Restless in a strange stall, the horse made a sudden move toward a new groom carrying a pitchfork. In a natural response from the groom, when the pitchfork was raised, it caught Calypso's upper lip, puncturing it. In spite of this misfortune, Calypso performed admirably at the Olympics and they earned the individual bronze medal. At the World Cup Finals the same year they took second place.

She and Calypso went on to claim even greater equestrian honors. They are the only horse and rider combination to win the Triple Crown of American Jumping, consisting of the American Gold Cup, the International Jumping Derby, and the American Invitational.

At the 1982 World Cup finals, they took the gold medal and two years later, at the 1984 Olympics in Los Angeles, they anchored the first U.S. team ever to win a gold medal for show jumping. Also, in 1982 Melanie was honored by the U.S. Olympic Committee as the 1982 Sportswoman of the Year. She was the first and only equestrian to date to ever be given that honor. She was also one of ten finalists for the Sullivan Award—the annual award given to the top U.S. athletes each year, and she was inducted into the Tennessee Sports Hall of Fame and named the AHSA Horsewoman of the Year. 1982 was indeed an outstanding year of honors for Melanie.

Melanie describes Calypso as being even more determined when the pressure was on. He was a horse that liked to please. He had tremendous desire and scope. She felt his greatest asset was his intelligence. He was a smart, level-headed horse, able to get himself out of problems and handle the pressure of international competition.

Before Calypso was retired in 1985, he went on to win some of the richest Grand Prix purses. He now grazes in Melanie's back pasture and is the resident "brood gelding." Her belief in him, and her abilities in training him, had turned him into one of the greatest horses in the world.

Melanie no longer competes. She does television commentaries, the highlights being her coverage of the 1988 Seoul Olympics and 1992 Barcelona Olympics. She still feels a part of the electric atmosphere. She is married to Lee Taylor and they raise and train Thoroughbreds as polo ponies and hunter prospects. Melanie especially loves working with young horses and seeing them progress.

She also judges and gives riding clinics. Part of her current farm family includes seven Long-Haired Dachshunds and a Golden Retriever. She lives three miles from where she grew up, bringing her full circle around the globe back to her home destination.

107

Courtesy Karen Stives

KAREN STIVES

Born November 3, 1950

The following account of the 1984 Los Angeles Olympic three-day-event competition was confirmed with Karen Stives as being "exactly the way it was." The account is taken from David Wallechinsky's outstanding book, *The Complete Book of the Olympics*. "Thirty three-year-old Karen Stives, the final rider of the competition, entered the arena knowing that her ride would decide both the individual and team gold medals. If she cleared all twelve obstacles without a fault, she would come away with both the golds. If she dislodged the rail of one fence, she would lose the individual gold medal to Mark Todd from New Zealand, but she would secure first place for the U.S. team. If she knocked down two fences, the team gold would be won by Great Britain. As the capacity crowd watched nervously, Stives successfully guided Ben Arthur over the first ten obstacles. But then, at the next to last obstacle, a triple jump, the horse nicked the top of the middle fence, sending the pole to the ground. Stives and Ben Arthur recovered to complete the course without incident." Talk about composure and grace under pressure!

When I asked Karen what she liked most about Ben Arthur, her immediate response was, "his incredible talent, scope and instinct." She went on, "While he was a great competitor, like so many other top athletes, he was very difficult from day to day. He was not an easy horse in the barn. He was afraid of his own shadow. When you gave him a bath, he didn't like the soap suds moving. He didn't like spray cans either, but put him on a cross-country course and he was a power machine."

According to Karen, Ben Arthur was a horse that made a lot of the executive decisions on the course and he was good at it when it came to the straightforward jumps. It was the jumps that called for a technical approach, a change of pace or collection, that Karen spent hours strategizing and worrying about, because this is where she had to organize and compress his enormous stride.

Ben Arthur was an Irish bred horse, living in England, being ridden by a New Zealander at the World Championships in Germany when Karen got word that he was for sale in 1982. The timing was right for her to make a change of horses after a bad fall in the World Championships selection trials on her horse, Silent Partner. Her mother urged her to get another horse and suggested that she ask for first refusal on Ben Arthur. In the end, after a lot of hard work, patience and determination, Ben Arthur turned out to be one of the best choices of her life.

In addition to her Olympic achievements, she takes much pride and enjoyment in having met one of her own personal self-challenges, that of being able to form a good partnership with several different horses and to help bring young horses along to a top level of competition. She more than proved herself with The Saint, Silent Partner, Yankee Girl, Flying Colors, and Chagall.

In cross-country competition, horses are required to carry 165 pounds to ensure a fairness in the load they carry in this grueling portion of eventing. As I sat next to this 100 to 105 pound woman, two things ran through my mind. The first was that this petite, slim lady had ridden an incredibly powerful horse to high Olympic honors, which certainly bears out the fact that this is one of very few sports where men and women compete on an equal basis. The second thing I thought about was the amount of weights she had been required to add in or on top of her saddle pad to compete in the cross-country and if it was as uncomfortable as I imagined, so I asked. She said, "When you're riding, if the weights are on right, the rider isn't aware of them. Where you notice the weights is when you've finished the cross-country and you're tired, you are required to carry the saddle, the weights and yourself over to the scale to weigh in!"

Karen was seven when she first started riding. Not being born into a horse family, she had to "nag and nag and nag" before her father finally relented, "probably just to keep me quiet," she says. Like so many other unsuspecting parents, who have no real concept of where it will all lead, he bought her first pony and made arrangements at a local barn for lessons. One pony led to another pony which led to a horse that she rode in hunter and equitation classes. She moved through the horse show circuit, riding every weekend until she left for college.

While in college, riding was placed on the sidelines, and she never entertained any conscious thought of making a future with horses. She stated that "Unlike many riders, I wasn't born with the goal of going to the Olympics in mind. As a matter of fact," she continued, " I never thought I'd be good enough to go to the Olympics."

Psychology was the major she started with in college, but in her junior year she changed to pre-med. Before developing her career choice at that time, she got married and moved into a new home that just happened to have a barn on the property. Enter horses back into her life. She began checking the area to see if anyone wanted to board their horses. This led to teaching, which led back to riding.

Karen related, "While I was in college, the horse shows progressed considerably in the level of sophistication required to be at the top. It called for more effort, money, and time than I was willing to give up at that time."

It took a dressage clinic with Michael Poulin, a well-known trainer and teacher, to get her enthused about the theory of putting a horse on the bit. She had taken one of her school ponies to the clinic, a 14.2 hand Appaloosa, and thought it was great fun. Shortly afterward, she returned to study with Michael Poulin for a couple of months to work on this new concept.

During this time in her life she got quite involved with dressage, but was also picking up a keen interest in eventing. She tried eventing at the preliminary level on her own for a year and came to the conclusion that she needed help. In the fall of 1978 she sought out the able assistance of J. Michael Plumb. In 1980, having been selected to go to the Olympics, she participated in the alternate Olympics held in Fontainbleau, France. The 1980 regular Olympics were held in Moscow. Part of the package to protest the Soviet invasion of Afghanistan was a boycott led by President Jimmy Carter against U.S. involvement in the Olympic events held in Russia.

It was at the Olympic Games in 1984 in Los Angeles, after she had acquired Ben Arthur, that she and her horse distinguished themselves by winning the individual silver medal and securing the team gold medal.

When I interviewed Karen at the Grand Hotel in Stockholm, Sweden at the 1990 World

Going cross country at the 1984 Games with Ben Arthur.   *Fred Newman*

109

Championships, she and her mother Lillian Malloney were there as owners of the versatile dark bay Holsteiner, Chagall, that Michael Plumb was competing on in the three day event. Since that time Karen has sold all of her horses, many of them going to other hopeful international competitors .

In 1990 Karen was just getting her feet on the ground learning the retail business in a shoe and sporting goods company which is a family business. She is a person who gives 100% to whatever her efforts are turned to, which left little time for riding at that time. She did, however, express her plans to stay involved through judging and committee work.

She has indeed followed through with her plans. In 1996 she continues to be active in the shoe business, in addition to keeping busy judging horse events locally, nationally, and internationally. Karen was chairman of the Selection Committee for the 1996 Olympic Games, Vice Chairman of the USET Three Day Event Planning Committee, and a member of the Board of Directors and Executive Committee of the USET. She is married to John Langermann.

In an exciting sport, this woman's energy and style have been missed in competition, but it is obvious that she's not yet finished making her mark in the horse world.

Tish Quirk

JOE FARGIS

Born April 2, 1948

Not all Olympic riders come from families with horses stabled in the barn behind the house. There are those whose natural desire to work with horses and whose innate ability and determination work together to move them up through the ranks with the passage of time. After moving from Norfolk, Virginia at age four, Joe Fargis began his riding career as a seven year-old, taking lessons at a local riding stable in the state of New York. He has been a competitive rider with the United States Equestrian Team since 1970. He has a refined, economical riding style and form that is envied around the world. He earned his way to the top and achieved both the individual and the team gold medals at the 1984 Olympics, and the team silver medal at the 1988 Olympics.

To win two gold medals at the Olympic level in any equestrian venue in the same year is a truly outstanding achievement. When Joe

and his horse, Touch of Class, won these honors in 1984, they became only the fourth partnership in 18 Olympic show jumping competitions to do so. At the 1984 Olympics, winning the two gold medals was not the only phenomenal thing that the Los Angeles spectators had the privilege to witness. Out of six rounds that Touch of Class jumped, only one rail fell to the ground. The athletic ability represented by this kind of breathtaking performance at the pinnacle of international competition cannot be overstated. To accomplish this kind of continuity of nearly flawless output, on difficult and demanding courses six times in a row, is a clear indicator of the athletic ability and exemplary communication between horse and rider.

Touch of Class had been brought to Sandron, Joe Fargis' and Conrad Homfeld's riding and training establishment, when Janet Nonni owned her and Debbie O'Connor was her rider. She stood out as being a good horse. She had been with a lot of good people who helped develop her sound basic training. She was easy to take

1984, Los Angeles, with the wonderful mare Touch of Class

Tish Quirk

care of, she was a good shipper, and she could be ridden by anyone. When Debbie stopped working for Janet, her owner put her up for sale. Joe and Conrad knew they wanted her to stay in their barn. So, in January of 1982, Mr. and Mrs. Patrick Butler, Mr. and Mrs. Brownlee Currey, Pam Hall, Earle Mack and Joe and Conrad's business, Sandron, bought the mare. Just before the Olympics, Pam had to sell out, so she missed having her name listed as an owner, but she was with them in spirit for sure. Joe began working with the horse and when they rode for the USET at the World Championships in Dublin, things were looking very positive for this new partnership. However, when they went to Hickstead in England for a warm-up show, Joe took a fall at the first fence in the first class and broke his leg. At the time it seemed like the end of the world to him. He was extremely disappointed. He describes himself as being a really cranky patient who was not at all easy to be around. The truth was that all he wanted to do was ride, but this he could not do. It took more than six months for his leg to heal.

When he returned to riding in 1983 in Florida, he started out by riding all of the horses too cautiously for a while, subconsciously wor-

rying about taking another fall. Eventually, time helped overcome this fear and he regained his usual assertiveness and form. In 1983, at the Nations Cup competitions in Rome and Calgary, Joe and Touch of Class competed as members of the U.S. Team and were strong contributors to the U.S. victories at both of these events. Joe began to seriously consider the possibility of competing at the Olympics.

So, in 1984, they entered the early selection trials to determine the Olympic Team. Off to a slow start, they steadily improved. Touch of Class became consistent and reliable. At the last trial in Lake Placid, New York, Touch of Class had four faults in the first round and jumped clear in the second one. Joe, however, continued to have his doubts about making the team. It was one of those years when there were eight to ten top contenders all vying for a position on the team. With so many good riders in contention, everyone knew the call was going to be close. When Joe and his friend and business partner, Conrad Homfeld, were confirmed as having made the team, it was a thrill of a lifetime to actually have qualified as an Olympic athlete. The selection trials had been really difficult and Joe was delighted to have made it this far.

111

Once again things looked very promising for Joe and Touch of Class, until another glitch presented itself when they arrived at Santa Anita Park, the site of the 1984 Olympic Show Jumping competition. The exercise area was on the race-track and Touch of Class responded in a way that any Thoroughbred might do under the circumstances—she remembered her racing days. The fact that she had started in seven races in her earlier career, and that she obviously had not forgotten what it was all about, became very apparent when Joe had trouble controlling her and she had worked herself into a lather within minutes.

Joe, who has a tendency to imagine things are worse than they are, began to question in his mind what he was doing at the Olympics, but he patiently worked through each day with the hope that it would all work out. It took at least a week for the mare to settle down to some semblance of her former self. Good advice came from veteran California horse trainer, Jimmy Williams, who suggested exercising and schooling Touch of Class as far away from the race track as possible. Fortunately, as the Olympics came closer, the track began to lose its look, little by little, as the stands were built in and the arena began to take shape. When there was no longer a homestretch that you had to walk by, Touch of Class started to calm down. Before then, her exercise consisted only of several long walks.

In the warm-up class, Touch of Class had a clear round. The mare was moving well and she was in tune with her rider. Joe does not believe in giving horses human qualities, so he did not feel that Touch of Class had any real sense about the importance of the occasion. However, he did feel that she had switched into gear and become very reliable and steady, doing everything that she had been trained to do. All her reactions were very straightforward. It is just such a two-way communication in a horse/rider partnership that can transform a competition into a brilliant performance.

It had never crossed Joe's mind that he might win two gold medals. He had just been thrilled to have made the Olympic team for the first time. His objective had simply been to do the very best that he and his horse were capable of doing. As it turned out, their very best was record-breaking.

In the team jumping competition, which took place before the individual competition, Joe was the first rider to go on course for the United States. He had watched the first two horses in the arena, and their rounds were not good. Thoughts of uncertainty began running through his mind again. He admits to being worried and of having recurring questions regarding his own presence at the Olympics.

However, the minute he started the warm-up, Touch of Class helped to reassure him; she was responding beautifully to years of training. By the time Joe rode the mare through the in-gate and onto the course, he believed that their preparation for that moment was as solid as it could possibly be. When they jumped the first jump, Joe was fully aware of how perfectly the horse was responding. This knowledge helped him to be more comfortable, both mentally and physically, and to begin enjoying the situation and the challenge of the course. Joe and his Thoroughbred mare had the first clear round of the day. The USET could not have had a better start. As the day progressed, Joe and Touch of Class took a commanding lead. Joe remembers that he was actually breathing when he rode in for the second round. Although usually not one to feel elated, by the time the USET won the team gold medal and had taken part in the medal ceremony, Joe admits that he was definitely "up." At an Olympic level particularly, there is nothing that can compare to the feeling of exhilaration when you have jumped clean throughout the competition.

There was no way anyone could have predicted that the individual competition would have ended in a jump-off between the USET members to determine the gold and silver medals. Joe Fargis and Conrad Homfeld were those two men. Joe would have won the gold medal without a jump-off had Touch of Class not knocked down the final rail in the second round. The two friends had a good time with the jump-off. The worst that could happen would be that one of them would get the silver medal. Certainly both men were already winners.

Conrad ended up getting the bad draw and had to go first. He pushed for speed and had two rails down. Joe opted not to go so fast and tried to finish clear. Touch of Class cooperated and Joe breathed a "thank you, God" when it was all over. Winning two gold medals in show jumping at the Olympics had only happened three other times since 1912 when equestrian events became an established part of the Games. In 1936, Kurt Hasse of Germany won both team and individual gold medals on Tora. In 1948, Humberto Mariles of Mexico won them on Arete. In 1956, Hans Gunter Winkler of Germany, on Halla, was the third show jumping rider to achieve a double gold medal, and in 1984 it was Joe Fargis on Touch of Class.

At the 1988 Olympics in Seoul, Joe was once again the anchor rider for the team. This time his mount was Mill Pearl, a chestnut, Irish-bred mare that Joe had trained from the ground up. Along with Greg Best on Gem Twist, Lisa Jacquin on For the Moment and Anne Kursinski on Starman, Joe and Mill Pearl won the team silver medal. Seven riders tied for seventh place in the individual standings. Joe was one of them. There is a special satisfaction in starting a horse at the beginning and training it to the Olympic level; it speaks volumes for the ability of the trainer.

Joe enjoys wearing the three hats of riding and training horses, and teaching students. He does all with a versatility and competence that marks him as the outstanding horseman he has proved himself to be.

CONRAD HOMFELD

Born December 25, 1951

Tish Quirk

The roads to achieving outstanding international equestrian wins are many and varied. Conrad Homfeld became a individual silver and a team gold medal winner at the 1984 Olympics. He also won the World Cup twice, in 1980 and in 1985. In 1987, after seventeen successful years as a competitive rider with the USET, he chose to turn his efforts to teaching and to training horses. It all started with his first exposure to horses through his parents' enjoyment of weekend riding. His natural ability, coupled with his parents' support, provided him with the opportunities necessary to progress as a young rider.

As his talent developed in his pre-teen years, Conrad made the transition from Western to English riding while competing in shows from his hometown of Houston, Texas. He was a rider full of energy and a desire to progress as a horseman. A turning point came for him when, at age thirteen, he attended a Texas riding clinic given by George Morris.

Morris's keen eye for talent and potential could not miss this young man who was out to make things happen in his own development as a rider. Conversation was initiated by George Morris with Conrad and his parents, and Conrad was invited to be a working student at George's barn in New York. So, Conrad went to the East Coast where George became his mentor and riding teacher.

The benefit of George's coaching was apparent two years later, when Conrad became one of the very few riders to win both the Medal and Maclay Horsemanship Champion Award and the AHSA Hunter Seat Medal Finals Competition in a single year. To win the two top junior awards in riding at age fifteen is no small accomplishment.

Conrad's years between age thirteen and seventeen provided some hectic but valuable riding experience. During this time he did a lot of catch-riding and showing and it was not uncommon for him to switch schools between Houston and New York three or four times a year.

Through George's network of horse people,

Aboard Abdullah at the 1984 Los Angeles Games.   *Tish Quirk*

Conrad had the good fortune to go to work at Frances Rowe's barn in Virginia. Where George is a teacher first and foremost, and approaches things from the rider's perspective, Frances was a trainer above all else, who always looked at things through the eyes of the horse. To have experienced both perspectives provided a balance that Conrad appreciated.

In 1970, as a result of Conrad's devotion to riding and Frances' help in loaning him one of her horses, Conrad reached one of the first goals in his natural progression as a horseman - to represent his country by riding for the USET at the 1970 Washington International Horse Show. The hectic pace of the next 18 months included competitions both at home and in Europe, where Conrad continued to make his mark both domestically and internationally.

His connection with Frances Rowe continued to be an ongoing influence upon his own growth and his maturing as a horseman. In addition to the many things she taught him about the care and management of horses, she also trusted him and gave him responsibility in

running the farm.

Three people who Conrad met at Frances's farm made a very positive difference to his life. The first were two clients there, Mr. and Mrs. Patrick Butler. Conrad, as well as many others, regards the Butlers as having been two of the greatest patrons of equestrian sport in this country. The Butlers were very generous with their thoughts, time and money. They enjoyed helping people and loved seeing them realize their dreams. It was Mr. and Mrs. Butler who opened the world of show jumping to riders of modest means, such as Conrad, by providing top level horses for them to ride. Balbuco was one of the Butlers' horses with whom Conrad did especially well.

The other major friendship that developed while Conrad was at Frances's farm was with Joe Fargis, with whom he shared riding assignments. The two not only became good friends, but also combined interests and knowledge to become business partners in establishing their own riding and training facility. Once again, this decision fell into the natural sequence of logical steps in the advancement of becoming horsemen. The transition from someone else making the final call to becoming one's own decision maker fits very naturally into the progression of events once sound knowledge has been acquired and if the willingness and commitment are there.

In 1978, Conrad and Joe changed locations and established "Sandron" in Southern Pines, North Carolina. The name of their business does not have any special meaning other than the fact that the words "pine" or "sand" are often incorporated into place names in the area.

It was while Conrad was at the Southern Pines location that he and Patrick Butler's South American Thoroughbred, Balbuco, continued to achieve some major wins. Balbuco was not an easy ride but, with Conrad in the saddle, they claimed the World Cup title in 1980 and two American Grand Prix Association Horse and Rider of the Year awards. These honors followed the record of wins that started when Conrad was still at Frances's farm when he and Balbuco won the AGA title in 1978.

Before Balbuco's career began to taper off, they had accumulated many significant wins. Eventually, however, Conrad found himself in a position that every competitive rider is required to face from time to time, and that was of wondering when and if another good horse would come along.

In December of 1983, the drought came to an end when Sue and Terry Williams gave Conrad a call to see if he would consider riding their Trakehner stallion, Abdullah. Terry and Sue were in active pursuit of a plan they had envisioned back in the 1970s, and that was of managing a stallion who would be both a show jumping competitor and a sire. Promoting a successful show jumper in the ring when it is also on the competitive market for breeding purposes has its obvious advantages; a mutual friend put Terry and Sue in touch with Conrad.

Conrad worked with the horse over the next year, producing some outstanding results. Three months into their new partnership, Conrad and Abdullah qualified for the 1984 World Cup finals. It was an insightful event.

This competition is held indoors and Conrad was soon to learn that Abdullah had a sense of confinement in indoor rings that magnified his problems. At the 1984 World Cup finals in Sweden, banners and huge banks of flowers enveloped the ends of the ring, adding to the horse's sense of claustrophobia. Conrad describes their performance at this event as being terrible. He fell off Abdullah twice and finished last. Although they were not off to a great start, awareness was at least quickly focused on issues that they needed to confront and work on.

The more Conrad worked with the stallion, the more he came to realize that the horse's quitting was not a sign of a complex temperament, but rather a concern for self-preservation.

Conrad does not view horses sentimentally, but he does believe that each one is unique and has an individual personality and talent. Beyond having a horse well-schooled, he never tries to make a horse conform to a pattern. He feels that part of the fun of working with horses is learning the personality of each one and trying to see things from their individual perspective. He then decides what can be improved and worked on and what he must accept.

Conrad's approach in working with Abdullah was much the same as he uses with all the horses he trains. It consisted of a lot of flat work. It also included setting up jumps that are progressive in their complexity and an organized system of schooling that strengthens the horse's weaknesses and develops his athletic ability.

When working on honesty, Conrad does not believe in clouding the issue with enormous fences. He schools over lower jumps, using variations in placement and sequence to present a test to the horse. His basis for choosing different sequences and methods is largely intuitive and is derived from years of experience in learning what works for different horses. He works on problems in a deliberate way that repeatedly reinforces for the horse the desired outcome.

Because Abdullah was a breeding stallion, between shows he was sent to Middleport, New York to fulfill his duties as a stud. Not all horses have the cooperative temperament that Abdullah had to allow the blending of these dual roles. Sue Williams worked with him on the flat and rode him cross-country to keep him fit between Grand Prix competitions.

Conrad had originally thought his performance at the World Cup in Sweden had ruined any chance he might have to make the Olympic team but, with his concentrated and well-chosen work with the stallion, things were now turning the corner. They were placing in every competition and won at Old Salem. By the time of the 1984 Olympic selection trials, they had developed a partnership that earned them a place on the Olympic jumping team.

The 1984 Los Angeles Olympics were a triumph for the American show jumping team. Course designer Bert de Nemethy's challenges in the Santa Anita arena were skillfully negotiated by the United States Equestrian Team members who won the gold medal. The Americans in the crowd showed great pride and appreciation during the medal ceremony. It was an outstanding and memorable event. Conrad and Abdullah made a strong contribution to claiming the team gold medal and then were involved in the jump-off for the individual gold medal with Joe Fargis, and his horse Touch of Class. In the draw, Conrad was the first to jump. He had the faster time of 51.03 seconds, but had two rails down for 8 faults compared to Joe's and Touch of Class's time of 58.06 seconds, but with no rails down. Both men were winners. Conrad took the individual silver medal, but also had the satisfaction of knowing that he had been instrumental in helping to bring Touch of Class along in her training at Sandron, and that he and Joe were members of the partnership that owned the double gold medal-winning horse.

After the Olympics, Sue, Terry, and Conrad decided that their next long-term goal would be to conquer the indoor arena problem with Abdullah and then to qualify and compete in the 1985 World Cup Finals in Berlin. Through carefully chosen shows to achieve this purpose, and by saving Abdullah only for those competitions that were very important, they gradually worked their way into a solid position. In preparation for the World Cup competition, Conrad repeated the same focus of schooling he had taken for the Los Angeles Olympics, only this time he concentrated on jumping indoors.

The first leg of the World Cup competition is a speed class. Not wanting to repeat his previous year's performance, Conrad's plan was very straightforward. He made a careful, deliberate goal of setting out to finish in the top ten. As it worked out, however, he did better than that; he had "his day" on all of the days of the competition! Conrad and Abdullah had one of the very few clear rounds in the second leg of the competition. Nick Skelton of Great Britain and Pierre Durand of France had to settle for second and third place respectively, for this was Conrad and Abdullah's year to take first place. Conrad and Abdullah had one of two double clear rounds on the third day. This also made Conrad a World Cup Champion for the second time, something that happens only very infrequently.

The gold-silver combination of the 1984 Olympics repeated itself for Conrad and Abdullah at the 1986 World Championships in Aachen, Germany.

In 1987, after recuperating from a broken leg, Conrad turned his efforts to teaching, training horses, and occasionally doing some course-designing and judging. After being a competitive rider since his pre-teen years, including representing the USET over a span of seventeen years, he enjoys the diversity of wearing more than one hat. Certainly, with his knowledge and skill as a rider and horseman, he is well equipped to undertake any equestrian endeavor that he chooses.

LESLIE BURR HOWARD

Born October 1, 1956

Tish Quirk

Leslie Burr Howard is currently one of the most sought-after riders and trainers in the country, as well as being a formidable competitor on the international Grand Prix circuit and in hunter divisions. She operates out of the Fairfield Hunt Club in Connecticut, where she gives lessons to many aspiring young riders. In 1985, six of her students won ribbons in the AHSA medal finals.

In her own progression as a young and developing rider, she broke a number of records which still generate a sense of awe and pride when she recalls them. 1983 was a stellar year for Leslie, when she accrued six Grand Prix wins in a single season. She had three of those wins in a row, and she took the first three places, riding three different horses at the Grand Prix in Upperville. All of these honors were unprecedented before she came on the scene. Also to her credit in 1983, she was American Grand Prix Association (AGA) Rider of the Year and a member of the gold medal-winning U.S. team at the Pan-American Games in Caracus, Venezuela.

Leslie is the daughter of professional actors. Her love of horses dates back to age four, when she spent hours riding a pony chained to a turnstile and equipped with a Western saddle that her parents had leased for her. By her early teens, riding rather than the theater became her career choice. She considers herself very fortunate to have had the best of equestrian training right from the beginning. Inspired by show jumping riders Frank Chapot, Bill Steinkraus, George Morris, and Kathy Kusner, by the age of 21 riding had become her first choice.

Her first Grand Prix horse was a great grey gelding named Chase the Clouds. After Chase the Clouds suffered an untimely death due to complications from colic, she was fortunate to acquire three successors that were also quality animals. They were Corsair, Boing and Albany.

It was the eight-year-old, brown Thoroughbred, Albany, that was her mount for the 1984 Olympics in Los Angeles when the USET claimed America's first gold medal in the team jumping competition. With Leslie as his rider, Albany had also distinguished himself as Horse of the Year both in 1983 and 1984. Owned by Debbie Dolan, Leslie describes him as a "scopey horse who was very fast and incredibly careful."

With Frank Chapot as coach, the 1984 USET jumping team generated some spectacular memories for all of its followers. The two clear rounds by Touch of Class and Joe Fargis certainly gave the USET the edge in obtaining the gold medal but, without the morale and strong contribution of each member of the team that day, America's national anthem could not have been played.

Leslie's strategy when she walks the course prior to the competition is typically to cover the ground twice, paying special attention to any troublesome-looking combinations or special efforts that will be required by her horse. She does not believe in strict adherence to one plan because she prefers to allow herself the choice of adapting to situations that might arise during the actual round.

Just before the U.S. team members were getting ready to walk the 1984 Olympic course, created by Bert de Nemethy, Leslie discovered that she had forgotten something that the crowd surely would have noticed. Her riding breeches had been left lying on the bed back at the hotel! Fortunately, a generous, unknown man at the barn overheard the dilemma and offered to drive to the motel to retrieve them for her. His offer was accepted, allowing her to be in full correct riding attire just in the nick

On Albany, Leslie's partner on the gold medal team at Los Angeles 1984.

Courtesy USET

of time!

As much of a thrill as the Olympic gold medal was for her, Leslie feels that the individual gold medal she won at the World Cup in Goteborg, Sweden was more of a personal victory. Achieving this medal entirely on her own is what makes this honor so special for her.

A series of providential events occurred to place Leslie at the Goteborg competition. In 1986, the year in which she won the World Cup, she had placed fourteenth in the qualifying try-outs. It was only by default, when some of the other riders dropped out, that she moved up the list and was able to compete.

Her goal at previous World Cup Championships had always been to finish in the top ten. Her placings ran the full spectrum from finishing last to having placed twice in the middle, three times in the top ten and finally, in 1986, as the winner.

After the first day of competition, Leslie was in fourth place and a contender for a medal. After winning the second leg, she was nicely in the lead. This brought back memories of 1984, when she had been in second place and then lost it. She knew she wanted the outcome to be different this time. She had to balance her confidence with careful decisions. She had great faith in her horse, McLain, and has always felt that if you do not believe you can make it happen, then you should not be there at all.

McLain, an Oldenburg stallion, had been imported into America, where the Dolans had purchased him and loaned him to the USET. Leslie felt that he had always been underesti-

mated. He was very fast and careful and had an incredible technique of being very quick with his front end, and really folding his knees at the take-off. The 1986 World Cup course was well suited to McLain's long stride, his balance, his steadiness and his scope. His athletic talents were particularly brought into play negotiating the difficult final line of the course.

A big smile came over Leslie's face when she and McLain were clear coming into the final line. This sent up a caution flag in her mind and she remembers thinking, "Honey, you'd better stop smiling, because you could fall off at the next jump and it will be all over." She did not fall, however, and the smile quickly returned and stayed with her for several days.

"The most difficult thing about going to the

118

Olympics or the World Championships," says Leslie, "is qualifying to get there. Once you are there, you know exactly what your focus is and you strive to accomplish it."

One of the highlights in Leslie's career came when she was named as Gem Twist's rider after his previous rider Greg Best sustained a broken shoulder in a fall while competing. She and Gem Twist were on the winning 1993 Nations' Cup team at the National Horse Show.

1993 was also the year in which she discovered the horse she would ride in the 1996 Atlanta Games: Extreme. Leslie was at the World Cup Finals in Gotenburg, Sweden when her friend Gabriel Coumans wanted her to come look at "this fabulous young horse" he had found. Since Gabriel had found about 90% of her horses and has a keen eye for them, Leslie flew from the show to go see the horse. She tried the chestnut Dutch-bred mare once and talked with Frank Chapot when she returned to the show. He then went with her to see the horse and loved the mare. Arrangements were made shortly after for her purchase.

At the 1996 Olympics, Extreme was only nine years-old. Leslie says of her, "She gives an extremely strong effort to the jumps. She is very scopey and extremely careful." Leslie continued, "She's a real freak of talent. Her temperament and rideability have gotten so much better over this last year." When I confirmed with Leslie that the horse was a Dutch Warmblood, Leslie replied, "Yes, with a tendency to be a Dutch Hot-blood!"

Much to everyone's alarm, Extreme was a very sick horse in early July. She had come down with a virus after the last trial at the Lake Placid Horse Show. She then colicked from the virus. When she finally stabilized, she was shipped home but during her first light work afterwards, she "tied up." This is like a giant muscle cramp which affects the hindquarters most, making moving painful and next to impossible.

Leslie related that it was very difficult for all of them not knowing how it was going to turn out. But, she said, "Extreme is a tough mare with a very strong constitution. Everyday her bloodwork improved. Thanks to modern medicine and Federal Express, Extreme was able to make it to the Olympics. By the time she was shipped, her bloodwork was back to normal and she appeared to be feeling good. The first five days we just walked here. The other horses arrived in Georgia on July 8th; Extreme got there on the 15th." Leslie had high praise for Federal Express, who understood the situation and recognized Extreme as an Olympic athlete and acted accordingly.

In Atlanta, Leslie and Extreme put in a clear second round after a fourteen fault first round. It was a pivotal performance that helped secure the silver medal for the team. The little mare that had been sick and gotten such a late start acclimating to the Georgia weather did herself and Leslie proud. When the vets checked her after the second round, they were amazed that she had one of the lowest heart rates of the day, 50, which is one indicator of how athletic she is.

Leslie came to the 1996 Olympics as a seasoned veteran. At her second Olympics she expressed a better recognition of how strong the European teams are. Also, this time she felt she had a much greater appreciation of what goes into winning a medal.

As a trainer, Leslie starts most Thoroughbreds toward the end of their second year. She follows the same procedure with an inexperienced eight year-old horse as she does with an untrained young horse, because all horses must progress in a step-by-step manner. Once the horse walks, trots, and canters with the use of simple, direct rein aids, she starts them over small cross rails and very low single jumps. The horse is ready to progress to slightly bigger jumps and combinations when he demonstrates confidence or seems bored with the present level of work. The horse's attitude must be carefully gauged throughout its training. The summer of the horse's third year is when Leslie would begin showing the horse at pre-green level, if all has gone well in its training. By this time the horse should be cantering around small courses and ready to handle flying lead changes around the turns. Whenever the horse encounters problems in the progression to a more difficult level, she returns him to a less demanding level, builds

119

up his confidence and then re-presents the original challenge. If the horse had problems with the flying lead changes around the turns, for example, she would go back to simple lead changes through a few steps of the trot.

Leslie has been consistently successful in the three equestrian abilities that continue to occupy her time: training horses, teaching young riders, and competing on an international level. She moves with competency and ease in all three areas and plans to continue doing the same for years to come. The hallmarks of her riding career have always been her drive and determination. That, too, remains unchanged as can be seen by her ready smile and the positive energy that she directs into work she loves.

GREG BEST

Born July 23, 1964

Tish Quirk

Preparation for Olympic competition is a rigorous commitment. It involves a dedication and determination that requires thousands of hours of practice and hard work. The preparation trains you to give your all during your event. All athletes that make it to the Olympics share in this common ground. To excel in their chosen sport is what it's all about. To achieve high scores when you are in top physical condition is one thing, but to achieve a silver medal when you are enduring adverse physical conditions places an athlete in a category of second mile - giving above and beyond all expectations. Such was the case with Greg Best at the Seoul Olympics in 1988. The story began years ago.

"Every little boy has a dream. Some dream of pitching in the World Series, some of playing in the Super Bowl. My dream was to ride in the Olympics." Greg started riding and showing at the age of four and got his first taste of success in the lead-line class at the Hamburg Fair Horse Show. Horses have been a part of his life as far back as he can remember. Greg's mother, professional horsewoman Maxine Best, managed the barn at Neil Eustace's Stillmeadow Farm in Connecticut. She also taught riding lessons there and was Greg's first teacher. By age six he was riding competitively in lead-line classes on a pony named My Trinket. Along with his sister, Leigh Ann, he and his mother spent innumerable weekends on the road. There were times when they would hit as many as three shows in one day. As a result of this points chase, Greg ended up lead-line champion of Connecticut, Rhode Island and New England.

It was during this time, when he was having considerable success in the walk-trot and short-stirrup divisions, that he began to dream of Olympic stardom. The picture was vivid in his mind. Greg would imagine his pony, Trinket, galloping along, carrying him over huge fences and racing home to victory. His vision then was of Trinket with her long pinto coat, pink pom-poms in her meatball-size braids and himself in his little red, white and blue plaid jacket with a blue clip-on bow tie, soaring effortlessly over the course. Eventually, of course, Trinket was retired and he dreamed of new Olympic mounts.

It was during these pony years that Greg first received recognition as a rider. He also got to meet such famous riders as Melanie Smith, Joe Fargis and Leslie Burr and to share with them his dream of riding with the USET.

In 1977, when Greg was thirteen, he swept the Florida circuit before heading north to win more championships on a pony named Snow Goose. This was his most spectacular year in

pony competition.

In 1978, Greg's family moved from Connecticut to Flemington, New Jersey. It was a time when Greg was beginning to make the transition from pony to horse. His mother, Maxine, continued to teach, this time on a free-lance basis, but both Greg and his mother were beginning to feel that it was time for him to work under another instructor. Maxine helped make the connection for him to ride F. Eugene Dixon's horse, Rallydale in the Junior Hunter divisions at a horse show. Dixon's Erdenheim Farm trainer, Jerry Baker, and hunter-jumper rider Michael Matz, helped supervise his riding.

But while Greg and Rallydale did well at competitions all over the East Coast, the horse was not teaching the young rider enough. Mike and Jerry encouraged Greg to stay soft, and not interfere with the ride, and that was that. Greg would just sit in the saddle while Rallydale went on automatic pilot and "did his thing."

After that season with Rallydale, Greg began his freshman year of high school and discovered he had an aptitude and love for soccer that threatened to displace his interest in riding.

He was voted "Most Valuable Player" in his first year on the soccer team. It was the first time he ever resented the amount of time his riding required. It seemed to be keeping him from playing more in the sport in which he was more currently interested. He went on to play soccer again in his sophomore year, until a bout with mononucleosis made it necessary for him to drop his varsity athletics. Months later, when he recovered from the dis-

ease, he went back to riding because he had nothing else to do. For the next three years his riding was inconsistent, even though he placed in the top ten in all three years of the Maclay Finals.

Greg was sixteen when a determined campaign by his mother resulted in former USET rider, Frank Chapot, agreeing to be his teacher. Frank is a veteran show jumper. Training a rider as young as Greg was not something that normally would have been included in his commitments. Maxine's persistence was a factor in the final decision, plus the right blend of needs, abilities and knowledge. Greg was a talented young rider with limited financial means, but with a willing and positive attitude just waiting to be developed in exchange for his exercising and working with Frank's horses. Frank had the knowledge and ability to develop Greg's potential, and could also use additional help with his horses. After a couple of informal jumping sessions with Frank, a mutual agreement was worked out that started with Greg going to Frank's barn on weekends to ride a couple of young horses for him. This developed into a regular routine and, before long, Greg was going to Frank's barn before school two or three mornings a week also.

Frank's laconic and disciplined approach challenged Greg into setting some necessary goals in his transition to jumpers after coming from a pony-hunter background. Greg needed to develop a deeper, stronger seat. If he could learn to sit as Frank wanted him to, he could improve everything else - keeping his balance around the turns, keeping everything together before the fences, and getting it back after a jump. Coming from a pony background and making the transition to horses is a challenge for many junior riders. A horse's stride feels so much longer to someone who has competed on ponies, and the urge to try to shorten that stride on the line to a fence is almost irresistible. Realistically, however, if you pick at a horse all the way down to the jump, you will very frequently never see the other side of it.

As Greg improved, Frank began letting him ride more of the young horses on his place, horses that had been sired by his former Olympic jumper, Good Twist. With the improvement he made with his new coach, Greg qualified for the Medal Finals in 1982, but was eliminated at Harrisburg when he forgot the course. More positive experiences came with invitations to compete as a team rider at the 1982 National Sports Festival, with repeats in 1985 and 1986, and at the Young Rider Championships in 1983, 1984 and 1985. Along the way, Greg also managed to earn a BA in economics from the University of Pennsylvania in 1986.

Under Chapot's guidance, Greg's jumping ability improved steadily. Maintaining a deep, relaxed seat was beginning to feel more natural. Everything was moving into place for the next turning point to develop. Gem Twist, one of the colts that had been sired by Good Twist, had been sent back to Frank. Michael Golden had bought Gem Twist as a three year-old in 1981 and wanted advice from Frank on how to correct some of the horse's behavior. Obviously a

talented jumper, Gem Twist had a mind of his own; if a rider tried to boss him around too much, he would throw in an extra spook or leap straight up in the air over a fence.

Michael sent Gem Twist to Frank in the winter of 1984. He had been showing the horse as a preliminary jumper and wanted to see what could be done with him. Gem Twist liked to overjump his fences, and this big effort was uncomfortable for Frank, who had some back problems at that time. Like the other offspring of Good Twist, he was a very careful jumper but had a tendency to spook and change direction unexpectedly—traits that, in the other young horses, had forced Greg to maintain the deep seat that Frank had taught him. It was a pretty natural move for Frank to start Greg working with Gem Twist. After he graduated from college, and with Gem Twist

Aboard Gem Twist in Seoul 1988. With a truly courageous performance by Greg (a triumph over nature?), the team silver came to the U.S. team.

Tish Quirk

122

in the picture, Greg turned to riding as his main objective. If he was ever to achieve his dreams of going to the Olympics, here was the horse that he felt could take him there.

In 1985, their first full year together, Greg and the grey gelding won the $25,000 Rolex USET Show Jumping Talent Derby and the American Continental Young Riders individual show jumping championship. Gem Twist carried Greg smoothly into the open jumper division, where their rise through the ranks culminated in the pair being selected for the 1987 Pan-American Games. At this competition the U.S. won the team silver medal.

The fact that Greg and Gem Twist were brought together when they both had talent, but at the same time had some habits that needed to be corrected, forced them to take things a little more slowly. One of the most satisfying things to Greg is that he was the rider who allowed Gem Twist to become the great horse that he was destined to be.

In December of 1987, Greg and Gem Twist won the AGA Championship in Florida. Winning this event was his greatest achievement up to this point because he felt that he had ridden consistently well in a pressure situation. He believed that his lifetime dream to go to the Olympics had a chance of becoming a reality.

Old Salem was the first official Olympic selection trial. Gem Twist was great, and, by winning that day, Greg knew that they were at least going to be among the leading candidates for the team. At Oak Ridge and Lake Placid they placed in the Grand Prix and, after winning the final phase of the selection trials in Southampton, they secured a sure place on the team for the Seoul Olympics.

The trip to Seoul was a long one. On the way they stopped in Los Angeles for "processing." While there, they received everything from language lessons to a hair dryer. Processing began with a lecture on the anti-American protests, terrorism, and how not look like an American athlete. Next they moved on to a physical examination, where everything turned out just fine for Greg except that he found out that he was "a little bit flat-footed." Then came the fun part from Greg's perspective. They were given uniforms, shirts,

socks, shoes, shampoo, athlete's foot powder, cameras, sunglasses, hats, luggage and even underwear. Greg wondered why he had even bothered to bring any of his own things with him. He also wondered how he could look inconspicuous, wearing clothes that were red, white and blue and had USA written all over them. So Greg sent most of the items home, figuring that he would be patriotic later but, in the meantime, would concentrate on staying alive.

Once in Seoul, his roommate for the first couple of weeks was Joe Fargis. Greg considers his experiences with Joe to have been some of the funniest he can remember. For about the first week, the two of them were waking up at 3 or 4 a.m. because of the vast time difference between Korea and home. They would eat breakfast, go to the gym and then to the practice track to watch the track and field people work out. All of these activities were short-lived, except for breakfast. Greg describes Joe as a very realistic and modest person who has a great way of putting everything in perspective. The two, who are indeed ideal physical specimens for equestrian sports, would always find it a little humbling when they watched the track and field athletes go through their routines. For the next week, things were relatively quiet. The horses were being good and the riders were anxiously waiting for things to get started.

Greg recalls the opening ceremonies as being inspiring. He rode over on the bus next to John Thompson, the U.S. basketball coach. Greg did most of the talking and, finally, the coach asked him what he was doing at the Olympics. Greg told him that he rode horses, and he said, "Oh, you're one of those equitarians." Greg just smiled and nodded his head, figuring that his knowledge of basketball was about as good as Coach Thompson's knowledge of the equestrian world.

With the opening ceremonies behind them, the U.S. team riders had another week before starting to compete. Greg spent most of his time sick in bed with a severe intestinal bug. The closer it got to competition time, the worse he felt, and the doctors could not do much for him because so many medications are banned for athletes. The first two days of competition came and went without any disasters. Gem Twist was behaving well and Greg was "O.K., but not well." But the next two days before the Team Competition were miserable. Because Greg was not feeling well, he watched many of the events on television. He knew things were getting pretty bad when he moved the television out of the living room and into the bathroom!

On the day of the Team Competition, Greg could not ever remember feeling worse in his life. This was the day he had dreamed about when he was still riding Trinket, and now all he could think of was whether he could wait until finishing his round before a bathroom visit was required. Between rounds he took a short nap and felt a little better afterwards. He recalls that it was a heck of a way to keep from getting nervous, but it worked all the same.

The jumps, reflecting the artistic and historical heritage of Korea, were beautiful. While their beauty was impressive, what Greg was more concerned with was their dimensions - whether they were wide, or solid, or airy - because the colors and structures were not a big deal to Gem Twist.

Greg recalls that the competition was as much of a challenge within himself as it was with the jumps. The pressure and chaos involved with the Games, as well as handling the turbulent political situation in the country and the threat of terrorist activity, were all new and unsettling variables to him, as well as having to compete while at a physical low.

Greg was the first rider for the USET to jump the course. The young rookie with dysentery did well. He and Gem Twist finished with four faults in each round and the combined effort of his other teammates gave them the Olympic team silver medal.

All of the demanding training and hours of hard work that prepares an Olympic athlete surely were part of what helped Greg to maintain his concentration and skill, but then all athletes come with that training. The part that makes a true winner is being able to tap into the inner resources of determination and will, and being able to give that extra effort when it seems as though there is none for the taking. Without a great amount of personal integrity and perseverance on the part of this young

rider, the USET could not have attained the Grand Prix Jumping silver team medal at Seoul.

The bus trip back to his room was not an easy one, because he kept feeling ill all over again.

He did not ride the next two days before the final individual qualifier. He knew that all he had to do was to complete the course, and that was just about all he did. He only had four faults, but it was really worse than it sounds. Gem came into one of the jumps so close that he almost went straight up and down to clear it. It came to be referred to as the famous "chip" jump and was shown repeatedly on television every time they talked about the equestrian events, much to Greg's chagrin.

Two days later came the last day of the competition, the day of the closing ceremonies and, most importantly, the day of the individual finals. Greg finally felt great!

The riders had to get up early to go over to the main stadium. Arriving before the sun had risen, they saw the torch softly lighting the field. As the sun came up and the mist started to lift, the course became visible. It was a sight to remember.

Greg relates that Gem Twist just kept getting better and better the whole time they were in Korea. This was very typical of him; once he settles into a groove and once he starts to relax, he really jumps because he is less distracted and easier to control. The fact that they moved the individual competition from the Olympic Equestrian Center into the main stadium in Seoul about 40 minutes away was a factor in sparking Gem Twist's interest.

There is no doubt in Greg's mind that the horse understood how really special this last day was. Above all else, Greg says that Gem Twist was a great competitor. He knew when to turn on and give that extra effort when the situation called for it. He made a very special effort in Seoul, despite the fact that he was tired after all the jumping he had already done at the Games. It was as though he knew he was on stage and that this was his big moment. The course was extremely large and difficult. It rode differently for the two rounds; the distances were very complicated, and the horses who had also competed in the team competition were tired.

After a jump-off with West Germany's Karsten Huck on Nepomuk (who had the advantage of not having participated in the team competition), Greg went on to win the individual silver medal behind Pierre Durand of France on Jappeloup. Greg will always remember it as the greatest day of his life. The dream he had lived for had finally come true.

Greg's coach, Frank Chapot, was also the USET chef d'equipe at the Seoul Olympics. Their student-teacher relationship includes admiration, friendship, and a playful bantering. When Frank was asked to describe his protege, he replied (as quoted in *Practical Horseman,*) "Greg is naturally talented and he's aggressive. At the top end of this sport you can't be a wimp. He was already a good rider when he came to me, but with his pony background he rode in a hunter style. To make the transition to jumper he had to develop a much stronger seat. He's a committed rider and he's

lucky; he's done very well very quickly. He's also a nice person; a lot of riders wouldn't have handled success so gracefully. Of course," Frank added, "I make sure he stays humble."

At the news conference after the 1988 Olympics, Greg Best had his turn, "I'm in a unique situation," he said, "The chef d'equipe has been my coach for ten years." Then he added, smiling, "But, I've done well in spite of this fact." He then proceeded to give Frank a glowing tribute.

During my interview with Greg, I found him to have a nice blend of enthusiasm, humor and wisdom that belies his young age. He is currently teaching students and training horses out of the Greg Best Barn. After doing so much intensive training, freelance riding, and world travelling, it feels good to him to have a home base and a routine that he can count on. He is using this as a time to regroup and redirect his energy and talent.

ANNE KURSINSKI

Courtesy USET

Born April 16, 1959

At the very core of Anne Kursinski's participation as a respected and well-known international equestrian competitor lies a tremendous love and respect for horses. She feels that she has received so much from them over the years, that she wants to give back to them and to the sport. Campaigning fifteen horses on the circuit in preparation for the 1992 Olympics in Barcelona was just one indicator of how much love and dedication she has for what she does.

Anne began her career on the West Coast in her native California. Her mother's love of horses encouraged her own contact with them at the early age of four. By the time she was five, she was entering novice classes at the Flintridge Riding Club shows. Up until about the end of her ninth year, she competed mostly at club shows. It was then that Jimmy Williams became her instructor and she began making the transition from beginner to a more advanced rider. By the end of her junior year in high school, she was established as a strong and worthy competitor, and travelled to the East Coast to compete in the AHSA Medal and Maclay Finals.

While Anne did not regularly compete in East Coast events, a turning point came for her at the 1978 Spruce Meadows Horse Show. It was her first time riding as a U.S. team member and competing against famous international riders. She loved it and she knew then that she wanted to be a part of the U.S. equestrian team. Through her friendship with Melanie Smith, she was put in touch with George Morris, who helped her in her search for the right horse and who also became her mentor. George arranged for her to ride Third Man and she began multiple transcontinental flights from the West Coast to the East Coast. In the fall of 1981, she rode for the USET for the first

time on an East Coast team at the Washington International Horse Show.

Anne's decision to move to the East Coast in 1981 demonstrated her seriousness as a horsewoman in wanting to compete against the top horses and riders. While participating in the fall circuit there, George found a wonderful, big-hearted chestnut gelding named Livius that he felt would be ideal for her in her preparation for the 1983 Pan-American Games in Caracas, Venezuela.

Anne remembers arriving at the Caracus Airport to be greeted by soldiers with machine guns. Their presence at the equestrian facility was something she never did get used to. She describes the atmosphere at this event as "being alive with the sense of serious competition."

The first twist in her plans came when Livius developed a problem in one of his forelegs. Dr. Dan Marks advised her not to use him in the warm-up class and to save him for when it really counted.

The initial round of the Pan-American Games was scored against the clock. Livius passed the vet check and, even though speed classes were not Anne's strong suit, she and her horse went into the ring to do the best job they possibly could.

The jumps had a Latin American flavor and were decorated with tropical foliage. While they were not overly high, they did require careful riding if they were to be left standing. The crowd was massive and the press was everywhere. Anne felt herself tighten up. The course rode slow and stiff for her and Livius. They placed seventeenth. Her high expectations were dashed and she was flooded with a sense of having let everyone down—Livius, his owners, her teammates, George and the USET.

It was at this time that she tried to put into effect what she had learned from a USET sports psychology seminar that had been organized by Chrystine Jones just prior to the Games. She struggled to get control over her mind and put into use all that the speaker, Dr. Robert Rotella, had said about concentration, visualization, shutting things out of her mind and focusing. Anne believes that the positive power of these concepts, which embrace your inner resources, are what turned her week in Caracus around and which also continue to help her in her drive to always be and do her best.

Part of the Pan-American Games is the team competition. What this meant to Anne was that her score would affect the whole team and that she just had to ride well. She went in to the ring focused on a plan of attack and she stuck with it. She and Livius jumped two clear rounds. Anne had redeemed herself. She was totally thrilled when her score, along with those of her teammates, Michael Matz, Leslie Burr (Howard) and Donald Cheska, took them all to the podium to claim the team gold medal.

Anne's double clear rounds in the team event qualified her in the overall standings for an opportunity to compete for an individual medal. Only three riders from each country are allowed to participate in the individual medal competition. The chance of actually getting another medal seemed really remote to Anne, but she had a sense of excitement in getting the chance to compete for one.

At this point, her main concern was whether Livius would hold up physically for one more grueling day of jumping. When her number was called to go into the ring, her mind was set on wanting to ride well and make a good showing, not on winning. She hoped she could move up in the placings, but a medal appeared totally impossible.

The course for the individual test was enormous and very European in its dimensions, with scopey combinations and tall verticals. It was a course made for Livius' athletic abilities. They entered the stadium with the goal of jumping a clear round, and they did just as they planned. This moved them up dramatically in the standings. Suddenly an individual medal was within reach. Anne knew she could not think about it or she would tense up again.

In the final round, more horses had trouble. Many were tired from the demands of having jumped so many large courses. Anne sensed that Livius was ready to show his strength. She set her mind to stay with him, loose and relaxed. It proved to be the perfect strategy, for they scored another faultless round. The only trouble she had this time was believing that it had actually happened.

There were still great riders closer to a medal than Anne who were left to jump. She couldn't watch. She just listened to the crowd as the rails fell. When the final rider, Canadian Jim Elder, completed his round, Anne was walking in front of the grandstand toward the in-gate. The crowd cheered wildly as she passed, but it was unclear to her whether they were cheering for Jimmy or for her. Her answer came as she neared the in-gate. Everyone rushed over to congratulate her. Livius had outjumped them all to capture the gold medal for her. It seemed like a Walt Disney movie come true.

A partnership of friends from the Flintridge Riding Club had bought Livius for Anne, and this was certainly a fairy tale scenario of beginning in seventeenth place and working their way up to win two gold medals.

In 1984, Anne was awarded the "Up and Coming Athlete Award" by the Women's Sports Foundation. That same year she went to the Olympic Games in Los Angeles as the USET's alternate rider. The setting was just a matter of minutes from where she had grown up, and where she had friends and multiple riding connections. While it was exciting to be a part of what many consider to be the ultimate equestrian competition, for Anne it was also psychologically devastating to have such strong regional support, be so psyched to compete and yet, as an alternate, not be needed to ride.

Anne knew, as other successful athletes do, that no matter how well prepared you are, things do not always work out according to plan. That is why anticipating setbacks and preparing for them is part of the success formula. So is taking a disappointing situation and turning it around to your advantage, which is what Anne did with her 1984 Olympic experience. After all, she was the youngest one on the team. What she learned about participation at the Olympics in Los Angeles she used as an important foundation to make her better and stronger in her competition in the 1988 Olympics in Seoul.

Toward the end of 1986 Anne went to Europe looking for another Olympic caliber horse. While in Germany, Astrid Winkler, the former wife of Hans Günter Winkler, one of Germany's most outstanding Olympic riders, made the connection for Anne to see a Westphalian stallion named Calypso. Anne had an intuitive sense about this horse—it was one of the greatest horses she had ever sat on. The only problem was that he was not for sale.

Back at the Flintridge Riding Club, Anne's enthusiasm for this horse captured the attention of Frank Steinwedell, a lifelong friend and supporter. Frank made the necessary contacts and was eventually able to work out a purchase agreement. The horse was renamed Starman, so that he would not be confused with the horse that Melanie Smith rode in the 1984 Olympics. The horse was now ready for Anne to develop for, while he showed great potential, Starman was still somewhat green and needed experience at the international level before he would be ready to jump in the Olympics.

By the time the 1988 Olympics began in Seoul, Anne had brought him along very nicely, and they were the lead-off partnership for the USET. Along with teammates Greg Best, Lisa Jacquin and Joe Fargis, their strong team showing won them the team silver medal behind West Germany. In the individual competition, won by France's Pierre Durand, Anne tied with David Broome from Great Britain for fourth place, just out of the medals.

Anne describes Starman as having a presence about him. He is a big, powerful bay stallion, sometimes aloof, but always polite. He knows he is great. He is not intimidated by the crowd. On the contrary, he loves the excitement it generates and, if anything, it contributes to his jumping higher.

The experience that has given Anne the most personal satisfaction to date is winning the Grand Prix at Aachen in 1991. At this prestigious competition, she and Starman accomplished three clear rounds, a major feat when

you are faced with the pressure of riding against the best horses and riders in the world. She became the first U.S. rider in twenty years to achieve this honor, and only the second woman in the competition's history to do so. The year 1991 was also when she won the Equestrian Athlete of the Year Award from both the United States Olympic Committee and the Amateur Athletic Union.

When Starman was injured in the selection trials for the 1992 Barcelona Olympics, another horse named Cannonball, who had also qualified for Olympic participation, became Anne's mount in the Games. This Holsteiner gelding, owned by Robin Hill Farm, was nine years old when he trotted through the in-gate to compete on Spanish soil. Anne described him "first and foremost as a great athlete: careful, moody and temperamental."

In the first round, much to everyone's astonishment, Cannonball had three refusals and he and Anne were eliminated. Even though her high expectations were once again dashed, and she felt that she had started the team off poorly, she understood how green and inexperienced Cannonball was. As great an athlete as he was, and as many points as he had accrued in the selection trials, the steadiness and calm that only comes with experience was missing. Anne knew that the jumps at Barcelona were bigger and wider than anything Cannonball had been exposed to before. In the second round, Anne and Cannonball came back with an excellent four-fault performance and the U.S. team narrowly missed the bronze medal by less than a single rail.

The ability to hang in there in spite of setbacks is one of the hallmarks that separates winners from the rest of the crowd. Perseverance is the only quality that will reap the sweet satisfaction of overcoming a difficult challenge against all odds. Anne is a winner. Realism and love are interwoven in all she does in her striving to be a better horsewoman. She recognizes that, by anybody's standards, her life's choice to work with horses represents long and hard hours, rigorous efforts in finding owners and horses, and a very time-consuming and demanding training schedule. She believes that the inner desire of wanting to do what you are doing above all else has to be

At the 1988 Seoul Olympics,
Starman shines for Anne.

Tish Quirk

there if you are going to succeed. Her own riding experiences have taught her that patience and resilience are important in reaching goals. Goals are simply not going to be reached right away but, if you keep a positive attitude, even the problems and the mistakes that you encounter can inspire you to better choices for the future.

On Anne's way home from Barcelona, she was already planning how to make things better in the future. On the flight she drafted a letter based on her idea about getting a group together to share the expense of an international level horse. She sent the letter to friends and clients inviting them to help pave the way to finding another Olympic-caliber horse and be a part of this dream. Some people were keen on the idea and others not-so-keen; the idea was hard to sell without a specific horse in mind.

That problem, though, came to end Thanksgiving eve, 1992 when Anne went to wish George Morris a "Happy Thanksgiving." An Australian rider was working a horse in George's indoor arena, a horse who had lived in Anne's barn all summer long. Because her focus had been on preparing for the Olympics,

she had never paid any particular attention to the horse, nor had she ever seen him jump. "Who's that?" she asked. George's reply was, "His name is Eros and he's for sale. I'll give you one week if you'd like to try him." There was no doubt that she'd like to try him, but she was honest with George: she had no money.

After Thanksgiving, Anne came and rode the horse for the first time. "I have to have this horse! " she thought. She immediately contacted a number of the people she had originally written the letter to and, by Christmastime, The Eros Group had been formed. The dream was a reality.

129

Anne refers to her connection with Eros as one of those "very meant-to-be things." Many famous people had tried Eros over the summer and for one reason or another passed him by. After Anne rode him and knew she had to have him, she felt strongly that Eros was destined to become her next Olympic horse.

In 1995 Anne won the American Gold Cup for the fourth time and was named AHSA/Hertz Equestrian of the Year. She was also presented with the Whitney Stone Cup by the USET for her distinguished record in international competition.

Anne carefully and thoughtfully planned the training and competition schedule for Eros, to enable him to peak at the 1996 Atlanta Games. She felt for sure that he was one of the greatest horses she had ever ridden, a fact no one would argue with very much. Eros was a strong contributor to the team's silver medal win in show jumping.

Anne says of Eros, "He's got a big heart and tremendous self esteem. He thinks he's the greatest horse in the world and that he can do anything. And it appears he is capable of doing just that. He's very catty and he's never had a course that's too much for him. He's also very feisty and wears a red ribbon in his tail because he will sometimes kick and lash out. When he gets excited he'll move sideways and kick. I think he commands a great deal of respect."

"In the barn he'll nip a little or stomp his front foot if you get too close. He believes he is a very special horse. A cute trait he has, after I ride him, is that he will paw and rear up and do all these funny things that led me to believe he was sick —- but he wasn't. He was just trying to tell me 'Get off,' because he wanted to roll. In Australia, he lived out and that's one of the things that's a part of his routine. So even at the Olympics, we put him on a shank and let him go out and roll in the sand."

Anne would still like to have a team or individual gold medal. She believes that U.S. equestrians have come a long way, but still have a way to go to have a strong win, not just on a lucky day but on solid merit.

When Anne is not out on the campaign trail to continue representing the USET, she rides and trains horses at her stable, Market Street, Inc., located at George Morris' Hunterdon, Inc. in Pittstown, New Jersey. She also enjoys helping members of the three-day event team with their show jumping.

She derives a lot of satisfaction from bringing young horses along in their training. She has held riding clinics here in the United States as well as in Europe. She has a genuine desire to continue doing more of the same and to strive to do it better. Like several successful competitors before her, Anne has turned her hand to writing and her recently published book is entitled, "Anne Kursinski's Riding and Jumping Clinic."

Two quotes come to my mind as I spoke with Anne. One is by Vince Lombardi: "The quality of a person's life is in direct proportion to their commitment to excellence, regardless of their chosen field of endeavor." The other is by Willa Foster: "Quality is never an accident, it is always the result of high intention, sincere effort, intelligent direction and skillful execution. It represents the wise choice of many alternatives."

More power to this active competitor in her pursuit of equestrian excellence.

Tish Quirk

LISA JAQUIN

Born February 22, 1962

When Lisa Jacquin was at the point in her riding career when she was ready to buy her own horse, she had only a limited amount of money to spend. When she first saw For the Moment, she had no idea that he would turn out to be the horse who would carry her to the Olympic mountain top.

She was working at the Fairfield Hunt Club with Leslie Burr at the time and was riding some top jumpers, in addition to being in her first position as a teacher under Leslie's guidance. One of the veterinarian's assistants had brought over a six-year-old Thoroughbred gelding for Leslie to take a look at. The horse came with a hard luck story as a $5,000 claimer from the racetrack. His current owner had not shown him, but she thought he might have some potential as a children's hunter, and wanted Leslie's opinion. What caught Lisa's attention about the horse wasn't his grace or beauty, but rather his ungainly pogo-stick fashion of jumping every jump with room to spare, and the way he carried his head so high.

At Leslie's request, the horse's owner brought him back the next day. This time Lisa rode him and Leslie watched. Leslie continued to praise him. She felt he had a lot of spring and power. With Christmas only two weeks away, Lisa left for her home in Arizona without giving For the Moment another thought.

She had been home only a couple of days when Leslie surprised her with a telephone call, suggesting that she buy the horse. Leslie and Bruce Burr, Fairfield's manager, had continued to try him over fences up to three and a half feet, as well as over combinations, and he had looked better and better to them. Leslie suggested to Lisa that she could at least work on his schooling as a junior jumper prospect, whose resale would enable her to look for

something more expensive. In the end, Lisa agreed to buy him, more convinced by Leslie's enthusiasm than by any particular liking she had for the horse at the time. Once the check was in the mail, however, she did begin to feel excited about her purchase.

What she found out about the horse over the next few years of working with him was how many idiosyncrasies and insecurities he had, but she also came to realize that her own blend of patience and intuition in knowing what was right for him created the very formula which brought him to his full potential as an athletic show jumping competitor.

If For the Moment, who is known more affectionately as Fred, had come to Lisa earlier in her riding career when she was less experienced, she would not have been able to cope with him. Fortunately, her work back in Arizona dealing with sensitive Thoroughbreds during her junior years of training with Kaye Love had helped prepare her for this new challenge. Kaye's emphasis on communication—making sure that the horse understood what was being asked of him, and keeping his reactions and feelings in mind when planning his program--really came into play with her new charge. Lisa drew on all of the best that she had learned from all of the people she had trained with to come to an understanding with Fred.

Lisa had started riding at the age of eight, along with her brother. After her family had moved to Arizona, her father became a member of the House of Representatives in Phoenix and it was his colleagues who told him that every child in Arizona should be given the opportunity to learn to ride. And so it was, on the back of a little Connemara pony at a local riding stable, that Lisa had her first contact with horses.

She had a natural ability that responded well to instruction. She competed successfully in the junior divisions. When she was sixteen she went with her instructor, Kaye Love, to the East Coast to work with some of the top trainers. Their first stop was Joe Fargis and Conrad Homfeld's barn, "Sandron" in Petersburg, Virginia. When one of Kay's horses, named Black Irish, qualified for Harrisburg in the junior hunter division, Conrad suggested that Lisa, who had already also qualified for the Harrisburg Medal finals, should spend the remaining three weeks with George Morris at Hunterdon to add the final polish.

After the more relaxed approach she was used to back in Arizona, working with Conrad had been difficult enough. When she arrived at Hunterdon, where precision is emphasized even more, it was uncomfortable at first. She felt like a cowgirl. It seemed as though her shirt was always untucked and that her riding ability was uncertain. Even though she may not have been one of Hunterdon's top prospects that year, she did finish in second place at the Medal finals, riding Black Irish. The peak of Lisa's junior career was a trip with Hunterdon to France where, under George's coaching, they came in second.

After returning from Christmas vacation and beginning to work with Fred in all of her spare time, Lisa was grateful for the accumulated knowledge she had acquired and for Leslie's ongoing encouragement. In learning about Fred's personality, strengths, and weaknesses, she came to recognize that he was a complicated mixture of bravery combined with an aversion to situations that made him feel uncomfortable. He was very powerful and, if conditions were right, he could jump anything, albeit still with a kangaroo-like leap with his head held high in the air. His courage, however, evaporated if something upset him. During Lisa's first few months with Fred, she learned that the list of things that sent him into a tizzy was a long one. He was so temperamental and sensitive she realized that harnessing his jump was going to be a long-term project.

The going was tough before it got better.

At first Lisa discovered that not only was Fred stiff and tense, but sometimes he was also out of control. In the beginning he would not listen to her between fences. He refused to change leads in the corners. He was difficult to turn and it took a lot of room to bring him to a stop. But he hated having rails down. If Lisa could not adjust his stride and they came into a fence at an awkward distance, Fred would stop rather than attempt to jump it and hit it. With his sensitive nature, she felt a real crash would be devastating to his confidence. He also hated muddy or slippery rings, and one evening class they entered revealed that he didn't like the overhead lights and the shadows they cast on the jumps. He communicated his displeasure by stopping three times on that particular course.

More often than not, Lisa coped with Fred's problems by side-stepping them until she could build his confidence. She drew from the knowledge she had acquired from several different coaches and from her own intuition,

Lisa aboard For the Moment, 1988 Seoul Games.

Courtesy James Leslie Parker

in order to discover what would work best for this unusual horse. There were times when she found herself making decisions just opposite to accepted wisdom, such as when she chose to move him up through the divisions to keep him interested, even though he was barely rideable. The horse needed major work on the flat, which Lisa did proceed with. But she also competed him and moved him up through the ranks as a jumper. This did not happen without risks, but it did deal with the boredom and frustration they both would have encountered if the flatwork had to be mastered first.

Lisa's challenge was to design a show schedule for Fred that was also a training program, a schedule that would not frighten or discourage him, but which also allowed his turning and stride adjustments to be improved. She looked for classes in big arenas where there would be long galloping lines and the generous turns that he loved, as opposed to courses in cramped rings. Over the next four years (with some time out for corrective surgery on her knees), Lisa continued to develop the horse on a custom-made program that was building trust, communication and confidence.

She learned that Fred liked his warm-up to go a certain way. She learned to start with a vertical and work up to 4'3" fences by easy stages, making sure the ground lines were rolled out properly. Fred hated trotting fences. Even over the lowest practice jumps he simply stopped. Instead of fighting him about it, Lisa started his warm-up at a canter after a few suppling exercises.

There was no such thing as letting him hit a fence in the warm-up so that he would jump more carefully in the ring. He was already so careful that, if he bumped himself over one of the final practice fences, he would get so frustrated he would stop at the first fence on course.

Lisa learned that, if the class was on a grass field that seemed slippery, she needed to put caulks in his shoes and school him on similar footage so he would realize that he was secure. She always tried to anticipate situations that would make him feel uncomfortable and deal with them before they happened.

In the early 1980s, Lisa took a job in California with Bill Herring. Fred went with her and she competed him on the West Coast while she continued to work on his schooling. It was with the help of California hunter-jumper trainer, Judy Martin, that a breakthrough came in getting Fred to adjust his stride so that he could get to a vertical in a shorter frame. Lisa and Judy achieved this by spending hours on exercises with a pole on the ground in front of a small vertical, which was then followed by another pole on the ground. It was the pole on the ground, rather than Lisa's hand that forced Fred to alter his stride.

By the summer of 1982 he was ready for the Intermediate division at Lake Placid, which he won. Then they began to compete in the Modified division on the Arizona circuit in 1983. Fred was soon winning a class or two at every show. They did so well at the Griffith Park Show in Los Angeles, that several riders and trainers encouraged Lisa to enter Fred in the Mercedes International Grand Prix, which was a World Cup qualifier class with a huge course. He won yet again. She felt at this point that she had pushed him enough for a while and decided to stop competing him in 1983 while they were ahead.

Thanks to the Griffiths Park win, however, Lisa and Fred qualified for the 1984 World Cup Finals in Sweden. In retrospect, Lisa wishes she had declined. At the time, however, she was too inexperienced to recognize that, after just three years of working with Fred, he was still too green for the big jumps and difficult courses they would encounter there. The jumps at Goteborg were so big and came up so fast, especially in the jump-offs, that they never got around the course without a stop. Lisa's only consolation was that stops were better than a crash, for she believes that would have destroyed Fred's confidence.

By the time they started the 1985 season on the Arizona circuit, Fred was beginning to feel broken in on the flat. His stride was more adjustable. Lisa now had the option of adding strides in a line instead of always having to press forward and leave strides out. All of Fred's ribbons came in classes where the jump-offs happened to be designed with galloping lines rather than with tight turns. Their

Arizona season once again qualified them for the World Cup Finals. The results, to a casual observer, would not have stood out as much of an improvement over the disastrous 1984 effort. This time Fred had no refusals and his more adjustable stride enabled him to lengthen and shorten in response to the big international course. His turns were still rough and he did not handle the jumps in the smoothest style but, when he had an occasional rail down, it did not upset him the way it would have done a year earlier. This was one of Lisa's first hints that he was learning to accept things he once regarded as unbearable.

Year by year Lisa and Fred progressed as a partnership. Lisa's strategy was to ride Fred with confidence, trusting in his great ability. The bond between horse and rider had become strong. By 1986, whenever Fred and Lisa went into the ring, they had a reasonable chance of winning, and not everything had to be going Fred's way in order for this to happen now.

The ultimate goal was reached when their combined efforts earned them a place on the 1988 Olympic team. In preparation for Seoul, Lisa took Fred to Vintage Farm in Collegeville, Pennsylvania, where Michael Matz coached them. Lisa respected Michael's approach to training and teaching. He was able to help her improve her riding, without trying to change everything about her or revamping the system she had developed to fit Fred's unique personality.

Although heavily favored to be the gold medal winners at the 1988 Seoul Olympics, the American team placed as the silver medal winners instead. Lisa and Greg Best were the two rookies on the team. They both did exceptionally well. Lisa, who had taken a fall in the qualifying round, had abrasions on her face as she and Fred entered the ring for the first round of the team competition. They turned in a nearly perfect round, except that a light rub on fence 14b cost them a rail and Lisa incurred a one-quarter second time fault when she slowed down to line Fred up for the triple. In the second round, For the Moment, just like Greg Best's Gem Twist, had another light touch but it, too, brought the rail down for four

faults. But both of Fred's rounds counted in the U.S. silver medal result.

It was a proud time for Lisa at the Olympic ceremonies. She and the horse who had been her one chance to succeed had made it to the top of the mountain. He had been a difficult horse. Few other riders would have had the sensitivity, patience and love to develop his confidence and help him to become the great horse that he was meant to be.

For the Moment won two Grand Prix competitions in Toronto and then travelled to Florida in 1995 to compete in the AGA Championships. He is the oldest horse to win the Grand Prix. He won all three phases and became AGA Champion and Horse of the Year for the second time.

Fred has now been a competitor for fifteen years and has been a winner from day one to the present date. He has an enviably sound record as a jumper and, at age twenty, had just won a Grand Prix class a week prior to my interview with Lisa. Due to his longevity, soundness and athletic ability, he currently holds the record as the AGA's overall leading money winner. When Lisa describes him she says, "He is a horse that enjoys jumping and is very careful. From the beginning he has been a tough 'survivor.' He thrives on attention, rises to the occasion in the ring and gives 100%. He likes people and activity and he likes to please."

Lisa's dedication as a horsewoman is exemplary. Her work with another difficult horse that had been injured, Gigolo, establishes her as having a gift in building confidence in horses, for she brought him back to win again. She continues to keep a keen lookout for five and six year-old horses that show potential. She believes her ongoing career depends on doing the best job she can with whatever comes along. Fred is living proof that her positive attitude makes ambitious goals possible to reach.

Lisa is currently working out of a farm she leases in Valley Forge, Pennsylvania, where she is riding and training horses, and teaching. For the Moment was retired at rhe Devon Horse Show in June 1995 and relaxes these days.

NORMAN DELLO JOIO

Born June 12, 1956

Tish Quirk

Norman Dello Joio's attraction to horses took flight after he was a spectator at a horse show in Madison Square Garden when he was not yet a teenager. The vision of the magnificent efforts and skillful riding he witnessed there captured his heart and mind; he knew he wanted to be a part of the world of horses. It motivated him to seek out a job at a working stable. The fact that he had to take a train from New York to Long Island to get back and forth to the stable was not a deterrent to him in his goal to learn more about horses. He went to his first riding instructor, Wayne Carroll, at the Secor Riding Club. From thirteen to fifteen, he continued as a working student and began showing horses locally.

When his parents moved to Bedford, New York, he began taking lessons from Victor Hugo-Vidal, who now teaches in California. Progress became apparent the more training Norman received. When he started as a working student with Ronnie Mutch in Weston, Connecticut, Norman owned his first horse and had set up shop by renting a stall. During this time he did a lot of riding for other professionals on the East Coast. The catch-riding he did during this time helped him to develop the ability to adapt to a diverse variety of horses of different conformation and temperament.

Wanting to channel his energy into a purposeful outcome, he took lessons from George Morris at Hunterdon. In 1979 he achieved a goal that he had carried with him from the beginning; he was selected to be a member of the U.S. Equestrian Team and represented his country at the Pan-American Games. The U.S. team won the gold medal. It was a great beginning for Norman as a U.S. team rider. In 1979, Norman went to his first World Cup and, in 1980, he was selected to go to the "Alternate Games" when the Moscow Olympics were

boycotted by the United States. By this time he rightfully felt that he was part of the international show-jumping world

Norman has a special ability to instill confidence in the horses he works with. Horsewoman and friend Judy Richter tapped into this gift when she put Norman in charge of working with a horse named Johnny's Pockets who had at one time been successful but had been injured in competition at the World Cup. Within two years, the horse was once again placing at every show. In 1983 he was so consistent with Norman as his rider that he broke a record by winning five Grand Prixes in a row!

During the early to mid-80s, Norman leased stalls at Judy 's Wembley Farms which is a big training establishment. He rode many horses during this time, and it was not uncommon to trailer 30 to 40 horses in order to attend Grand Prix shows along the East Coast.

In 1983, Norman won the World Cup Final in Vienna, Austria on a horse named I Love You, and also won the Spruce Meadows du Mauriers International, which is the richest purse in show jumping and is about as close to the Olympics as a Grand Prix can be. In 1984, Norman went to his second World Cup Final. He and I Love You missed first place by a single rail. He did not make the 1984 Los Angeles Olympics due to what amounted to some miscalculation in the selection trials and points accumulation now required to qualify.

During the next three or four years, Norman devoted his time to riding and training. His reputation as an instructor was well established by the results of such students as George Lindemann, Martha Wachtel, Peter Wylde, and Jeffrey Welles. He did not have a world-class horse during this time but, like all other serious contenders, the search for potential is never-ending. Norman feels that the best equine competitor is an older horse that is physically sound and mentally fresh. In this

The 1992 Barcelona bronze medal rider on the very green Irish —- an amazing accomplishment. *Tish Quirk*

particular combination, the horse is both "course-wise" and a great competitor. Unfortunately, this combination is rare.

Irish, the horse Norman rode in the 1992 Olympics, was considered "pretty green" for that competition, for it was Irish's first major year at the Grand Prix level; earlier in the summer he had been in some smaller Grand Prix competitions in Texas. Norman first heard about Irish through Rodney Jenkins, who was judging in California when he came across this Thoroughbred from Ireland. At the end of his drive after his flight to California, Norman stood looking at the 16 hand chestnut horse with the white blaze and snip on his face. He was pleased with what he saw. The horse was very careful and had a style that Norman liked: he was a forward-going horse with a bit of a hot temperament. He had the nervous energy that Thoroughbreds are known to have and that riders like Norman are challenged to direct in positive ways.

At the 1992 Team Competition at the Barcelona Olympics, Norman was the second rider to go. Irish, who was then eight years old, exhibited some of his inexperience by accruing twelve faults but as Anne Kursinski's young horse Cannonball was eliminated, it meant that Irish's score had to count. In the second round, Norman and Irish had two fences down, putting pressure on Lisa Jacquin, Anne Kursinski and Michael Matz. They almost made it with only eight faults between them, but had one rail too many and the U.S. team had to be content with fifth place.

A storm with heavy rain, thunder, and lightning announced the beginning of the individual competition. Twenty-two riders with eight faults or less qualified for the afternoon's final round. Lisa Jacquin, Michael Matz and Norman all rode in the final round.

Only four riders and their horses jumped clear in the afternoon and Norman and Irish were one of the four. With only 4.75 faults after the second round, they took the lead with just two horses left to compete. They were assured of a medal, which could even be the gold, depending on the scores of Holland's Piet Raymaker and Germany's Ludger Beerbaum. The results were out of Norman's hands as he watched them, one at a time, go out on course. Raymaker rode a slow clear round, picking up one-quarter of a time fault to take the lead; but then Beerbaum won the gold medal when he turned in the day's only double clear rounds on his horse, Classic Touch. Norman was very proud of his young horse's performance and that, considering their competition, they had succeeded in winning the bronze medal.

USET chef d'equipe Frank Chapot was quoted in the *USET Newsletter* as saying, "Norman did a fantastic job of riding. Most of the experts considered his horse a little green for the Olympics, but Norman was able to build his confidence and bring out his ability much more quickly than we anticipated."

Norman has a quiet, modest way about him. He recalls feeling "honestly relieved when the Olympics were over." In preparation for and during the Olympics there is no let up. "It is a good and happy thing for most people to return to normal when the pressure is over."

Norman won the Pan-American trials in Palm Beach, Florida in 1995, on the mare S&L Second Honeymoon. He is in business for himself riding and training horses for several clients, and is based at Wembley Farm at the Palm Beach Polo Club.

CHARLOTTE BREDAHL

Born April 21, 1957

Courtesy USET

Charlotte Bredahl grew up on the small island of Moen in Denmark, which was largely rural. She remembers the huge draft horses on the island, plowing the fields, pulling wagons, and grazing on the hillsides. From the time she was seven years old, those farmers who lived within walking distance or were friends of the family knew her as the little girl who longed to ride horses, and they often made it possible for her to do so.

With an unshakable interest in horses, she proceeded to talk her parents into riding lessons. By age fifteen she was spending every free moment working at a farm that trained racing trotters. By age eighteen she had an amateur license as a sulky driver.

By the time she moved to the United States at the age of nineteen, she had ridden jumpers and dressage horses and raced trotters, and her desire to work with horses continued just as strongly as ever. Once in the United States, she began to specialize in the fine art of dressage.

Dressage is a sport in which competitors strive for perfection. This being impossible, they nevertheless make every effort to come as close as possible. A well-developed partnership between horse and rider is essential, along with meticulous attention to detail. The grace and beauty of a well executed performance has been known to take spectators' breath away and to bring tears to their eyes.

Charlotte enjoys working with young horses because their improvement rate is quicker and more exciting to her. With the very accomplished dressage horse, the progression is much more slow and subtle. Perseverance is the name of the game in developing a dressage horse, because it takes so long to produce results that enable a horse and rider to qualify for world-class competition.

When Charlotte met Stuart Miller, she found a kindred spirit and someone willing to assist her in buying horses to school and then re-sell. In 1987, with good contacts in her homeland, they purchased two Danish horses. Monsieur was one of these horses. He was a five-year-old at the time and barely broken. He ended up being a late bloomer. There were points along the way when they put him up for sale, but to no avail. They simply could not sell Monsieur! While this was unfortunate at

Riding to the team bronze in Barcelona on Monsieur.

Tish Quirk

the time, it definitely turned out to be well-fated for Charlotte in the end. The longer she continued to work with him, the better he became. The consistent, gradual improvement in this late blooming, chestnut Danish Warmblood gelding began to make its mark in the dressage world.

In 1989, Monsieur was runner-up as the Intermediaire I USDF Horse of the Year and first in the Prix St. Georges and Intermediaire I and II USDF All-Breeds award. These were the years when Charlotte's knowledge and skill as a dressage rider, and Monsieur's response in performance, prepared the way for them to try out and make the 1992 Olympic Dressage Team. It was an end toward which all efforts were directed.

Four years after Charlotte started working with Monsieur, he competed at the Grand Prix level as a nine year-old. In 1990, he was an alternate for the World Championships. In 1991, 1992 and 1993, Charlotte and Monsieur participated in international shows on a grant from the USET. Charlotte greatly appreciated these opportunities, because they exposed her to the top trainers in the world and to their insight and expertise as dressage specialists.

Going to the 1992 Olympics in Barcelona was something Charlotte loved. "Living in the Olympic Village, along with the other top athletes from around the world, was an incredible experience. The village was located right on the coast and, when you walked out of the door of your apartment, you were right on the beach." The pinnacle of the experience was, of course, ending up on a medal-winning team.

When the 1992 Olympic Dressage Team won the bronze medal, it announced to the world that, not only could the USET produce world-class dressage horses, but that its riders were also stronger than ever.

At those Olympics, the Grand Prix was the

138

team test and the Grand Prix Special was the individual test. Charlotte was the first U.S. rider to enter the Olympic dressage arena at Barcelona. While being the first rider has its disadvantages, Charlotte felt that, once her ride was over, the pressure was off and she was able to relax and enjoy the rest of the competition. She got the team off to a great start with a score of 1507.

Charlotte describes Monsieur as "quite a character. He is very happy with himself. He has to believe he is doing what he wants to do." He was especially difficult at competitions when Charlotte first started working with him, because there were so many things that frightened him. Quite often Charlotte had to hand-walk him and talk to him to calm him down. To this day, participating in award ceremonies remains one of the least favorite settings for Monsieur and he is still apt to do a few spins if there is an outburst of loud, spontaneous clapping. The memory of one award ceremony, at which a band started playing abruptly and several horses in the line bolted,

is an experience that has been hard for Monsieur to forget.

In 1994 Monsieur was USDF Horse of the Year at the Grand Prix and Grand Prix Freestyle levels. In the same year Charlotte and Monsieur were also one of the five finalists at the World Cup League Finals in Washington, D.C.

Charlotte is a multi-faceted and interesting individual. In addition to leasing a training facility, Bredahl Dressage Center, where she trains both horses and riders, she also enjoys using her equestrian knowledge to serve as a horse show judge. She is a real estate agent in Solvang, California, and she enjoys tennis and ballroom dancing.

Charlotte believes that patience and persistence are the two qualities that are most essential in dressage, which is the most demanding and disciplined of all the equestrian sports. She stresses the importance of striving to do your very best at all times, showing love and respect for the horses, and really caring about what you are doing.

ROBERT DOVER

Born June 7, 1956

Mary Phelps

Robert Dover has the energy and capability to have multiple equestrian projects going on simultaneously. He trains horses and riders. He has both short-term and long-term goals for all of them, in addition to having them for himself. When I first interviewed him, he had just returned from being on the 1994 World Equestrian Games bronze medal winning team at The Hague, in Holland, where the USET had achieved some of its highest scores. Robert and Deveraux were given over 70%. With this win, the United States Dressage Team took even greater steps forward in securing a solid position as a world power in this discipline. The U.S. currently has the greatest depth it has ever had, with reserve horses ready to go that have the potential to do exceptionally well if one of the frontline regulars encounters a soundness problem or illness.

Robert's riding skills and versatility allow him to bring several horses along at one time and compete on them at different levels. Having now trained and competed on over 20 internationally competitive Grand Prix horses, he has achieved a world-wide reputation of being a top trainer and rider.

Robert grew up as a city boy whose family did a great deal of moving and travelling. Chicago, Toronto, the Bahamas and Florida were all homes to him before he was fifteen. It was in the summer when he was twelve years old, that he started taking riding lessons with his next-door neighbor at Trakanen Farms, just outside Toronto where he was staying for the season. For his thirteenth birthday, Robert's family bought him his first horse, Ebony Cash, which was shipped from Florida to Freeport in the Grand Bahama Islands where they had recently moved. A horsewoman named Myra Wagner was his first real riding instructor.

Robert has maintained his friendship and connection with her and enjoys seeing her in Florida each winter.

Two years later, when Robert was fifteen and his family was living in Florida, he went to a riding clinic presented by the late Colonel Bengt Ljungquist, who became his trainer and mentor for many years and who was very influential in getting Robert serious and focused on dressage. A year and a half later he went to Elizabeth Lewis's stable in Georgia. She was then one of the star American dressage riders and is still a wonderful rider today. Robert was always very fortunate to find worthy people who influenced his development as a dressage rider. His personal initiative and ability to negotiate always made the most of those connections.

In 1977 he was long-listed as a member of the USET on a horse named Johnathan Livingston Seagull. He worked with Colonel Ljungquist in preparation to secure a position on the team. Then suddenly, without warning, the horse dropped dead of a heart attack while Robert was riding him. To have this magnificent animal go down while he was riding him was devastating to Robert. He could not bring himself to ride for awhile, and even considered giving it all up but, fortunately, there were consoling friends who urged him to continue and he made a comeback.

In 1980 Robert did a great deal of "catch riding." He rode everything and anything. During this period he worked with three notable horses. One of these was a problem horse, Blue Monday, that he brought to the Intermediaire I level. His work with another horse, Apollo, also brought good results. But it was a young Danish stallion named Chablis, that Robert was able to train to the Grand Prix level.

In 1980 Robert had the good fortune to ride Lago Maggiore, an older horse that had been

Lectron and Robert in Barcelona, riding through a nightmare. Their brave effort, though, helped gain the bronze for the U.S.   *Tish Quirk*

trained in Germany by the master, Willi Schultheis. This wise old dressage horse proved to be one of Robert's best teachers. In the early part of the 1980s, it became more and more clear that, if Robert was going to excel, he needed to gain more European competitive experience and also acquire a new Grand Prix horse. Chablis was now eight years old and was being sold, and his other horse, Federleicht, was at the Prix St. George level. Robert made a connection in Boston which put him in touch with two representatives from the German-based Performance Sales International. When they saw Robert ride they asked him to work for them at their U.S. headquarters in Virginia. Although Robert did not particularly want to live in Virginia, they made him an offer that he could not refuse, which included getting a Grand Prix horse. The horse he acquired from this transaction was

Romantico.

Robert's first international event was representing the USET at the 1984 Olympics, riding Romantico. The U.S. team placed sixth. Robert's successes in the 1980s continued to skyrocket and included being the 1983 National Dressage Champion, riding in the 1986 World Championship Team, and being a five-time winner of the National Freestyle Championship.

Between the fall of 1986 and the spring of 1988, Robert competed in 35 international competitions. At the time he was training seven horses, and he literally started at the bottom and ended up by winning six Grand Prix competitions and going into the World Cup Finals as the European League leader. During this period, Federleicht won the Grand Prix Freestyle in Aachen. Robert was the first American in 27 years to have won a Grand

Prix at Aachen in dressage.

After riding for the USET at two Olympics (1984 and 1988), two World Championships and two World Cup competitions, Robert left competition to coach and to train. When he was helping Melinda McPhail in 1991 with her Dutch Warmblood, Lectron, she and her mother, Mary Anne McPhail, suggested that Robert try out for the Olympics with their horse. He thought that the opportunity to work with the stallion for this purpose was too good to pass up, so he came out of his retirement from competition.

In 1992, when the dark brown Dutch stallion was eleven years old, Robert and Lectron went to Barcelona to compete in the Olympics. They had indeed made it on the team. Robert describes Lectron as a beautiful, sensitive, intelligent horse who was an inspiration to ride.

The Olympic year was also Lectron's first year at the Grand Prix level. He actually evolved into an Olympic contender during the qualifiers and the selection trials. Robert rode a fine line in 1992, making Lectron think he was playing when he was actually working, because Robert felt that was when he was at his most brilliant. Robert schooled him in the arena only about three times a week, taking him to other areas in between to keep him fresh; before one test in Florida, he had the horse do piaffes on a race track! He kept his pre-test warm-up light and as free as possible of repetitions, so that the horse came into the arena prepared, but not drilled. Then, instead of the safe, conservative test you might expect of an inexperienced horse, Robert went all out to display the horse's strongest point - the scope of his gaits. He showed the biggest extended trot, the most collected piaffe, the most collected canter to a pirouette, and the biggest extended canter. By doing this, Robert allowed Lectron to treat the movements as a game, instead of concentrating on making every single thing happen without a glitch. It was a real balancing act according to Robert for, in allowing the horse to be more extravagant in his movements, he also opened the door for errors to creep in, especially in the transitions.

As Robert was warming Lectron up at the

Olympics, he felt that the horse was more supple and lighter than ever, which confirmed his earlier belief that Lectron was as good a horse as any in the world. He also felt a sense of gratitude for all the help that trainer Herbert Rehbein of Germany had given him during the previous month.

Customarily, ten minutes before the Olympic riders leave for the main arena, the steward advises the rider that he must have his groom give the final touches, and after that, neither horse nor rider may be touched by anyone.

At this point at other shows, it was normal for Robert to get off and tighten Lectron's noseband one more notch, but the stallion was being so light and obedient that owner, rider and trainer agreed to leave it and head toward the ring. When Lectron entered the arena the added tension made him flinch, and at that moment, for the first and hopefully the only time in his life, the horse put his tongue over the bit.

This is a dressage rider's nightmare. With the bit under the tongue the horse sticks his tongue out, searching for a way to get comfortable. It also makes the horse feel like stopping whenever the rider touches the reins. Many thoughts ran through Robert's mind at that moment, not the least of them being, "Should I just stop and give up?" "Maybe he'll fix this himself, but I doubt it." And finally, "Okay, Robert, the worst has happened (again!) but you have to make the best of it. Ride with your seat and legs and absolute minimal contact with the reins, and hope for as few mistakes and disruptions as possible." And that is just what he did.

Lectron, in every way, did just as well as he could and, all things considered, pulled off quite an amazing score of 1507 and 64.12%. Though this was quite a let-down, considering Robert's expectations, he knew that the wonderful stallion had managed to keep the U.S. team within striking range to capture the bronze medal and that the team's final rider, Carol Lavell, would only need 1522 points to make that dream a reality. Carol exceeded the required points she needed and the U.S. secured the bronze medal, breaking a sixteen-year period in which the Americans had not claimed any Olympic medals in dressage.

The entire Barcelona experience was a good and an interesting one once the team had arrived. The U.S. dressage team settled nicely at the Royal Barcelona Polo Club, the beautiful club which was the main equestrian venue. Stabling was excellent, according to Robert, as was all the footing in all of the practice arenas. Life at the Olympic Village was absolutely wonderful. The apartments were very nice and the food and other facilities that were available to the athletes were excellent.

In the 1992 Olympic issue of *Horses Magazine*, Robert describes two interesting, but frustrating situations. The first had to do with bus transportation to and from the stable. In order to accommodate all the athletes, the Organizing Committee had hired drivers from all over Spain. The result was that few, if any, of the drivers knew how to get to and from the venues. This changed what should have been a twenty-minute drive into sometimes a two-hour scenic detour. Fortunately, after the first week this problem seemed to resolve itself.

Not unlike the problem with the buses was that of the stewards, who are responsible for upholding all rules of conduct in the practice and stable areas. Rather than hiring experienced stewards from around the world, as has been the case at past Olympics, the organizers decided to accept volunteers from the local Catalan community. Although they had the best of intentions, they were, for the most part, unaware of the normal procedures. When Carol Lavell went to work Gifted in hand, they swarmed around her like bees around honey, ready to prevent her from lungeing or other "crimes." Carol tried to explain her intentions but, to her dismay, most of the stewards spoke no English. Confusion like this was more the rule than the exception.

When it came time for the veterinary inspection, it seemed that luck was running out for Lectron. A few days earlier, a clod of dirt had lodged under his pad and had bruised his sole. Although he was 98% healed, the Ground Jury, for some reason, was extraordinarily critical and seven horses, including Lectron, were called back for a re-jog the next morning. All concerned felt there would be no problem, and indeed there was none, though

they all swear that he moved exactly as he had the day before—-which was perfectly.

Others were not so fortunate. The great Corlandus that, among other things, had been European Champion, and that was to compete one final time before retiring, was not allowed to start. Leonie Brahmal, who was to ride her horse for Canada, also had a ruling that the horse was not sound. Although the veterinary inspections are essential and very much a part of all Olympics, the decisions that come from them can severely weaken teams. Such was the case for both France and Canada in Barcelona.

Robert has a very positive attitude, whether or not things go well for him in his competitions. Life will go on because he is a happy person and he loves what he does. And for some reason, he relates, it is at the biggest international competitions where things tend to go the worst for him. Medals have eluded him in international events. When he went to the 1990 Pan-American Games in Cuba as chef d'equipe, he watched the dressage team win a silver medal and thought, "Gee, that's pretty nice! I certainly wouldn't mind if once, out of all these competitions, a medal came my way."

In spite of Lectron's problem with the bit in Barcelona, 1992 was a turning-point year. Two years later he had another bronze-medal year, this time at the 1994 World Championships riding Susanne Dausby-Phelps' horse, Devereaux. Here Robert not only achieved a very high score, but also placed fifth in the individual world standings.

1994 was also the year the U.S. Olympic Committee awarded him the "Male Equestrian Athlete of the Year" title.

Robert's horse for the 1996 Games was a gray Dutch Warmblood gelding owned by Anne Gribbons. Anne had been deliberating about aiming for the Olympics with her horse Metallic, but had experienced some health problems and the horse was just starting Grand Prix. Fate stepped in, in the person of Jane Clark, AHSA president, who made an offer to lease Metallic from Anne for Robert to ride in the Olympics. Jane's proposal was motivated by a desire to do anything she could to assure a medal for the U.S. Anne agreed and Robert got Metallic in March of '96 to begin fine tuning their partnership.

He had four months to do with Metallic what he would have preferred to have had a year to do, to evolve into a horse and rider partnership that harnessed Metallic's strong will and equally strong movements into something presentable in the Olympic ring. Robert would have liked to have reached the level where the horse could feel the composure that an experienced and seasoned animal would feel going into an Olympic test.

It was a tall order to achieve in such a short time. Changing riders and the even slightly different signals and aids can be confusing to a horse. Also, Robert was always balancing what would be best for the team against what would be fair for the horse. He feels he was never able to achieve that settled, confident feeling that the timing of their partnership was right for this Olympics. Nonetheless, the remarkable rider and the stunning horse had a solid consistent ride, scored a 65.96, and contributed to the U.S. team's win of the bronze medal.

Robert, who has known Metallic since he was three years-old, has always loved him. "He has an extremely strong character. When he comes into the ring, he all but says 'Don't you think I'm wonderful?' He has such power in him and is impressive because he is a strong mover and has very strong legs. His strong will has certainly made things challenging, and yet he has some very endearing qualities. He's a bit of a clown in the stable area. When you raise your index finger, he'll stick out his tongue and bring up his lip. So he's got a cute side, too, and enjoys people playing with him."

Robert praised the 1996 dressage team as being the best the U.S. has ever had. His own influence within the group was integral. He had supervised the training of Michelle Gibson's horse Peron from the time he was three until he was nine and doing Grand Prix work with his previous rider Ken Acebal. He was Guenter Seidel's mentor for several years, and Steffan Peters praises him as one of the people who has made a real difference in Steffan's own career.

Since 1984, Robert has captained all four Olympic dressage teams. He had a twinkle in his eye when he explained that his team members in Atlanta felt he should be captain because he is the most vocal, assertive one. One of the main jobs he described is going to the captain's meeting to get the flag bearer nominated. The fact that Michael Matz, the first equestrian ever to bear the flag in the Olympic closing ceremonies was nominated and got the honor in 1996, has to be a testament to Robert's ability to persuade and convince.

Robert feels there are two things that riders have a hard time realizing. First, that it is a reality that no one can stay at the top forever and, when the downside begins, a person is far better off to take it with grace than to be bitter and act as if life has dealt an unfair blow. And, second, that one's value as a horseman will be judged by other horsemen not only by what we do when things are going great, but also how we rode and how we treated our horse when things aren't going so well.

CAROL LAVELL

Born April 8, 1943

Mary Phelps

Carol Lavell 's first requests for a horse of her own began when she was around six years old and lived on a family acreage in Rhode Island. Because she was the only one in her family that had a passion for horses, the recurrent theme of getting her own horse went unanswered. When the family moved to East Greenwich, there was no space to have one, but she was given permission to start riding lessons. Thus began an even greater love for horses while learning more about them.

Through her teens and twenties, her natural riding ability and her competitive spirit moved her up through the ranks. She was active for a long time as a three-day- event rider. During this time she was involved in the training of the event horse, Better and Better, that J. Michael Plumb rode in the 1976 Olympics in Montreal to win the silver individual medal and the gold team medal.

As Carol continued eventing in the late '70's and early '80's, she became more aware that, due to her very competitive nature, she had the inclination to over-ride her horse. Choosing not to allow this to happen, she eventually made the transition away from three-day eventing and into the dressage arena.

While training with Michael Poulin, her talents as a horsewoman were soon turned to training horses to the Grand Prix level in dressage. By 1983, she was showing at Grand Prix level, and by 1984 she had three horses that were in the upper levels as FEI horses. None of them, however, had the potential to be an international star.

Carol's search for a world class dressage horse took her to Europe in 1984. She knew that the purchase was going to be an expensive one because she was looking for a horse that

had already been well started in the intricasies and precision of dressage. Part of the package would be paying for all the training and work that had brought the horse along that far.

When she found Gifted, it took a whole box of Maalox before she made the final decision. It is never an easy decision when you start with a plan that you think you should follow and end up wanting to do something else. She ended up purchasing two horses. Neither of them had been trained, but her intuition told her that they had the qualities she was looking for. She was right.

Gifted was one of the horses and was only 4 years old at the time. When she called her father to wire the price of the purchase to her, there was a silence on the other end of the line and then a collected, quiet voice that asked, "Now how many horses did you say you were buying?"

Next year, as Carol undertook the patient job of bringing Gifted along, she would call her father and invite him to "Come and see your horse." All through the years, neither one of her parents had shown any real interest in the horses themselves. Her father did, however, begin turning up more and more frequently as Gifted began winning at higher and more significant events. Unfortunately, he discovered that he was allergic to either the horses or something in the barn. This suited him just fine. His preference was to watch them from a distance, as he still regarded them as "big and dangerous."

When it came time for Carol to pay him back for the money he had wired to her, he said, "No, you can't pay me back for 'my horse.'" The father that had said "no" to his little girl now made a special gift to her. From that time on, Carol has referred to Gifted as his horse.

As Gifted improved with Carol's training, she and her husband, Tom, had to make the

With the wonderful Gifted in Barcelona, in a beautiful partnership that brought home the team bronze.

Tish Quirk

decision whether they were willing to commit to the time and effort of developing the horse to it's maximum potential. They chose to do so. They both believe in allowing the horse's potential and ability to be the guide in making the decision of how far one can go—and also when it's time to stop.

Once the decision is made to go forward with the career of a horse, there is no real let up in the pressure. It places you in a "Catch 22" of needing to improve your own riding skills and stay in top physical and mental condition while, at the same time, pursuing the competitive career of your horses. Add to that juggling your finances to cover everything, and you have created a very rigorous and demanding schedule for yourselves and your horses.

Carol is very grateful for the USET grants that have enabled her to study and compete in Europe. Being involved in European competition is a vital piece in the preparation for world class events. The sources for the financial backing for American riders come from their own pockets, sponsors (if they are lucky), as much assistance as the USET can give them and from patrons of equestrian sports. This is

in contrast to the German team, for example, whose expenses are all paid for.

Carol began riding as a teenager. 1985 marked her first year of riding for the USET in the Prix St. George/Intermediate I level at the North American Continental Dressage Championship. In 1986, she was a competitor at the same dressage level at the World Championships. At the Pan American Games in 1987 she rode on the USET silver medal winning team on a horse named In the Black, placing fourth individually.

At the 1989 North American Continental Dressage Championship, which was the same event at which she made her USET debut four years earlier, she and Gifted won the individual and team gold medals. They were the first Americans to win both the individual and team gold medals at this event.

At the 1990 World Equestrian Games, Carol and Gifted were the highest ranking American partnership. The United States Olympic Committee commended her as the Female Equestrian Athlete of the Year. In 1992, the U.S. Olympic Committee bestowed the same honor to her when she and Gifted once again were the leaders for the USET, this time at the

Olympics in Barcelona.

As the highest-placed U.S. dressage rider at the 1992 Olympic Games, Carol was also named the 1992 Miller's/USET National Dressage Champion. She had won the same title in 1991 and was Reserve Champion in 1989.

Carol and Gifted's partnership reached a spectacular year in 1992. Prior to the Olympics, they had placed fourth in the Volvo Dressage World Cup Finals in Goteburg, Sweden, making their World Cup finish there the best ever by an American rider. Following the World Cup ride, Carol went on to win the Grand Prix at the CDI-W Goodwood in England.

As a rider, Carol's goal has always been to be the best she can possibly be. She believes that by keeping focused on that singular goal, it has helped her to be able to perform at her optimum both as an individual and as a team member.

Carol describes Gifted as being impatient and too intelligent for a horse. When he moves, he is so full of energy and power that he has never been easy to keep round and steady on the bit and through to the aids. He is highly opinionated and territorial. If you go into his stall and awaken him before he is ready, he is apt to put his ears straight back and bare his teeth at you. He doesn't like loud noises, but he can respond beautifully to music in freestyle competition.

Carol believes that Gifted had some of his finest hours at the 1992 Olympics in Barcelona. They were the last and the strongest USET partnership to compete in the team event. Just before they entered the ring to salute the judge and begin their test, quick calculations revealed that they needed a score of 1524 to move the USET past Sweden to claim the bronze medal. Germany and the Netherlands had already secured the gold and silver medals respectively.

In the evening twilight of the Barcelona Polo Club, the spectators in the crowded stands were soon treated to a stunning performance by Carol and Gifted. Their final score was 1629. They had exceeded the score they needed by over 100 points. Their success was cause for celebration by Americans on both sides of the Atlantic. It was the first time in 16 years that the United States Dressage Team had won a medal at the Olympics.

Carol's team score placed her among the top 16 riders who advanced to the Grand Prix Special to determine the individual medals. She and Gifted placed sixth, which was the USET's best dressage finish since the 1976 Olympic Games in Montreal, where Dorothy Morkis and Monaco placed fifth.

A strong feeling of pride filled Carol during the medal presentation. All the effort, endurance and encouragement that had brought them this far had also enabled them to make a great contribution in securing the team bronze medal at the 1992 Olympics. The positive feelings of such a significant achievement were increased even more for Carol when the American flag was displayed on the flagpole at the awards ceremony announcing their accomplishment. Carol is from a generation of people who swell with pride whenever they see Old Glory flying. She recognizes that lives were given to ensure our freedom, and she has an appreciation of all that our flag stands for. After the victory gallop, Carol paused one more time to look back at the flag to lock the beautiful memory in her mind.

In speaking about her chosen discipline of dressage, Carol is right up front about the long hours that go into the preparation of dressage horses. Sometimes the repetition of exercises gives you the feeling of rediscovering the wheel over and over again. And yet there are those times when you achieve that moment of perfection, that one moment of time when it all goes together. It is those special times that make up for all the rest. Carol believes in holding on to the good things and savoring the satisfactions that can only emerge with dedication and hard work.

1993 at Wellington is one of those special times that Carol likes to recall. It was the time when her Hanoverian gelding lived up to his name and was letter perfect for three tests. Carol describes the rides as being comparable to driving a really expensive sports car. It was above and beyond in terms of smoothness and energy. Gifted scored straight 70's at this competition.

Another special memory for Carol was when she did a benefit ride for the USET at the

New York Horse Show. A man who had been both a judge and special mentor to her when she began her career in eventing, General Jonathan Burton, was there to represent the judge at the benefit. He was spectacular in his full Army dress uniform. It gave Carol much pleasure to present Gifted to him at the salute and to give the performance as a tribute to him.

Due to injury, 1994 was not a good year for Gifted. Carol has nothing but praise for Marty Simensen, DVM, and for several other vets who have offered their advice and time in working with Gifted. World class horses command the same kind of respect and honor from the medical community as do their athletic human counterparts.

At the 1994 World Championships, even though the USET won the bronze medal, Gifted's performance didn't contribute the highest score as it had done so many times before in recent years. And even though his performance was admirable and his second piaffe letter perfect at the Hague, Carol has had to face the sad fact that her prize horse may be in the transition down from his peak years.

Carol is very proud of Gifted. His accomplishments stand as being exceptional. He has been at Olympic level for six years and has represented the USET in Europe five of those years. If he never does another thing, he will still remain outstanding in his achievements.

Whatever Gifted's future is, there is no doubt that Carol will remain a shining star in the dressage world. One of her pet projects is underwriting talented riders in their late teens and early 20's who do not have the financial ability to pursue their riding talent on their own. This age represents a time when many talented riders fall through the cracks. It is the time of transition between being a junior rider and competing with adults. It is a time when support and encouragement can make all the difference in the world.

Carol continues to work with young dressage horses in a progressive system to help bring them along. She remains hopeful that, once again, she will have that intuitive feeling or see that special brilliance that distinguishes another Olympic potential. When her busy schedule permits, she enjoys going on a cooking frenzy or sailing at the lake with her husband and friends.

Carol Lavell has a sense of humor and an appreciation of life as it comes to her. She has a distinguished record in international competition, and she has always been a fine ambassador for the USET and equestrian sports. The Whitney Stone Cup that she received in 1993 recognized all of these qualities.

MICHAEL POULIN

Mary Phelps

Born June 10, 1945

Michael Poulin has been teaching for many years and has literally touched and changed countless riders' attitudes towards riding. While a significant amount of his time is aimed at helping dressage riders to improve their abilities, his teaching about communication between horse and rider benefits participants in all aspects of horsemanship. Karen Stives, the three-day event medal winner from the 1984 Olympic Games, sought Michael's help for many years before her Olympic experience, and learned to work her horse "on the bit."

Michael's most noteworthy student to date is Carol Lavell, who shared a place with him on the 1992 Olympic dressage team in Barcelona and who had the highest American score, enabling the American team to capture the bronze medal.

Michael Poulin's clinics are aimed at getting riders to understand their horse and to learn how to use the aids (hands, legs and weight) in order to give clear and consistent direction to the horse. His premise is that a willing partnership is built on achieving good communication between the horse and the rider, and this can only happen when the rider seeks to understand the animal. He frequently will ask the rider, "Can you feel him relax? Do you sense that he didn't understand what you wanted before?"

Michael makes a strong point of teaching riders to pat their horses when they feel the horse yielding to the bit and responding well to the aids. "Praise him. He needs to know he's doing it right," is a frequent statement.

Michael Poulin is dignified, patient, and fair in dealing with both horses and riders. He is quiet and firm and has a charming sense of humor and love of life. He grew up on a farm in Maine as one of eleven children without a

father. From the day he was born, work horses were as much as part of his growing up as were hand-me-down clothes and shared responsibility. Family values included a strong work ethic and honesty. The plowing, planting and harvesting at the Poulin farm were accomplished with the help of the horses. There was something about the honesty and forthrightness of the horses, coupled with the teamwork between man and animal, that attracted Michael early in this life. If a horse did not like you, you were the first to know. To win him over you had to learn to understand him before any willing communicating could develop.

When Michael was about eight years old, he started working with the horses on the farm. At around eleven, he began taking riding lessons and to this day he has always found working with horses to be very satisfying. He believes in taking things as they come and making the most out of them. As an Olympic rider he is grateful for the people who recognized his talent and dedication in working with horses, and who were willing to offer him financial and emotional support with no guarantee of return or success.

Barbara Westerlund, Joan Bessey, Linda Pinto, his wife, Sharon, and Harry Jones have been major contributors to Poulin's effort. Harry donated money and set up a foundation to enable Michael to continue learning, competing, and teaching. Harry, in particular, went above and beyond to ensure that Michael's limited funds were supplemented to enable him to develop, teach, and compete to the maximum of his ability. It was Harry Jones who united with Dee Muma in the purchase of Graf George for Michael, so that he could continue to work with him and, hopefully, take him to the Olympics.

Originally purchased at an auction in Germany, the grey Hanoverian gelding was

Aboard Graf
George, at the 1992
Barcelona Games.

Karl Lech

brought to Michael's barn by Meg Hamilton
for him to train. He was a sensitive horse with
a hot temperament that would blow up if a
whip was used on him. Michael was inspired
by Meg's belief that he would be able to do
something very positive with the horse and he
put extra effort into working with the magnificent animal. When Meg put the horse up for
sale, it was Harry Jones and Dee Muma who
made it possible for Michael to continue his
ongoing progress with Graf George.

Michael was understandably touched by
such generosity, and for Harry to have a direct
link with a world-class horse was a dream
come true. Michael believes that, when you
are given this kind of trust, you are motivated
to give your very best in return.

In the training of Graf George, Michael recognized the hot, sensitive nature of this young
gelding. He knew that if the horse were to be
pushed too hard, or placed under pressure to
progress too soon, it could break his spirit. As
a firm believer in working in harmony with

the nature of the horse, his strategy was to dis-
sipate the horse's tension through progressive
exposure, not by adding more pressure.
Michael described Graf George as a beautiful
animal who loves to play; both the clown and
the actor are part of his personality. He was
nine years old when he competed in the 1992
Olympics in Barcelona.

In 1992, Michael was able to appreciate the
accomplishment of achieving Olympic status.
For many years he had believed in himself,
and felt that his abilities were competitive
enough to take him to the top. Although
proud of his riding achievements, his greatest
accomplishment comes from his family and the
valuable time he spends with them. Incentive
or motivation to reach Olympic status comes
from several different individual drives to succeed. For Michael, who is essentially a non-
political, hard-working rider, teacher, and
trainer, his satisfaction comes from the accomplishment of a job well done.

MICHELLE GIBSON

Born February 25, 1969

Mary Phelps

Michelle Gibson's Olympic story is truly one of desire, determination, dedication, love and support. The youngest daughter of Marshall and Marie Gibson was horse crazy since she was placed on her big sister's horse as a toddler. She started taking lessons at 10, when she became a working student. She did some jumping and some cross country, but was drawn to the educating of horses in the classical movements by the time she was in her early teens. She liked working with the horses and seeing them improve.

Her desire to be very good at the sport she loves gave her the drive and ambition to be a working student for 17 years. She gave up many of the comforts, securities and pleasures of her youth to study away from home. She first trained with Michael Poulin for a year and a half; he'd invited her after seeing her ride at a horse show in Georgia. Later, she twice went abroad to study in Germany for a total of six years. Almost all of that time was spent with the respected German trainer, Rudolph Zeilinger. She endured homesickness, adaptation to a new culture, and frostbitten toes working horses during Germany's harsh winters in exchange for dressage lessons. Through that perseverance, she achieved a polished and elegant ride at the 1996 Olympics and posted 1880, the highest score by any dressage rider in U.S. Olympic equestrian history. She was only 27 years old at the time.

When she returned from Germany the first time, she had the skills to go with her love of dressage. She began campaigning for a horse and a sponsor to make her Olympic dream come true, a dream she had had for many years. In her high school yearbook it was written that she would one day "go for the gold." Her father, Marshall, had kidded her that by

the time she made the USET, the Olympics would be in Atlanta.

An article about her in the *Atlanta Journal* caught the eye of Carole Meyer-Webster's husband Russell, who immediately faxed the article to his wife. Carole owned a stallion, Peron, for which she was looking for a new rider. The horse had been trained to Prix St. Georges and Intermediare I by Ken Acebal under Robert Dover's supervision.

Michelle and Carole hit it off immediately, and Michelle loved Peron from the beginning. She said of him, "He's a fantastic horse, an exceptional stallion with a big heart. He's willing, dependable, and very good to work with." Peron is a 12-year-old bay Trakehner stallion, standing 16.2 hands, with three white socks and a star on his forehead. Michelle developed a special bond with Peron, as they worked to achieve the unity of a dressage partnership. She never regarded him as a pet. " He likes to have his space. He's not one that likes to have people come in his stall to play with him or stroke him. He's not one who shows his personality to just anyone. He has to know you and trust you first. He likes Granny Smith apples above the rest because they are more crunchy."

Michelle's parents willingly helped her career as a horse trainer and international competitor. They have been her spokesmen, letting friends and community activists know of their daughter's efforts and successes. Marshall is a contractor and his wife, Marie, is a real-estate broker. Financial constraints have always been a struggle. When Michelle was in Germany," her mother related, "she was so homesick, I couldn't hang up. Phone bills of $600 a month were not uncommon and one time our phone even got disconnected." Nor was it uncommon over the years for Marshall to go straight from his job to pick up Michelle to get her to the barn to work or have a lesson.

At the 1996 Atlanta Games, Michelle and Peron achieved the highest score by any U.S. dressage rider at the Olympics.

Cheryl Bender

Michelle has said, "My family has been a huge encouragement to me. Their moral support saw me through some tough times. My Mom, my Dad and my sisters have always been there for me. And of course Rudolph Zeilinger made a huge impression on my riding career. Without him, I wouldn't be where I am today. And, of course, without Peron I wouldn't be here today either. I am very grateful to everyone who has been there for us along the way."

As the reality of Michelle's going to the Olympics began to materialize, expenses and needs also increased. Friends of the Gibson's who believed in their daughter began to make donations. They recognized a young woman who had drive and talent that money couldn't buy, but who needed financial assistance to help her realize her potential. Between donations and grants, the gaps were bridged.

In the fall of '93, Atlantan Dan Fritz, a non-horse person who is president of a large corporation, sat down with Michelle and her mother to put together a portfolio to represent Michelle's riding goals. At this time, she was intent on taking Peron to a Zeilinger clinic in New Jersey, so she could get her former trainer's thoughts on Peron. With portfolio in hand, Michelle and her mother went door to door seeking financial aid. Barkley Burkes forever endeared himself to them by being the one who gave the first contribution. He was so moved by Michelle's efforts that he went to his company and came back with significant assistance.

In the months following Michelle's matching with Peron, she had been schooling him on her own and recognized that his piaffe, passage, and extensions needed to be confirmed and made more brilliant. When Zeilinger saw them at the clinic, he felt there was excellent potential with Michelle and Peron's partnership, and urged her to return to Germany with Peron for training. Laura and Brad Thatcher held a barbecue at their Applewood Farm near Atlanta, to raise money to pay for the trip. A band played and Michelle rode a musical freestyle as a commentator described to the crowd of people what she was doing and something about the history of dressage.

Michelle also successfully applied for a Carl Heinrich-Asmis Scholarship. This fund was set up to help deserving U.S. riders train in Europe and is administered by the late trainer's widow and a USET Committee.

Before Michelle returned to Germany in May of 1994, she and Peron competed on the Florida circuit, a trip made possible by the fund raising efforts of Ben and Connie Kushner. Although Michelle and Peron competed in no other U.S. shows, their scores on the Florida Circuit earned Peron the U.S. Dressage Federation's Intermediare II Horse of the Year title for 1994.

As the pair began to score well at the European competitions, they gained respect and attention in the dressage community. The U.S. Olympic Committee eventually awarded Michelle close to $12,000 in subsistence grants and paid for insurance. In Germany, she worked to pay for Peron's board and training, and her own board. She rode eight to eleven horses a day and worked six to seven days a week.

While in Germany, Michelle enjoyed several important wins and awards. In Dusseldorf, the judges awarded her the Best Seat Award, the highest compliment anAmerican rider could receive from the German dressage judges. In Munster, she won the Grand Prix Special over Olympians Reiner Klimke and Isabell Werth. In Darmstadt, she placed first in the Grand Prix over thirty-four other competitors. She won the Grand Prix Special in Bad Honnef. In Dortmund, she won the Best Foreign Rider Award. Peron held up his end in this remarkable partnership by being named Trakehner

Stallion of 1995 by the German and American Trakehner Associations.

Michelle said she will always remember and be grateful for her time in Germany with the top riders and their companionship. The CHIO at Aachen in June of 1995 was one of the most memorable events for her. At the end of the week, when the nations say goodbye, the audience waves white handkerchiefs. With over 50,000 people in the audience, it was definitely one of those "never- to-be- forgotten moments."

When it was time for Michelle and Peron to come home for the GMC/USET Festival of Champions in Gladstone, New Jersey, the final qualifying event for Olympic participation, the Thatchers held another barbecue, and once again raised enough money to make it happen. The Klatte Corporation of Germany and the Dutta Corporation, horse transportation companies, offered to bring Peron back to the United States, and to pick up the plane fare for Michelle, Rudolph Zeilinger, and Peron's groom. In New Jersey, driving competitor Sharon Chesson opened her home to Michelle, and Jennifer Baumert, a young dressage rider, loaned her car for Michelle's use. Michelle won first place at the Festival of Champions in Gladstone, and became the dressage team's anchor, as well as its best hope for an individual medal.

Col. Hiram Tuttle is the only American to have ever won an individual medal in dressage; in 1932, he won the individual bronze, as well as the team bronze. Michelle had her heart set on claiming an individual medal, and it seemed that for the first time in many years, an American had the chance to end the drought.

And, indeed, under the old system, Michelle would have secured the individual bronze medal on the strength of her scores after the second round, the Grand Prix Special. However, at the 1996 Games, the rules of the competition for the individual dressage medal were changed. In an effort to increase public interest, an additional test called the Grand Prix Freestyle was added, and the top 25 riders from the Grand Prix Special were allowed to ride for the individual medal honors. Also called a "kur," the freestyle is a ride choreo-

153

graphed to music.

Michelle had won in Munich earlier in the summer with the same routine. She wanted to do it again, for herself, for all the people that had helped her, and for her nation. Unfortunately, though, Peron resisted momentarily during a piaffe. Michelle remained composed and had him back on the bit in the next instant, bringing Peron to a strong finish. But, sadly for her and the American crowd rooting for her, that resistance of just a few seconds dropped her from third to fifth place. Such is this level of competition! But Michelle realized that she was new in the Olympic ring compared to the big-named, experienced riders. She believed then and believes now in focusing on doing her best and learning from each competition; that's what she did in Atlanta.

And, her outstanding performance in the Grand Prix helped the U.S. earn the bronze medal in team dressage.

On the last day of the 1996 Olympics, Michelle received the prestigious German Golden Rider Award. This award goes to riders who win 10 Grand Prix events during the season. Michelle is the first American recipient of this award which has, up until this time, never been presented outside of Germany.

After the Olympics, Michelle returned to Germany for more training and competition, while Peron began his career as a breeding stallion in the U.S. Although this Olympic partnership may be over, one thing is for certain: Michelle Gibson has a important role to play in the future successes of U.S. dressage.

STEFFAN PETERS

Born September 18, 1964

Cheryl Bender

Steffan Peters had mixed emotions immediately after the 1996 Olympics, great happiness tinged with a bit of sadness as well. His beautiful chestnut gelding had produced a personal best score in his dressage test and helped push the United States ahead of France to claim the team bronze medal. But, at 18, it was time for the big Dutch Warmblood to retire. Steffan and Udon had been partners for 15 years. "Udon had been going so incredibly well. To retire him when he's the best he's ever been is hard. The decision was, however, one that all of us who love him and are invested in him made unanimously. We wanted him retired while he was at the top."

Steffan was born and grew up in Germany, the center of dressage excellence. His love of horses began at an early age and was encour-

aged by his parents' interest and support. He and his sister got started with ponies when they went to their parent's weekend house near the Dutch border. Steffan was around seven years old at the time. A few years later, their parents bought them two ponies that were quite talented in dressage. They competed with the ponies through the Young Riders Club, which took them to other European countries to compete. After the Young Riders program, Steffan worked for six years in Johann Hinneman's barn. He completed his mandatory Army duty in late 1986.

The family acquired Udon when he was a three-year-old. Steffan and his sister broke Udon; both landed on the ground more than once! After Udon was broken, however, he was a wonderful horse. The whole family owned him until 1991. Then, Steffan met Lila Kommerstad through a clinic that he taught in Los Angeles. She shared her dream with him

Steffan Peters aboard
his marvelous cam-
paigner Udon.
Tish Quirk

that she would like to own a grand prix dressage horse and a grand prix jumper. She
thought she would have to go to Europe to
acquire them. Steffan said, "You don't have to
go to Europe for the dressage horse; I've got
one in my barn." The purchase was made, and
the arrangement that Steffan would continue
to be his rider was a part of the agreement.

In 1992 Steffan had a chance to try out for
the U.S. dressage team, but was prevented
from competing because his American citizen-
ship was still pending. The paperwork was
completed two weeks after the Games ended.
He took the setback with grace, and related to
me that without the European experience he
had between then and now, he might not have
been as prepared as he was for Atlanta.

In 1992 he had a series of victories on both
the east and west coasts of the U. S. with
Udon, but an injury to Udon's front tendon
prevented them from qualifying for the World
Championships that year. In 1993 Steffan and
Udon finished second at the Miller/USET
Grand Prix Championship, an event he then
won in 1995. In the summer of 1995, Steffan
was selected by the USET to ride Animation at
the U. S. Olympic Festival. In Los Angeles at
the Mid-Winter CDI-W in February, he won
the Grand Prix Freestyle on Udon with a score
of 70.958, and was second on Akeena and third
on Udon in the Grand Prix.

The Olympics asks a tremendous amount

of a horse, but Steffan's old campaigner saved
his best till last. Steffan described the chestnut
gelding with the white blaze down his face,
"Udon would definitely do it for you all the
way. We've had many tests where it really
counted. I always felt like he was saying to
me, 'OK, you tell me how much you want and
I'll try to give it to you.'" Jessica Ransehousen
described Udon, "Although the horse is not
brilliant, he's smooth and fluid. Steffan and he
create the kind of impression that really counts
with the judges." Their 1996 Olympic performance confirmed Jessica's insightful observation.

Steffan feels he is one of the really fortunate people who have very supportive sponsors. He credited several people as important
members of his support network: his wife,
Janet, his parents and sister, his assistant,
Allison Rogers and his sponsors, Lila and Bob
Kommerstad. He added that without the
training advice of Johann Hinneman, Dietrich
von Hopffgarten, and clinics with Robert
Dover, he would not have attained the success
he has at this point in his life. He said,
"Without all of these people, all of this never
would have happened."

This native of Germany who now wears
the colors of the U.S.A. has been an active part
of our international competition efforts since
1992. Steffan was and is a welcome addition to
"our team."

GUENTER SEIDEL

Born September 23, 1960

Cheryl Bender

Guenter Seidel and his Olympic horse Graf George were referred to as "one of the season's most important mergers," when this partnership began competing to qualify for Atlanta.

Graf George was in Robert Dover's barn when he was offered for sale. With Michael Poulin in the saddle, Graf George helped win the team bronze medal at the 1992 Olympics in Barcelona. Robert called Dick and Jane Brown to suggest that Guenter and the horse would make a good partnership. When the Browns heard that a rider from the Netherlands was going to try him, they put Guenter on a plane the next morning. While the Browns did not have a burning desire to own Graf George, they felt very strongly about keeping a horse of his caliber in the United States. After they saw the video of Guenter's ride on Graf George, a deal was made.

Guenter grew up in Fischen, Germany, south of Munich in the German Alps. He was attracted to horses, and by age ten he had started to ride. When he was 14, an uncle who was associated with a dressage barn took Guenter along a couple of times.

His first trainer was a woman named Herta Beck. While she was not one of the well-known "name" trainers in Germany, she was a respected teacher who provided him with a solid classical background and taught him the German system of dressage.

Guenter took lessons at the same barn until age 18, when he fulfilled his country's requirement to serve in the Army. During that time, his riding was limited to weekends. After the Army, Guenter took a job preparing and showing horses at a large breeding farm, staying there for a couple of years. It was hard for him, though, to bring up the young horses and then watch them be sold. And, the job did not

allow him to really ride and pursue his interest in dressage. The combination of those two facts probably accounted for his reaching a point of feeling "burned out and needing a break."

So, he sold his car and took off for Munich, where he managed a disco and waited tables. The money was good, and after a few months he bought a ticket to Los Angeles for a vacation. His plan was to stay there as long as his money lasted, come back home, get reorganized and look for another job.

At this time he spoke hardly any English and he had no contacts whatsoever in the U.S. But on the flight to Los Angeles, he met some people with whom he was able to communicate about himself, his love of horses, and his vacation plans. From that point on, he never stayed in any hotels; he was put in touch with "friends of friends of friends." He traveled around for a while, but then the inevitable happened: he ran out of money. By this time he was in love with the balmy year-round weather. He loved the beach and he loved the people. He started looking for work; he was even willing to muck stables or whatever it took because he wanted to stay so badly. But before he could set down roots, he returned to Germany to get needed papers and put his life in order before returning to California on a more permanent basis. Coming to the U.S. was much easier this time than was that first visit because he already had friends and contacts here. Shortly after arriving in California the second time, he found work at a hunter jumper barn.

He began pursuing his education in dressage, this time with "I" judge, Dietrich von Hopffgarten. When von Hopffgarten asked him who he had studied with in Germany, it was a surprise to learn that von Hopffgarten had worked at the same stables as Herta Beck.

For the past six years, Robert Dover has

been his friend and mentor, and has helped Guenter shape his training and showing strategy. Guenter first rode for the USET at the 1995 Pan American Games in Buenos Aires, Argentina where he helped win the team's silver medal. At the Los Angeles Mid-Winter CDI-W, Guenter and Graf George showed the success of this merger with wins in Grand Prix (67.267) and the Grand Prix Special (70.233), as well as posting the highest score in the Grand Prix Freestyle (73.917). Guenter thoroughly enjoys the freestyle. While fun to ride, he especially likes it for the audience, and believes that choreographing the horse's classical movements to music of the rider's choosing will draw more public attention to dressage. Perhaps someday it will even receive television coverage, as it does in Germany and, indeed, much of Europe.

The 1996 Games at Atlanta were Guenter's first Olympic experience and only his second international competition. His personal goal was that he and Graf George place in the top ten horses overall —- no mean feat considering the level of competition. They did just that, after completing the three tests: the Grand Prix, which decided the team medal standings, the Grand Prix Special, in which the top 25 riders from the Grand Prix rode, and then the Grand Prix Freestyle, which decided the individual medal winners from the 13 riders who qualified to compete in this last test. The 6' 2" man on the 17 hand horse presented a beautiful, fluid ride and were strong contributors in the winning of the team's bronze medal. In addition, Guenter placed 7th in the Freestyle, the highest ranking American.

Guenter said of his Olympic partner, "Graf George is willing to work all the time. He can get explosive and full of himself, and that can be a drawback.

Graf George and Guenter Seidel helped bring home the team bronze medal and were 7th in the individual standings, the highest ranking U.S. rider at the '96 Games.

Cheryl Bender

But he has so much talent for the upper level movements —- his body can do just about everything. He's confirmed in everything, but his strongest points are piaffe, passage, and extensions."

Guenter's integrity and love of horses is genuine. He campaigned three horses for the 1996 Olympics, Numir, Tanzen and Graf George. When Numir's legs ulcerated after a strangles shot, Guenter and the horse's owner, Jennifer Lee, led the big horse to the beach every day for hours so that the soothing surf could help with the healing. While Guenter loves horses, they aren't the only thing he loves. He has always tried to have a break in his workday so he could go to the beach to go "boogie-boarding" (you lie down, not stand, on this small, light surf board and catch the waves). He works out and attends practices for his masters' competitive swim team. He is the resident dressage trainer at the Rancho Riding Club and runs his other part of the training business out of nearby Rockridge Farm. He has nine to twelve horses in training and teaches a small group of students up to Grand Prix.

Guenter Seidel's career as an international competitor in dressage has just begun, but his fans and supporters look forward to an exciting future for him. And our U.S. dressage community has had a most welcome addition!

DAVID O'CONNOR

Brant Gamma

Born January 19, 1962

It was at the 1990 Rolex/Kentucky International Three-Day Event that I first had the privilege of watching this handsome man and his wonderful horse Wilton Fair negotiate the challenging course in terrible weather conditions and win the event. This victory qualified David to ride in the 1990 World Equestrian Games in Stockholm where I saw him again. He is a natural and talented rider. One can't help but notice his focus and horsemanship.

Since then, David has gone on to compete with the 1994 World Equestrian Team. He finished second to Bruce Davidson in the 1995 FEI North American Three-Day Event Rider rankings. 1996 was a stellar year for him: he placed 3rd at Badminton, and then went on to be a major contributor, riding Giltedge, to the U.S.'s silver medal win at his first Olympics. In the individual three-day competition, David placed fifth despite his horse, Custom Made, throwing a shoe on the cross country course (which may have also cost David a medal).

With the win of the team silver medal, the 1996 Three-Day Event Team broke a 12-year drought in eventing medals for the U.S. At these Games, the USET took home medals in all three disciplines: eventing, dressage and show jumping. The last time the U.S. won medals in all three competitions was in 1932, when only military officers competed in equestrian events. On the first day of the 1996 Games, in the dressage test, David and Giltedge had one of the best dressage scores they had ever achieved, 40.80. They rode a clear round on cross-country with only a time penalty and, in the show jumping ring on the final day, brought the crowd to their feet when he followed the faultless round of his wife Karen with one of his own.

David described the 10-year-old Irish Thoroughbred, Giltedge, owned by Jacqueline Mars, as being very much a technician in every thing he does. "He's reserved and careful. He's not a very social horse and only relates to two or three people. He is an accurate horse in everything he does." David feels Giltedge is sometimes underrated because he's so quietly consistent.

David described his horse for the individual Three-Day competition, the Irish-bred Thoroughbred Custom Made owned by Joseph Zada, as being "a bit of a paradox. He's quite reserved and independent to work around. He's gentle and sweet, but not a social horse either, with horses or people. Once you get on him, put him in front of a crowd and have him jump, he changes into this outgoing, exuberant horse with tons of flair." He concluded by saying, "Both of these horses have such exceptional talent, and the diversity required to ride them is fun."

David started riding at eight years old. His mother, equestrian author Sally O'Connor, loved horses and gave David and his brother Brian (a well-known announcer at equestrian events), lessons at the Potomac Horse Center in Maryland where she was a teacher. He started in Pony Club when he was ten years old and progressed from there. His first pony was 12.2 hands and was named Bramble.

A turning point came for him when he went to Radnor in 1979 and did well in his competition. He knew then he wanted "a piece of three-day eventing," but he didn't have the money. As he was starting college to study veterinary medicine, he was invited to train at the USET headquarters. He was asked to continue as a resident rider and stayed there for four years. His pursuit of a career with horses took off.

In 1993, the USET made a significant rebuilding move in eventing by hiring two-time British Olympian and four-time

David and Giltedge help clinch an eventing team silver medal at the '96 Olympics.
Brant Gamma

things through. That's what I like best about him."

David and his wife Karen are the second husband and wife team to ride for the USET on an Olympic team; the first was Frank and Mary Chapot at the 1968 Olympics in Mexico. David and Karen, however, are the first husband and wife team to win an Olympic medal. David says, "It's great when you are married and you both do something that you love for a living."

David manages a farm in The Plains, Virginia, where his job description includes everything from riding and training the horses to mowing the fields and being sure the cattle are where they are supposed to be. He and Karen have a number of young horses in training. He serves as president of the USET Active Riders Committee, and is also chairman of the AHSA Combined Training Events Committee. David believes it is important to be active in improving communication between riders and governing bodies, and in helping the sport grow. He is a committed and articulate spokesman for the sport.

As the sport does grow, there is no doubt that one of the individuals who will continue to give horsemanship a good name is David O'Connor.

Badminton winner, Mark Phillips, as U.S. chef d' equipe. David said, "Mark has been a great influence on all of us. He thinks like a competitor, and knows what's going on in a competitor's mind. Not only is he a very, very good technical horseman, but he's also a real sports psychologist. He is able to come at things from different angles with different people in order for them to feel confident and do their best. He's not one of these people that says, 'You have to do it my way'; we talk

Karen Lende. It was the year she married David. It was also the year that she placed first and third in the 1993 Punchestown CCI in Ireland, and the U.S. Olympic Committee named her the 1993 "Female Equestrian Athlete of the Year." 1993 was also the year she was ranked 3rd in the FEI world rankings, and was the top woman to finish since the first two places were held by men.

At the 1994 World Championships, Karen finished 8th. In 1995 she placed 3rd at the Badminton CCI, a feat her husband accomplished in 1996. 1995 was also the year she tied for fifth place with riders from Great Britain, Australia and New Zealand in the European Open Three-Day Event Championship.

The 1996 Olympic medal ceremony was very special for the O'Connors, because they became the first husband and wife team in U.S. equestrian history to win a medal. Afterwards, Karen said something both she and David feel very strongly about: "We are the lucky ones who get to stand up on the podium to receive the medal, but second to the horses, which are by far the most important part of the program, it's essential to have a strong supportive group behind you. We have such a group who have so much heart and want to be a part of our 'O'Connor Event Team.' Especially with two of us involved, we have so many people invested in getting it all done. That includes everyone from the owners, to the grooms, to the management people, to the bookkeepers, to the blacksmiths, vets, parents and family. They are with us in our victories and they are with us through the worst of times. It's that kind of dedication to the 'O'Connor Event Team' that has enabled us to be as successful as we are and that will carry us into the future.

Karen and Biko, on course at the 1996 Atlanta Games and making history as part of the first husband and wife team to win a medal (silver).

Brant Gamma

JILL HENNEBERG

Born September 22, 1974

Brant Gamma

To make it to the Olympic level takes outstanding horsemanship. To qualify at only 21 is a more remarkable achievement, and that is exactly what Jill Henneberg did! Although none of Jill's family were horse people, she was drawn to horses at an early age. By the time she was nine years old, she had started once-a-week lessons. She rode hunters, but by age eleven realized she preferred the excitement of eventing.

Kathy Adams Makin was her first eventing instructor, and, once again, her lessons were of the "once-a-week" sort. Two years passed on this program, and then discussions about buying a horse took on a more serious tone; they often bordered on begging. Jill began looking for a novice horse with some experience in eventing.

One day when Jill was in the local tack shop, she saw a mare's picture on the bulletin board with a note: "For Sale —- $2,000." She called the owner, who was going through a difficult divorce and needed the money to pay for overdue boarding bills.

The horse happened to be in the same barn where Jill had first taken riding lessons. The mare had not been ridden for six months, and the owner was not about to get on to show the horse. The comments that followed were also less than reassuring to her parents, who were along. Someone mentioned that the horse had tried to kick the farrier and would not hold still for the vet. Jill was told the horse would be hard to catch out in the field. But when she went out with saddle and bridle in hand, the three-year-old gray mare came right up to her. Her name was Nirvana II.

Jill talked a more experienced rider at the barn into riding Nirvana II first. The horse did a few crow hops and then settled down. Jill rode the mare for the first time later that night. In retrospect, she now understands that the comments made earlier were about the horse's young age and lack of being handled and ridden, rather than temperament or ability. Before Jill and her parents left that night, the owner made the offer that if they could have the horse out of the barn by the end of the month, she would sell the young mare for $600.

Jill took Kathy, her eventing instructor, out to see the horse. When Jill asked Kathy whether she should buy the horse, Kathy replied, "Well, I wouldn't pay a million dollars for her." Jill said, "How about $600?" Kathy's immediate response was, "Sold!" The purchase of the former race horse and granddaughter of the famous Native Dancer was made

Jill could not have even imagined at the time that her patient work with the horse over the next eight years would end up qualifying her to be on the USET Three-Day Event Team to go to the 1996 Olympics in Atlanta. As their partnership progressed, however, that possibility became not only a dream, it became a reality.

Sometimes there is a unique meshing of human and horse personalities; Jill and Nirvana II have this meshing. Perhaps this partnership began that first night when the mare came right up to Jill in the field. The fast, careful and brave little mare was a good combination for this gutsy young rider. They made a name for themselves as they frequently had the fastest time without a fault on cross-country in qualifying events for the 1996 Olympics. Nirvana II was one that did not like to touch show jumping rails. As is often the case, dressage is the part of the test that had given this twosome the most difficulty. Their dressage test at the 1996 Olympics went well; they scored a 57.0, a personal best for them. It was cross-country on the second day that gave them their problems. The luck of the draw was not with them: they were 29th of 30 riders on Richard Haller's test that had serious challenges for each partnership to overcome.

It was the 13th obstacle on the course that was their undoing. It was a jump with two options. Jill was confident that she could go right down the middle of the covered bridge. Her coach and teammates urged her to take an alternate approach over a fence to the right of the bridge. The second choice would require a little more time, but was less risky.

Her's was the same intuition and self-confidence that often makes a winner. But as Jill said, "Sometimes it works and sometimes it doesn't."

They rode boldly into the obstacle, but Nirvana II misjudged the landing point, going head first into the jump and unseating Jill. They retired from the course but, fortunately, neither was too badly hurt.

There's no doubt that this particular fence was tricky, with shadows creating part of the difficulties. Karen O'Connor on Biko had already encountered a refusal. Seasoned veterans have that same self-confidence as Jill, but they have one thing that a 22-year-old rookie does not have yet, and that is experience, which only time can give. And although their elimination was a disappointment, Jill and Nirvana II were part of the silver-medal-winning team that ended the twelve-year run of "no medals" for U.S. eventing in the Olympics. To be a part of this "comeback" in eventing was an invaluable experience for Jill.

When I asked Jill to pick out two or three people who have helped her the most or that she particularly admired or was inspired by, she mentioned her parents first and foremost. She said, "They have always been there for me, both financially and emotionally." She has deep respect for Michael Godfrey, her eventing coach for several years now and the person who helped her become an advanced event rider. His support with dressage and his presence at the 1996 Olympics were very important to her. Brendan Furlong, the USET vet was the third person she mentioned with respect and gratitude. He helped bring Nirvana II back from a fractured splint bone injury in 1994 and has always been supportive and concerned about her mare's well being.

After the Atlanta Games, Jill started a job as a resident trainer at the Hillsborough Equestrian Center in Flemington, New Jersey. Jill has always looked ahead with confidence and conviction, and her story as an Olympic level competitor is likely only in the opening chapters.

Jill Henneberg and Nirvana II in their dressage test at Atlanta. Jill was one of the youngest riders ever to qualify for the Olympics.

Brant Gamma

Brant Gamma

KERRY MILLIKIN

Born December 10, 1961

Eventing in the 1996 Atlanta Olympics experienced a major change in how the individual and team medals were determined. For the first time since the "military" began in the 1912 Stockholm Games, different horse and rider combinations were required for both the individual and team categories. Previously, the final scores of each rider contributed to both categories, but the International Olympic Committee mandated that a separate competition be held for the respective categories. The idea was that this would prevent two medals being awarded for one effort. Whatever one's view might be of the decision, it's clear that it opened up the competition for more riders and that Kerry Millikin made wonderful use of the opportunity.

Kerry's participation in the 1996 Atlanta Olympics began with a bit of luck. Only one month before the Games began, she was added to the Three-Day Team as an alternate. Kerry's opportunity came when another country's rider pulled out and an extra spot became available, enabling Kerry to compete in the individual competition. She and her nine-year old Thoroughbred gelding Out and About were ready!

Their solid dressage score and cross country ride with only time faults brought them into the third day's stadium jumping tied for third place with Jean Teulere from France. When she finished to the roar of approval from the "home team" crowd, she had held on to the bronze medal. The dry spell in claiming an individual medal in eventing since 1984 had been broken, once again by a woman (Karen Stives won the individual silver medal in 1984).

Kerry was always passionate about horses. As a child of seven or eight years old, she would walk down to a local horse farm, sit on the fence and just wait to touch the horses as they came up to visit. She loved looking at their pictures in the horse magazines her mother subscribed to. So it wasn't any real

The future event rider in 1973, with braids flying!

Stacy Holmes

surprise to anyone the day she ran home to tell her mother a pony had been put up for sale at the farm for $150. "It's with foal and its name is Kismet," she said. What horse-loving mother could say no to that information?

In 1974, at 13, Kerry took part in her first event and fell in love with the running and jumping; as she says, she always liked best that "go-fast stuff." 1975 was a turning point for her when she went with a friend to the Ledyard International Three-Day Event in South Hamilton: she thought it was the most exciting thing she had ever seen. "It was nerve-racking, awesome and a little scary, but it was a challenge I knew I wanted to take."

Out and About became her horse when he was three years old. He had one or two unsuccessful starts at the track and had been turned out. She first saw him out in the field, and remembers thinking he was just a scrawny little horse. But while his physical appearance at that time wasn't anything to write home about, when she put tack on him and put him on the lungeline, the way he moved got her attention right away. He moved well in all three gaits, and absolutely floated in his canter. Plus, he had a great attitude. Kerry recognized his potential and purchased him immediately. The scrawny little horse grew up into a beautiful 16.2 hand horse.

It was apparent early on that the horse liked being "out and about," which is how he got his name. Kerry said of Out and About, "He's a very complicated personality. He is an intense horse, and also very aggressive. But he also has a sweet side to him where he'll oftentimes just put his head up against you. He used to worry about a lot of things, but I worked to channel that energy into helping him feel really confident about himself. Sometimes he gets too aggressive and too confident, and that's when we have a clash of wills. When he was younger, I would refer to our rides as the 'clash of the Titans.' One of the main things about him is that he is a good worker and that's why I persevered with him." At the 1996 Olympics, that perseverance certainly paid off.

Kerry made her entry into international eventing in 1987, when she became the first and only rider to win the USET's Spring and Fall Championships on the same horse, The Pirate, in the same year. She accomplished this double victory by winning the Advanced Division of the Rolex/Kentucky International Three-Day Event in May and the Rolex/Chesterland Three-Day Event in September.

Kerry ended the twelve-year drought of individual medals in eventing with her bronze medal win in Atlanta.

Brant Gamma

To prepare for the 1996 Olympics, Kerry had to sell her other horse and take a long leave from her profession as a registered nurse. In 1995, she was the recipient of the Jackie Vogel grant, which enabled her to train in Europe. She is grateful and appreciative for the investment the USET has made in riders through training sessions and grants. As one who has benefited from this support, she is pleased that she was able to help make it pay off. Kerry felt the European exposure was especially helpful. "When you get to learn from and compete with the 'best of the best,' you gain confidence in handling pressure and foreign situations," she related.

Three people stood out as role models in the eventing world forKerry: J. Michael Plumb, Bruce Davidson and Lucinda Green. Kerry relates to Lucinda the most, probably because she is a woman: "Lucinda has won the Badminton Three-Day Event. She has a poise and a humility about her that makes her a very likeable and respected horsewoman. She can ride several different types of horses, and she shows a lot of consideration for her animals."

Although balancing two careers is certainly not easy, Kerry likes being both a horsewoman and a nurse. After the 1996 Games, she returned to work as a respiratory neuro-surgical nurse at St. Luke's Hospital in Medford, Massachusetts —- but, of course, all future plans include eventing!

Cheryl Bender

PETER LEONE

Born August 1, 1960

August 1st is Peter Leone's birthday. It was also the day of the team competition in Show Jumping for the 1996 Olympics. "Traditionally," Peter related, "I haven't done that well on my birthday. So, the way I looked at it, I had a job to do first and then I could celebrate my birthday." It wasn't until the U.S. team was on the podium to receive the silver medal that his teammates wished him "Happy Birthday!" in one unanimous voice. Winning a silver medal at the Olympics on your 36th birthday is probably right up there with the all-time best birthday gifts.

Peter was 5 years old when his parents introduced his two brothers, Mark and Armand, and him to ponies. All three of the brothers took to riding then and there. Three years later, when his parents bought a farm in Oakland, New Jersey, they bought ponies for the boys. Little did anyone know at that time that the three good-looking brothers would grow up to ride on the circuit as "Team Leone." All members of "Team Leone" were at the '96 Olympics but, as Peter put it, "Today, I just happened to be the lucky one was who was riding." The support they give one another when they are in competition is invaluable to Peter.

Peter has competed successfully on the Grand Prix circuit since the late '70's. He has represented the United States in international competition many times, including the 1982 World Championships in Dublin, Ireland, when he helped the U. S. finish fourth. As Peter grew up, there were four people that were particularly inspirational to him: Rodney Jenkins, Bernie Traurig, George Morris and

Peter Leone and Legato. Peter's birthday fell on the same day as the team show jumping competition at the Atlanta Games. Winning the team silver medal has to be up there with the all-time best birthday presents!

Cheryl Bender

Eddie Mackin." To this day I still wear green socks when I compete in honor of Eddie Mackin from Ireland." Peter quickly added that he is not superstitious, but neither does he think that it can hurt to wear the green socks.

For Peter, watching the '76 Olympic Games in Montreal had a profound effect. Nor would he ever forget going to the '78 World Championships and staying at Qualinhoff with the other riders. Michael Matz was there riding Jet Run from Erdenheim Farms. At the celebration in the Qualinhoff bar after the World Championships, the new World Champion Grover Gerd Wolfgang moved around the crowd inviting them all to share a drink from the Championship cup filled with champagne. At 18, this heady atmosphere and experience had a lasting effect on Peter. Having been "included" made him want to be a part of that atmosphere of competitive camaraderie even more.

Prior to making the switch to a career with

horses, Peter went to Drew University, graduating with a major in economics and a minor in psychology. He then worked five years as a financial consultant for Merrill Lynch. Choosing to go to a smaller company, Liberty Travel, where he felt he could make more of a difference, he progressed through the ranks to Vice President of Sales, covering 80 offices in 30 states.

In the travel business he met only a few successful people who were able to say, "I love what I do for work." Applying that statement to his own life, he knew he liked what he did and he knew he was good at it — he just didn't *love* it. Working and competing with horses was what he loved This awareness and honesty led him to leave the business world and do what he loved most as his chosen career. He now owns his own farm in Greenwich, Connecticut, where he continues to develop his career as a horseman in addition to coaching, riding and developing horses for sale. And, as Peter leaned down to have the silver medal placed around his neck in Atlanta in 1996, he felt the correctness of his choice had been confirmed: he was indeed doing what he was meant to do with his life.

Coming to the 1996 Olympics certainly hadn't happened without incredible perseverance and determination on his part, however. At the Garden State Horse Show on May 3rd, just a little less than three months from the Atlanta Games, his collarbone was shattered when the preliminary horse he was riding had a freaky accident at a jump, fell and slammed Peter into the ground. He had already had orthopedic surgery on his hand in February; now he underwent more with the surgical repair of his right collarbone. Five screws were inserted and Peter had to miss the third

168

Olympic qualifier because of the surgery.

Ten days later he rode Crown Royal Legato in the next Olympic qualifier.

After he walked the course, Peter drove to the nearest hospital, met with the anesthesiologist, got anesthetized, drove back, got there 10 minutes before his round and climbed on his horse to warm up. His Olympic hopes were kept alive with just one rail down. He then refractured his collar bone at the fourth qualifier on May 19, but continued competing with the help of a local anesthetic (within the parameters allowed by the Olympic Committee, you are allowed a local anesthetic injection at a fracture site). By the time of the second round, however, the effect of the medication had worn off and he was barely able to salvage a 12 fault round.

By the time Peter reached the fifth qualifier, he had already used the two discards allowed under the rules, and he knew he wasn't going to make the team if things continued to go in the same direction. But, with true Olympic grit and determination, Peter and Legato went on to ride four rounds with no faults and only one round with more than four faults in the selection trials.

On the day of the team show jumping competition at the Olympics, Peter competed without an anesthetic for the first time in months, although there was an anesthesiologist on hand as a backup if needed. Peter, along with Leslie Burr Howard, moved into high gear during the second round, both managing no-fault rides of the challenging course to clinch the silver medal for the U.S.

Legato, the beautiful bay French/German cross gelding Peter rode to victory on Linda Allen's course in the Olympics, is one of the most special horses he has ever ridden according to Peter. "Legato is such a powerful jumper, but also very clever and careful, in addition to being light on his feet for his 17 hand size. He has the spark and character that is so important to consistent performance. When I rode him as a 4-year-old, he just had that special look about him —- it was the look of a winner. He has been an outstanding horse from day one."

With the conviction he made the right choice when it came to his life's work, and the perseverance, dedication and courage he brings to the sport of show jumping, it is certain that Peter Leone will add more exciting chapters to his equestrian resume.

Cheryl Bender

MICHAEL MATZ

Born January 23, 1951

Michael Matz carried the American flag in the closing ceremonies of the 1996 Olympic Games in Atlanta, the first time in Olympic history that an equestrian athlete had been chosen to represent our nation in this way.

An honorable man and highly respected horseman, Michael carried the flag with pride, humility and awe. Over the years, Michael developed some of the top Grand Prix jumpers in the U.S. He rapidly became one of the country's most successful grand prix show jumping competitors. He tops the American Grand Prix Association's all-time standings with close to $1 million in career winnings since he entered the sport in 1972.

Michael's ability to maintain a cool head under fierce pressure has been apparent both in the show jumping arena at international competitions and also in his personal life. One harrowing episode for him was the emergency crash landing of DC-10 Flight 232 in Sioux City, Iowa in 1989, in which 112 people lost their lives. Michael was a passenger on the ill-fated plane, and in the mayhem that followed the crash, led two small children out of the wreckage to safety, despite fire and heavy smoke. This true hero was awarded ABC-TV's "Man of the Week" award for his quick action after the crash.

The story of how he became a horseman began when he was 15 years old. He had a job cutting grass for a friend of his father's every weekend. The friend bought two horses, one for himself and one for his wife. When his wife didn't want to go riding, he would invite Michael to go. Michael remembers the very first time: when asked if he knew how to ride, he replied confidently, "Oh, sure." He really just wanted to keep his lawn mowing job, so he was quite relieved when he found out it

was an older, quiet horse.

As Michael tells the story, "One thing led to another and the rides became more expected and looked forward to. Then his Dad's friend bought a younger horse. Michael was asked to ride it, even when his father's friend was unable to join them. He and the young horse would go on trail rides, and a horseman was born. Eventually, this same man got Michael started in the Pony Club, and three years later, at 18, he began to compete.

After graduating from high school, he found a job grooming horses at a farm, and learned the rudiments of horsemanship from Bernie Traurig. But he wanted to have more opportunities to ride, so he moved on to a job with Vince Dugan in Westchester at a sales stable. Here Michael rode all different types of horses, and he loved it. Michael then took a job riding for J. Basil Ward in Ohio. Working at Ward's Hound's Hill Farm offered him his first opportunity to ride some really top horses.

Throughout his career, Michael Matz has gained respect as an international competitor and a consummate horseman. He has won eight medals in the Pan American Games, including five gold. He earned the USET Show Jumping Championship a record six times. He claimed the championship at the 1981 Volvo World Cup on the American Grand Prix Association Horse of the Year, Jet Run. He is a veteran of three World Championships, winning team and individual bronze medals in 1978 with Jet Run, and the team gold medal in 1986 aboard Chef. He has been the American Grand Prix Association Rider of the Year twice.

An Olympic medal had eluded him, though, both in the 1976 Montreal and 1992 Barcelona Games when he rode for the USET. But when he rode in his third Olympics in Atlanta 1996, he gave credence to the old saying, "the third time is the lucky one" when the

170

Michael and Rhum
IV at the '96 games.
Maximum effort
helped bring home
the
team silver medal!

Cheryl Bender

Americans claimed the silver team medal. Although Michael had three rails down in the first round which put him out of the final round, his presence and encouragement as team captain offered strong moral support to his fellow team members.

His Olympic mount Rhum IV, a 13-year-old bay Selle Francais gelding, was sent to Michael eight years ago for training by another rider who eventually ended up selling him to Mr. and Mrs. F. Eugene Dixon. Michael said of his Olympic partner, "To look at him, you might think he was just a 'plain little bay horse,' but when he gets in that ring, he gives me everything he's got. Nobody could ask for more than that. It's something you can't pick out in a horse. That quality comes from within the animal itself. Rhum IV happens to have it."

Michael and his wife D.D. run Vintage

Farm in Collegeville, Pennsylvania. They operate a small business and have all kinds of horses. D.D. came from a family that has bred and campaigned racehorses for decades, and she and Michael share an interest in racing. It is possible that this may be a future direction for the Matz's.

He and D.D. have served on the USET Board and look at it as both a responsibility and an opportunity to have input and serve as problem solvers for current issues in the horse world. They both bring a strong sense of what is right and fair to their duties on the Board.

It was a high honor to carry the American flag in the closing ceremonies of the 1996 Olympics. In this age when heroes are conspicuously absent, Michael Matz truly deserved the honor.

MEDALS WON BY U.S. RIDERS IN THE OLYMPICS

Medals Won By U.S. Military Riders

1912 Olympics
Stockholm, Sweden
Three-Day Event Team Bronze Medal:
 Lt. Benjamin Lear on Poppy
 Lt. John Carter Montgomery on Deceive
 Capt. Guy V. Henry, Jr. on Chiswell
 Lt. Ephraim Foster Graham on Connie

1924 Olympic Games
Paris, France
Individual Three-Day Event Bronze Medal:
 Maj. Sloan Doak on Pathfinder

1932 Olympic Games
Los Angeles, California
Three-Day Event Individual Silver Medal:
 Lt. Earl F. "Tommy" Thomson on
 Jenny Camp

Three-Day Event Team Gold Medal:
 Lt. Earl F. "Tommy" Thomson on
 Jenny Camp
 Maj. Harry D. Chamberlin on
 Pleasant Smiles
 Capt. Edwin Yancy Argo on Honolulu
 Tomboy

Dressage Individual Bronze Medal:
 Capt. Hiram E. Tuttle on Olympic

Dressage Team Bronze Medal:
 Capt. Hiram E. Tuttle on Olympic
 Capt. Isaac Leonard Kitts on American Lady
 Capt. Alvin Moore on Water Pat

Show Jumping Individual Silver Medal:
 Maj. Harry D. Chamberlin on Show Girl

1936 Olympics
Berlin, West Germany
Three-Day Event Individual Silver Medal:
 Capt. Earl F. " Tommy" Thomson on
 Jenny Camp

1948 Olympics
London, England
Three-Day Event Individual Silver Medal:
 Lt. Col. Frank Sherman Henry

Three-Day Team Gold Medal:
 Lt. Col. Frank Sherman Henry on
 Swing Low
 Lt. Col. Charles Anderson on Reno Palisade
 Col. Earl F. "Tommy" Thomson on
 Reno Rhythm

Dressage Team Silver Medal:
 Lt. Col. Frank Sherman Henry on
 Reno Overdo
 Col. Earl F. "Tommy" Thomson on Pancraft
 Lt. Robert Borg on Klingsor

Medals Won By USET Riders

1952 Olympics
Helsinki, Finland
Three-Day Event Team Bronze Medal:
 Charles "Champ" Hough on Cassavellanus
 Walter G. Staley, Jr. on Craigwood Park
 John Edward Brown "Jeb" Wofford on
 Benny Grimes

Show Jumping Team Bronze Medal:
 William Steinkraus on Hollandia
 Arthur McCashin on Miss Budweiser
 John Russell on Democrat

1960 Olympics
Rome, Italy
Show Jumping Silver Team Medal:
 George Morris on Sinjon
 Frank Chapot on Trail Guide
 William Steinkraus on Ksar d' Esprit

1964 Olympics
Tokyo, Japan
Three-Day Event Team Silver Medal:
 Michael Page on Grasshopper
 Kevin Freeman on Gallopade
 J. Michael Plumb on Bold Minstrel
 Helena "Lana" duPont on Mr. Wister

1968 Olympics
Mexico City, Mexico
Three-Day Event Team Silver Medal:
 Michael Page on Foster
 James Wofford on Kilkenny
 J. Michael Plumb on Plain Sailing
 Kevin Freeman on Chalan

Show Jumping Individual Gold Medal:
   William Steinkraus on Snowbound

1972 Olympics
Munich, West Germany
   Three-Day Event Team Silver Medal:
   Kevin Freeman on Good Mixture
   Bruce Davidson on Plain Sailing
   J. Michael Plumb on Free and Easy
   James Wofford on Kilkenny

Show Jumping Individual Bronze Medal:
   Neal Shapiro on Sloopy

Show Jumping Team Silver Medal
   Neal Shapiro on Sloopy
   Kathy Kusner on Fleet Apple
   Frank Chapot on White Lightning
   William Steinkraus on Main Spring

1976 Olympic Games
Montreal, Canada
Three-Day Event Individual Gold Medal:
   Edmund "Tad" Coffin on Bally Cor

Three-Day Event Individual Silver Medal:
   J. Michael Plumb on Better and Better

Three-Day Event Team Gold Medal:
   Edmund "Tad" Coffin on Bally Cor
   J. Michael Plumb on Better and Better
   Bruce Davidson on Irish Cap
   Mary Anne Tauskey on Marcus Aurelius

Dressage Team Bronze Medal:
   Dorothy Morkis on Monaco
   Hilda Gurney on Keen
   Edith Master on Dahlwitz

1980 Alternate Olympics
Rotterdam, Holland
Three-Day Event Individual Silver Medal:
   James Wofford on Carawich

Three-Day Event Individual Bronze Medal:
   Torrance Watkins on Poltroon

Show Jumping Individual Bronze Medal:
   Melanie Smith on Calypso

1984 Olympics
Los Angeles, California
Three-Day Event Individual Silver Medal:
   Karen Stives on Ben Arthur

Three-Day Event Team Gold Medal:
   Karen Stives on Ben Arthur
   Torrance Watkins Fleishmann on Finvarra
   J. Michael Plumb on Blue Stone
   Bruce Davidson on J.J. Babu

Show Jumping Individual Gold Medal:
   Joe Fargis on Touch of Class

Show Jumping Individual Silver Medal:
   Conrad Homfeld on Abdullah

Show Jumping Team Gold Medal:
   Joe Fargis on Touch of Class
   Conrad Homfeld on Abdullah
   Melanie Smith on Calypso
   Leslie Burr on Albany

1988 Olympics
Seoul, South Korea
Show Jumping Individual Silver Medal:
   Greg Best on Gem Twist

Show Jumping Team Silver Medal:
   Greg Best on Gem Twist
   Anne Kursinski on Starman
   Joe Fargis on Mill Pearl
   Lisa Jacquin on For the Moment

1992 Olympics
Barcelona, Spain
Dressage Team Bronze Medal:
   Carol Lavell on Gifted
   Robert Dover on Lectron
   Charlotte Bredahl on Monsieur
   Michael Poulin on Graf George

Show Jumping Individual Bronze Medal:
   Norman Dello Joio on Irish

1996 Olympics
Atlanta, Georgia
Three-Day Event Individual Bronze Medal:
   Kerry Millikin on Out and About

Three-Day Event Team Silver Medal:
   David O'Connor on Giltedge
   Karen O'Connor on Biko
   Bruce Davidson on Heyday
   Jill Henneberg on Nirvana II

Dressage Team Bronze Medal:
   Michelle Gibson on Peron
   Guenter Seidel on Graf George
   Steffan Peters on Udon
   Robert Dover on Metallic

Show Jumping Team Silver Medal:
   Anne Kursinski on Eros
   Peter Leone on Legato
   Leslie Burr Howard on Extreme
   Michael Matz on Rhum IV